DEPARTMENT OF HEALTH

The Children Act
Guidance and
Regulations

Volume 4
Residential Care

THE CHILDREN · ACT 1989 ·

A NEW FRAMEWORK FOR THE CARE
AND UPBRINGING OF CHILDREN

© Crown copyright 1991
Applications for reproduction should be made to HMSO Copyright Unit, Norwich NR3 1PD
Fifth impression 1996

ISBN 0 11 321430 8

Preface

The guidance in this volume is issued under section 7 of the Local Authority Social Services Act 1970 which requires local authorities in the exercise of their social services functions to act under the general guidance of the Secretary of State. It is the fourth volume in a series designed to bring to managers and practitioners an understanding of the principles of the Children Act and associated regulations, to identify areas of change and to assist discussion of the implications for policies, procedures and practice. It is not intended that any one handbook should be read by people in local authority social services departments, and others carrying on children's homes, as a discrete entity. The Children Act was conceived as a cohesive legal framework for the care and protection of children. Each volume of guidance should therefore be read in conjunction with the others in the series and cross-references are entered where appropriate. However, for the convenience of users who have responsibility for, or are responsible for, or share in the responsibility for, or otherwise work in, children's homes, most of the content of Volume 3 (Family Placements) is replicated in this volume slightly amended where appropriate, given that this volume is about *residential* care.

The need to build on sound practice and the multi-agency, multi-disciplinary co-operation identified as crucial in **Working Together — A guide to arrangements for inter-agency co-operation for the protection of children from Abuse** and in the **Principles and Practice Guide** in the Children Act series is also reinforced wherever appropriate in the Act, Regulations and Guidance.

A glossary of terms and index will be provided separately for this series as a whole.

The masculine gender is employed throughout in this volume and should be read as including the feminine.

Contents

2   ARRANGEMENTS FOR PLACEMENT OF CHILDREN

3   REVIEW OF CHILDREN'S CASES

4   CONTACT

5   REPRESENTATIONS PROCEDURE

6   INDEPENDENT VISITORS

7   AFTER CARE – ADVICE AND ASSISTANCE

8   SECURE ACCOMMODATION

9   REFUGES FOR CHILDREN AT RISK

ANNEXES

CHAPTER 1 CHILDREN'S HOMES

1. INTRODUCTION

General

1.1. The regulations and guidance in this volume are concerned with the care of children in residential homes of various kinds. They supersede previous regulations and guidance issued some 20 years ago and the opportunity has been taken to adopt a radically new approach to what is needed based on the principles of the Children Act 1989 and the changing tasks of homes. Residential care is a positive and desirable way of providing stability and care for some children which they themselves often prefer to other kinds of placement. Homes should set out to treat each child as an individual person and to promote and safeguard his welfare in every way. In part this will be achieved by planning and review of each child's case as required by the guidance and regulations covering Arrangement of Placements and Review included in later chapters. But homes themselves must exercise the concern that a good parent would by providing a safe environment which promotes the child's development and protects him from exposure to harm in his contacts with other people or experiences in the community. Responsible authorities need to be continually aware of practice in each home and how it contributes to the children's well-being. They should define the principles upon which each home operates and establish standards for practice. The operation of the home must be regularly and carefully monitored. Local authorities and other organisations responsible for several homes should have effective management structures which guide, support, monitor and control all aspects of their work.

1.2. Residential care remains a vital resource, but it is essential to see it as part of the overall network of services for children, used in a planned way and when it is in the best interests of the individual child. The major principles underlying the Children Act about partnership with parents, involvement of children and those with parental responsibility in decision making, proper planning and review, the right to make representations and so on, apply equally to children in residential settings and should help to ensure that their placement there is not seen in isolation from overall services to provide support to families and to children in need.

1.3. The way in which children's homes are used in the care of children has changed greatly in recent years. Whilst residential solutions are used less frequently overall, the young people in the homes are older than before, and older than other young people in care. Placements are frequently of short duration and some are made at critical times when other arrangements are changing or have broken down. Changes elsewhere in the care system, such as the efforts to reduce the use of custody for young offenders, may also have an effect on the use of children's homes. Children's homes are provided for a range of purposes: some are a long-term base for a child growing up; others provide accommodation for a period while specific tasks are achieved. Some of the children have suffered the most distressing life experiences and working with them calls for skills of the highest order.

1.4. The Act and Regulations, as well as the guidance, make significant demands on those responsible for children's homes and it is hoped that the new legislative provisions will help bring about important improvements in the level of service provided in homes. This guidance describes the basic requirements for providing good child care in general, but different aspects of the provision will require different emphasis depending on the nature of each home and the needs of the children.

1.5. The Regulations and Guidance are designed to provide a framework of practice for the running of children's homes which emphasises the importance of safeguarding and promoting the welfare of individual children. They are not intended to be a detailed guide to good practice. The National Institute of Social Work (NISW) has been commissioned to produce with the Wagner Development Group further guidance on residential services for children and young people, along the lines of "Home Life – a Code of Practice for Residential Care" (published by the Centre for Policy on Ageing in 1984) which deals with adult residential care. This is expected to be available in 1992.

1.6. Although the administrative arrangements for the different kinds of homes governed by the Regulations are different, the aim is that the requirements with regard to the welfare of each child in the home and the conduct of the home should be subject to the same standards of provision and child care practices.

1.7. Good practice encompasses both the running of the home and individual care and planning for each child. There is a need to be particularly sensitive to some issues in group care. Children being looked after will have very different family backgrounds and different needs and will be subject to individual child care plans. Homes must be run so as to be able to respond to each child as an individual. Whilst there is a need for each child to conform to shared "house rules" which foster mutual respect within group living, the institutional needs of the Home should never be allowed to dominate the lives of children and staff. Safeguarding the child's personal possessions and encouraging the child to develop ownership of some part of their surroundings is extremely important.

1.8. The concept of *partnership* between parents, children, Local Authorities and voluntary organisations is central to the Act and Regulations. Particular guidance is given in Chapter 4 – Contact.

Scope

1.9(i) The primary legislation on children's homes is in Parts VI, VII and VIII of the Children Act 1989. Parts VI and VII replace the provisions of Parts IV and VI of the Child Care Act 1980 on community homes (ie homes which local authorities either directly provide or share responsibility for with a voluntary organisation or trust) and voluntary homes respectively. Part VIII on registered (ie private) children's homes replaces the unimplemented, and now repealed, Childrens Home's Act 1982. Guidance on definitions of homes is provided below.

(ii) The children's homes referred to in this volume are children's homes as defined in sections 53, 60 and 63 of the Children Act 1989 ie:

local authority homes (maintained, controlled and assisted community homes)

voluntary homes ie homes carried on by non-profit-making organisations

registered children's homes, that is homes carried on by persons or by organisations which are not non-profit-making. This means a home which is not carried on by a local authority or a voluntary organisation. A voluntary organisation would usually be expected to be a registered charity or friendly society or a limited company whose accounts show that it is non-profit-making.

(iii) Independent schools accommodating from 4 to 50 boarders and not approved under section 11(3)(a) of the Education Act 1981 (for special education) are required to register as registered children's homes under the Children Act 1989. This applies regardless of whether the school also has day pupils. Independent schools are subject to Education legislation, so that those schools that are also homes are required to be dually registered.

(iv) Where voluntary or private homes accommodate 4 or more children provided with personal care by reason of *disablement* they come under the Registered Homes Act 1984, not the Children Act. This also applies to schools which would otherwise be children's homes within the meaning of the Children Act.

(v) The following Regulations apply to those responsible for *all children's homes* within the meaning of the Children Act:

Children's Homes Regulations 1991 (Annex A to this Volume)

Arrangements for Placement of Children (General) Regulations 1991 (Annex B)

Review of Children's Cases Regulations 1991 (Annex C)

Representation Procedures (Children) Regulations 1991 (Annex E)

(vi) In addition the following regulations apply to *all local authority children's homes* and in respect of *all children looked after by local authorities* including those placed by them in voluntary or registered children's homes:

Contact with Children Regulations 1991 (Annex D)
Definition of Independent Visitors (Children) Regulations 1991 (Annex F)

(vii) The following regulations apply in the special circumstances indicated:

Children (Secure Accommodation) Regulations 1991 (Annex G). These apply to children looked after by local authorities placed in secure accommodation, – usually in community homes. Secure accommodation can not be provided in a voluntary or registered children's home. They apply also to children accommodated by health authorities, NHS Trusts, or local education authorities or in residential care homes, nursing homes or mental nursing homes.

Refuges (Children's Homes and Foster Placements) Regulations 1991 (Annex H). These apply to homes providing refuges for children at risk (section 51 of the Children Act).

Inspection of Premises, Children and Records (Independent Schools) Regulations 1991. These apply to independent schools with boarding governed by section 87 of the Act. (Welfare of children in independent schools.) These regulations and guidance on section 87 are in Volume 5 in this series.

Schools

1.10. Guidance on the provisions regarding residential provision in most independent boarding schools will be found in Volume 5 in this series. Independent boarding schools with 50 or fewer boarders, unless they are approved under section 11(3)(a) of the Education Act 1981 (for special education), are required (by section 63 of the Children Act 1989) to register as children's homes. They will be subject to the Children's Homes Regulations (Annex A) and the guidance given in this chapter. However it must be recognised that a measure of flexibility will be expected in the application of the Regulations and Guidance to such establishments. Independent schools usually have a very different ethos from children's homes. Local authorites are asked to exercise discretion and to be sensitive to the special position of schools in exercising their registration and inspection functions under the Children's Homes Regulations and Guidance. For example some small independent schools whose boarders are all, or almost all, SSD or LEA placements will need to be looked at as rigorously as any private children's home and close attention will have to be given to schools accommodating pupils 52 weeks a year or specialising in catering for children whose parents are overseas and do not have a lot of contact with their children. On the other hand in schools where all the children go home at least at half-term and at holiday times a somewhat less rigorous approach might be appropriate. The same might apply to some schools where there is a large number – possibly hundreds – of day-pupils and 50 or fewer boarders. Similar discretion and sensitivity will be required in the case of the other regulations and guidance that apply to all Children's homes – see para 1.9(v) above. Whether a school is also a home under Section 63 of the Children Act depends on the number of boarders, regardless of number of day-pupils. <u>Non-maintained special schools</u> are not independent schools and do not fall within the ambit of either section 63 or section 87. They do however fall within the ambit of sections 61 and 62 – see paragraph 1.177 below. They are also subject to the Regulations at Annexes B, C and E (and the related provisions in the Children Act) as well as the guidance in chapters 2, 3 and 5 in this volume.

Children with Disability

1.11. References to the needs of children with disability are included (paragraph 1.78 to 1.81 and 1.32) in the paragraphs on accommodation (paragraphs 1.54 to 1.81) and staffing (paragraphs 1.27 to 1.53) below. Separate guidance – in the Children Act series – on Services for Children with Disabilities is in preparation. Local authority homes for children that accommodate children with disability are governed by the Children's Homes Regulations. Voluntary and private children's homes accommodating and providing personal care for four or more children with disability are not governed by these Regulations: they are governed by the Registered Homes Regulations 1984. Voluntary and private children's homes accommodating four or more children of whom three or fewer are children with disability are governed by the Children's Homes Regulations.

Short term care

1.12(i) These Regulations also apply in respect of children placed for short periods in children's homes, either as a 'respite care' arrangement or otherwise (and in respect of the homes).

(ii) Regulation 3(2) exempts from the provisions of the Children's Homes Regulations premises used to accommodate children for the purpose of a holiday for periods of less than 28 days at a time.

Inspection

1.13. The document "Community Care In the Next Decade and Beyond – Policy Guidance" indicated (in paragraph 5.15) that further advice would need to be issued on the particular considerations that need to be borne in mind in applying the principles of free-standing inspection units to children's services.

1.14. In the interests of ensuring that good practice is consistently sustained in the home and of demonstrating that the well-being of children is protected the work of all homes should be regularly inspected. Registered children's homes are subject to formal inspection by social services departments and voluntary homes by the Social Services Inspectorate on behalf of the Secretary of State. Local authorities should ensure that similar procedures are in place for their own homes. Regulation 22 requires responsible authorities to visit each home monthly and to receive a written report on the visit. Guidance is given later (paragraph 1.170) about such visits. Beyond this however there is need for a system of formal and thorough inspection which considers the operation of the home in the light of its statement of purpose, the framework of guidance and procedure laid down by the local authority for its daily conduct, and the implementation of the guidance and regulations in this volume. Care should be taken that the inspection process supports the staff of the home while retaining independence and objectivity to ensure that information is gathered and practice and assessment of quality and safety made independently of the home's management and staff.

1.15. Ideally, inspection is one part of a comprehensive system of quality assurance to make sure that the service delivered meets its intended objectives and standards. Inspections should normally be carried out by the Social Services Department's independent unit. However, inspection does not diminish the duty of the department's managers to be fully aware of practice in the homes and to monitor their operation regularly and carefully. Neither should it detract from the authority's duty to review the case of each individual child under the Review regulations and guidance. Authorities setting up independent inspection units which include in their remit children's homes as well as adult services will need to ensure that staff in the units have appropriate skills and experience for the work they are required to do. This will usually mean that those carrying out inspections of children's homes (including those in the independent sector) should be qualified and experienced in child care services and able to take account of the range of circumstances of children growing up. It is crucial that they are able to assess the quality and impact of the individual care planning for the child as well as the quality of the residential environment.

REGULATIONS

Statement of Purpose and Function of Children's Home

1.16. Regulation 4 requires the responsible authority to compile and maintain a statement of the purpose and functions of the home. The particulars to be included in the statement are listed in Part I of Schedule 1 to the Regulations.

1.17. As regards the purpose and objectives of the home it may be helpful to note that, in general, children no longer spend a large proportion of their childhood growing up in residential care. Increasingly, homes have adjusted to meet the particular needs of children during a phase of their career in care and have adopted various approaches to the care of children. For example, some homes work with children to prepare for a definite goal in a task centred manner; other homes attempt to reproduce family life and support children into adulthood; certain homes attempt to create a therapeutic milieu and work with children psychologically damaged by abuse; still other homes are geared to addressing a child's unacceptable behaviour by means of a systematic behavioural regime. The statement of purpose should describe what the home sets out to do, but should not unduly restrict the possibility of development of good practice. It is hoped that an increasing variety of imaginative and positive approaches to the residential care of children will develop.

1.18. The overall purpose of the statement is to describe what the home sets out to do for children and the manner in which care is provided. The statement of aims and objectives is intended to be designed for those making placements, staff and parents. It is also directed at those responsible for managing the home in order that they have a clear basis for making management decisions.

1.19. The purpose of the home should be set out in a brief statement of broad intentions or aims. In boarding schools such statements are often written into the school's prospectus. Wherever possible consistent with the stated intentions, the aims and objectives should be as concrete as possible, clearly attainable and capable of being measured or evaluated. One yardstick of success for a home should be the extent to which it meets its stated objectives. It is also necessary to recognise that other factors, eg the wishes of children and parents, need to be taken into consideration in measuring success. The statement should describe what the home is to do, the manner in which care is provided, and the plan for moving on at the end of the placement. Guidance on leaving care is given in Chapter 7.

1.20. The statement would be expected to include a description of the intended ethos of the home. This is primarily a statement of the values the approach to care emphasises. The document may embrace a philosophy or set of guiding principles which may be derived from the founding principles of the organisation running the home. It may give expression to the religious orientation of a particular home. It may reflect the policy of the Authority running a community home or the contribution the home makes to a wider network of care alternatives. It should convey some idea of the "feel" of the home. For example an approach to the care of young people moving into independence may involve minimal staff intervention and put a heavy onus on residents accepting responsibility for the consequences of their actions, even where this may detract from the comfort of the surroundings. Such an ethos is very different from one in which care staff work very intensively with a child and take the main responsibility for the living environment and for keeping it in good repair.

1.21. A further section should describe the practical arrangements which follow from the home's aims, objectives and ethos. A written admissions policy should describe the age range, sex, and the particular needs for care of the children the home sets out to look after. If the home is, for example, attuned to the care of children with learning difficulties, then this should be clear from the statement. It should define the limitations on the home's care provision and should be sufficiently specific to be of value in regulating admissions without being so rigid as to preclude flexibility. Admissions should take careful account of the suitability of the home and its current staff and residents, to the needs of the child to be placed. For example it would be inappropriate to place a sexually abused child in a home accommodating children who are themselves abusers.

1.22. The statement should describe the procedures for admission which stem from the policy. Some homes will need to have extensive and detailed pre-admission procedures, particularly if the care needs which the home addresses are specialised and precise. Other homes may be geared up to admit in emergencies in which case procedures are likely to concentrate on the admission process itself and immediate follow up. In these cases it is extremely important for the referring agencies to be in possession of the home's written admissions policy in order that they refer the right children, and it is equally important that the staff on duty responsible for the admission are very clear that the admission is a correct one.

1.23. The numbers, relevant experience and qualifications of staff in post should be stated. In larger homes, children may be cared for in small groupings with their own special group of staff probably headed by a group or unit leader. The statement should indicate the deployment of staff. Staff with particular responsibilities should be identified together with a brief description of those responsibilities.

1.24. When the person running the home – ie the person with day to day responsibility for the running of the home, the head of the home, the officer in charge – is not the responsible authority (as defined in Regulation 2) this is to be included in the statement. In boarding schools, day to day running of the boarding houses often rests with housemasters and housemistresses and their names as well as the name of the headteacher should be included in the statement. If a home is privately owned, then the statement should specify the owner and the (managerial) relationship between the owner and the person in charge (Children Act 1989 Sch 6 para 10(2)(k)) of the home. If the home is run by a voluntary organisation, then the statement should specify the voluntary organisation and the managerial relationship between the organisation's governing body and the head of the home. It may need to describe briefly the intervening managerial layers. Similarly in the case of a community home the statement should describe where the head of the home or officer in charge fits into the managerial structure of the social services department.

1.25. The statement should detail the facilities and services the home provides. The home may provide for children with special difficulties. The home may offer a particular programme or regime to help with developmental delay. Guidance on other matters included in this Chapter, eg health, education, fire precautions, discipline, complaints, reviews, will assist responsible authorities in covering these aspects in the statement. Again, in boarding schools the information required to be provided would normally be expected to appear in the school prospectus available to parents, governors and all staff.

1.26. Part II of Sch 1 to the Regulations lists the persons to whom the statement is to be made available.

Staffing of Children's Homes

1.27. Regulation 5 provides that homes should be adequately staffed.

Establishment numbers

1.28. The staff of a home should be engaged in numbers which are at least adequate to support the aims and objectives of the home and to provide both adequate supervision and activities appropriate to the age, sex and characteristics of the children concerned. The number of staff employed will depend not simply on the number and ages of children being cared for, but also on what is hoped to be achieved for the children and the working methods used. This means, for example, that residential care which aims to provide minimal support for young people approaching independence will require rather fewer staff than residential care for similar aged young people where more extensive work is being undertaken with them. In those homes which are also boarding schools, numbers of staff refer to all those staff with specific responsibility for the welfare of boarders whether or not they also have teaching responsibilities.

1.29. It is not appropriate to specify one set of staff ratios for the differing kinds of children catered for in residential care. At one end these may include some very young children or children with disability, needing close supervision. At the other end there may be teenagers needing a period of freedom from the more intense demands of family life, and with less close supervision – though some teenagers needing a lot of rehabilitative work will involve intensive staffing. Those responsible will have to make judgements on staffing complements based on the needs of the children in the home and the task assigned to the home to do. The forthcoming guidance referred to in paragraph 1.5 above may provide further advice on this.

Qualifications, competence, experience

1.30. Adequate staffing means the competence of staff as well as the number in post. Staff need to be appropriately competent, experienced, and qualified for their work. Exactly what is appropriate will depend upon the aims and methods of the home. Those responsible for running a children's home must decide the qualifications and experience that are appropriate for posts carrying different responsibilities within the staff establishment. Recruitment should then be directed at engaging those possessing the appropriate qualifications and experience. When a qualified person cannot be recruited homes might consider taking a long term view and paying for staff to obtain external qualifications. A wide range of professional and vocational qualifications is relevant to residential care and the developing structure of the *National Vocational Qualification* (NVQ) may be particularly relevant for some staff. It may not always be possible to employ staff who match up to these requirements. It is important for children and staff that homes do not attempt to use methods to care for children which require a level of competence, experience and qualification which the staff complement does not, in fact, possess. It would not, for instance, be appropriate for a home to attempt to engage in "family therapy" unless the staff involved are properly qualified and trained. In such cases, the objectives of the home should be changed to reflect what realistically can be achieved or additional support provided from outside the home's establishment to secure the necessary skills.

Staff development and training

1.31. All staff, even those who are appropriately qualified, need on-going training to ensure that a body of competence and expertise is maintained. Those in charge of the home are recommended to arrange training programmes for staff which are appropriate to the home's aims and methods and to the individual needs of staff. Training needs are likely to include developing basic childcare skills together with more specific awareness training in such matters as culture, religion and race; child protection; HIV/AIDS. Staff should be expected to develop a range of techniques for working with children as well as specific skills required by the home's aims and methods. The managers of homes should consider supporting staff to study in many ways: on distance learning courses (for example the Open University), by attending external short courses or part-time courses as well as in-house training. Joint training with other groups of staff and carers will often be relevant.

1.32. Attention will also need to be given to additional staff training where residential care staff are looking after children with disabilities. The training should seek to instil a positive attitude and approach to dealing with particular disabilities, and should emphasise the importance of seeking to enable the child to achieve maximum independence within his capabilities, and of the promotion of feelings of self-confidence and self-worth within the child. Staff should not be over-protective and should try to treat the child as they would any child.

1.33. Importance should also be placed on training in communication skills for care staff, which will of course be of especial importance when caring for children who may suffer from visual or hearing impairment. Again the particular needs of individual children will vary greatly, and each will have to be specifically addressed. For example a deaf child may use sign language, and will therefore need carers with whom he can communicate. A hearing impaired child may need encouragement to use a personal hearing aid or a radio microphone aid. Visually handicapped children may need assistance with low vision aids, large print books, audio tapes or braille material where appropriate.

Vetting Staff and Others in regular contact with children

1.34. Those managing residential care for children must take particular care in selecting staff. They will be expected to carry out thorough checks on the suitability of staff prior to appointment for the responsibilities they will be required to undertake. The DH consultancy list should be checked in order to screen out people known not to be suitable to work with children. The DH consultancy service is available to any employer in the child care field, whether a local authority or in the voluntary or private sector. The DH list contains details of people whose fitness to care for children is in doubt. The information in the DH list derives from information provided by employers and the police. Full information about the service is provided in the joint circular LAC 88/19, DES Circ 12/88, obtainable from the Executive Officer, Department of Health, CS2B, Room 213, Wellington House, 133–155 Waterloo Road, London SE1 8UG. SSDs should also check with the police for any criminal records of prospective employees as should independent schools through the DES. Part-time as well as full-time staff need to be carefully checked out, also people placed by training schemes, volunteers and in some circumstances regular visitors to the home. The home's daily log should always include an accurate record of the names of all visitors to the home each day. Responsible bodies should give clear written guidance to staff covering the regulation and vetting of visitors to the home to ensure that children are not exposed to potential harm. Similarly, where, for example, children are to be placed in lodgings to enable them to enter work or further education the person or persons who own, or manage, or are otherwise responsible for, the lodgings should be checked out. The premises should be visited, the landlady or landlord interviewed, and a written report prepared. In the case of schools which are homes proprietors should check DES list 99 before confirming any appointment. List 99 is a confidential list of persons who have been determined by the Secretary of State for Education and Science to be unsuitable for employment in schools – not just as teachers. The DES strongly advise all employers to check list 99 before confirming any appointment to a post at a school. School proprietors should ask DES to check people against the DH consultancy service at the same time as they do their List 99 and criminal records checks. Arrangements have been made to enable this to be done. Independent schools were strongly advised to use the arrangements whereby checks can be made on the background of prospective employees in a letter from the Registrar of Independent Schools in England dated 30 April 1990. Checks should be made only on people short-listed for appointment, not on all applicants for a post. Requests for references from previous employers or other referees should include a specific enquiry as to whether there is any impediment to the prospective staff member being employed in a situation where he or she will have some responsibility for the care of, or substantial access to, children living away from home. Proof of qualifications should be required to be produced. Gaps in CVs should be required to be satisfactorily explained. Amongst other things, selection methods must test for maturity, sound judgement and a realistic understanding of the needs of children and young people. Experience may not of itself be a commendation unless it can be shown that it has enhanced the candidate's understanding and skill. Selection should also test a candidate's ability to withstand personal stress and willingness to receive support. Staff should be able to provide a good example to the children. Those inspecting homes are expected to pay particular attention to checking that all action advised in this paragraph is undertaken as appropriate.

1.35. Responsible authorities are required (Regulation 19(2)(b) and paragraph 1.167(b) below) to notify the Secretary of State of conduct suggesting a person may not be suitable for work with children.

1.36. Those responsible for recruiting staff to children's homes should seek to ensure that the composition of the staff group reflects the racial, cultural and linguistic background of the children being cared for. It is important that black children should have positive experience of being cared for by black care givers. It is usually possible to invoke the genuine occupational qualification exemption to the Race Relations Act 1976 (section 5(2)(d)), to recruit staff from a particular racial background.

1.37. Similarly there should be a proper balance of male and female staff and it may be appropriate to use the exemption in the Sex Discrimination Act 1975 section 7(2)(e) to take positive steps in recruitment to ensure the appropriate balance, where it would be in the children's interest to do so.

Staff support

1.38. Caring for children in any residential setting is demanding and in some cases can be a singularly stressful and isolating experience. It is essential that those responsible for running children's homes ensure that staff are properly supported by means of written guidance, staff supervision, staff meetings, training and external consultancy. Where the officer in charge does not have access to a line manager, consideration should be given to appointing a "mentor" who can provide professional support. In boarding schools, housemasters and mistresses need someone to turn to for advice and support.

Written guidance

1.39. Staff in all homes should clearly understand their duties and should have, as a minimum, a written job description. In addition they should receive written guidance on important procedures. Depending on the nature of the home, guidance may be required on such matters as:—

Admission and reception of children

Methods of Care and Control

Case recording and access to records

Care planning

Log book and diary recording

Confidentiality

Administration of finance (petty cash) and security

Purchasing

Repairs and maintenance

Fire precautions and emergency procedures

The extent to which all, or any part of, the premises may be locked as a security measure

Statement of safety policy

Child Protection

Arrangements for regulating and vetting visitors to the home

Arrangements for checking lodgings and vetting landladies and landlords

HIV/AIDS awareness, confidentiality and infection control

Dealing with disclosure of sexual abuse

Treatment of children who have been abused

Rostering shift handovers

Sleeping-in, bed-time and night supervision

Care practices towards children of the opposite sex to staff

The particular care needs of children from minority ethnic groups and practices within the home to combat racism

Disciplinary and Grievance procedures

Delegated authority and notifications to senior staff

Placements

Reviews

Dealing with aggression and violence

Risk taking

Dealing with sexuality and personal relationships

Working with parents

1.40. This written guidance should be available to all staff at all times either in a handbook or other suitable form.

1.41. Guidance should be kept up to date and it is recommended that the way in which guidance documents are assembled should be amenable to easy revision.

Staff Supervision

1.42. All staff should receive individual supervision from their line manager. This includes those who are not employed as care staff but, by virtue of the fact that they work in a home, will come into contact with children. All staff will have emotional demands made upon them by the children, and will be obliged to respond.

1.43. Supervision should be on a one-to-one basis, in private, and so far as is practicable free from interruption. Staff should be afforded the opportunity to express their feelings as invoked by the care of the children, and be helped to understand those feelings. Supervising staff should ascertain that the staff member's responses to children are appropriate to the methods employed, and that their degree of personal involvement with children is appropriate. Wherever possible staff should receive direct practical guidance.

1.44. The frequency of supervision sessions should be defined in writing, taking account of the nature of the home and demands placed on staff. Care staff should ideally receive supervision for one to one and a half hours, not less frequently than once every two to three weeks. Other staff should be seen just as frequently but the length of each session would not normally need to be as long.

1.45. Notes of the issues covered in supervision should be made by the supervisor and a copy provided for the staff member. These notes should contribute to identifying the training and staff developmental needs of the staff member.

Staff meetings

1.46. Staff rotas should be organised in such a way as to allow the staff, or as many as possible, to meet together. Such meetings are important for the cohesion of the staff as a group and for group supervision and to help combat the fragmented experience the children will have of the staff group as a result of staff working shifts. There should be regular meetings of all staff responsible for the welfare of the children. This will allow staff members to contribute to decisions affecting the running of the home and encourage the development of a common awareness of the needs of the children. Meetings should be timed so that, as far as possible, part-time staff may attend. They should also be a forum for mutual support through the sharing of experience.

External consultancy

1.47. Residential care staff often find the services of an external consultant to the home particularly helpful. Such interest serves to reduce the sense of isolation and is a source of support not associated with line management accountability. It is for those running a home to decide whether to seek consultancy support and if so whether this engages directly with the needs of the children or concentrates on staff support. It is essential that there is a written agreement with any external consultant engaged which clearly defines the role and distinguishes it from the management function.

1.48. Homes which employ behavioural or psychotherapeutic methods must ensure that senior staff are properly qualified and that they directly lead the practice in the home. In these homes it is particularly important that on-going, in-house training for staff should be part of the regime and ethos. It is expected that external consultants with specialist expertise in these methods will be engaged to provide additional support to staff and guidance in the treatment of particular children.

Organisation of care in homes

1.49. The responsible authority must create an appropriate management structure within the home to ensure that staff are deployed and responsibilities divided to best meet the care needs of the children. There must be clear arrangements to designate a member of staff to deputise when the person in charge is absent. Where possible this should be the same person each time and the task should be included in his job description. Attention will need to be given to maximizing the numbers of staff on duty at times when there is the greatest demand from the children. However, staff will also need time free from direct contact with children to make entries in records, to plan activities, treatment or care programmes, and to receive supervision. Such times should be scheduled when rotas are prepared. In boarding schools the deployment of staff must take account of any teaching responsibilities they have.

1.50. The requisite number of staff on duty at night, whether they remain awake or can sleep in, will need to be decided by those responsible for managing the home. This will have implications for the staff establishment.

1.51. Consideration should be given to the way staff come on and go off duty and how information is passed between them. This is important to achieving continuity of care and maximizing the effectiveness of staff coming on duty.

1.52. The way the responsibility for particular children is allocated to staff must be clearly established by the person in charge. He may for example favour a key-worker system or, in boarding schools, the allocation of a personal tutor. The allocation of such responsibilities should not restrict a child from developing relationships with other staff members with whom they have regular contact. A child must not feel forced to form a special relationship with a certain staff member when that is not of the child's choosing. A child may wish to relate to a range of staff in different ways, and the fact that a staff member has been asked to undertake certain responsibilities in relation to a child does not necessarily require the child to form a special relationship with him.

1.53. The responsible authority is required to ensure that all those working at the home are informed of various matters referred to in Schedule 1 to the Regulations.

Accommodation

1.54. Regulation 6 requires suitable and properly equipped and furnished accommodation to be provided for each child in a home including disabled children accommodated in children's homes (see paragraph 1.78 et seq below).

1.55. Regulation 7 requires the responsible authority to ensure the provision of sufficient washing, bathing and toilet facilities, adequate heating, lighting, decoration, maintenance etc, facilities for children to meet privately with parents and others, laundering facilities, including those to enable children to wash and iron their own clothing, and access to a private pay telephone.

1.56. It is not possible to give specific guidance here on the wide range of children's homes which exist, but the question of appropriate standards will be further addressed in the material commissioned from NISW referred to in paragraph 1.5 above.

1.57. The welfare of each child accommodated in a home is to be provided for. Those responsible for the home must make sure that each child's accommodation is designed to secure the child's welfare and development, as well as taking account of general management needs. In the statement describing the aims and objectives of the home the accommodation provision should feature as it contributes to the achievement of those aims and objectives.

Planning for Location of Home

1.58. A children's home should, as far as practicable, be situated in a location which supports the aims and objectives of the home. Clearly, when planning for a new home the location should be a primary consideration. An urban or rural setting may be appropriate depending on the area served and the present and future needs and background of the child. However, a site shared with other social services facilities, eg next door to a home for the elderly and infirm would not be likely to be suitable. In boarding schools easy access to the main school facilities out of school hours is also important. The importance of being able to get to the schools, shops, youth clubs and other facilities in the community cannot be overestimated. Particular thought should be given to the suitability of location to provide the sort of environment most helpful to each child's development. Where young children are involved, matters of security and safety should be considered. Easy access to the home by public transport is essential to enable family links to be maintained, encouraged and developed.

1.59. If possible a home should be indistinguishable from an ordinary family residence in outward appearance and siting. Whilst recognising that there are sometimes difficulties of control with some children and that the need to cope with these may inform a decision as to the character of premises, the decision should balance such considerations with the need to avoid the stigmatisation that would be automatic from a home which had the outward appearance of an institution.

1.60. Due consideration should also be given to the optimum size of the home, bearing in mind the principle that as far as possible conditions in the home should reflect those in an ordinary domestic environment.

1.61. Consideration should be given to good relationships with neighbours at the planning stage and thereafter when the home becomes operational. Children living in children's homes have as much right to live in a neighbourhood as other residents. By the same token the staff and children in a home have responsibilities as good neighbours and due consideration must be given to neighbours' privacy, property and way of life. It is important therefore to consider at the planning stage any aspects of design and siting which might assist in maintaining a responsible and positive relationship with the neighbourhood.

Structure and Layout of Home

1.62. When accommodation is being planned or an existing home adapted, the accommodation should, as far as practicable, be able to meet the needs of individual children. It is useful to have variety in the size, shape and location of bedrooms and other rooms. There must be sufficient space for children to exercise choice as to where they spend their leisure time. There should be opportunities for contact with the whole community, involvement with small groups of children and/or adults, as well as opportunities for complete privacy. The design of the home must recognise the need for both companionship and privacy. A flexible approach is needed to take into account the children's wishes to make sure that personal items of furniture, personal pictures, possessions, ornaments or models can be kept to enhance and personalise that child's surroundings.

1.63. Hard and fast rules (over and above the minimum requirements of the regulations) would not be helpful, because the needs of each child will be different. The choice, for example, of whether a child has a separate room or shares with siblings should only be made after careful consideration of all available facts. There will always have to be considerable thought given to balancing the individual needs of each child with those of others and with the practical limitations of available resources.

1.64. Homes are required (Regulation 7(5)) to make available a place where a child can make and receive telephone calls in private. This facility should be available for ordinary everyday use and not restricted or treated as being available as if it were a privilege.

1.65. Regulation 7(3) requires those running the home to provide facilities for visits to the children by family or friends. These should be in a welcoming, congenial setting. This is necessary to enable each child to maintain links with family and others; visitors should not be made to feel that they are intruding, nor, for example, should a child have to feel self conscious because his/her visitors are occupying the only room available and thereby excluding routine activities of other children such as watching the television.

1.66. It may sometimes be necessary for those responsible to have private discussions with a child, and consideration should be given to the availability of suitable accommodation for this purpose. In some homes staff will need office space.

1.67. Consideration should also be given to the availability of accommodation for staff performing sleeping-in duties. The need for such accommodation will to a large extent depend on the size and type of the home, and the numbers, age and sex of the children resident in it. Where for example a home contains children of both sexes, both male and female staff should sleep in, and two sleeping-in rooms would therefore need to be provided. Where, however, a home has only a very few children, or where all the children in the home are of the same sex, it may be appropriate for only one member of staff to sleep in. In all cases emergency cover must be allowed for so that an adult is always available even when, for example, a child needs escorting to hospital.

1.68. Regulation 7(2)(a) requires that adequate levels of lighting, heating and ventilation be provided in all parts of the home used or occupied by children. These basic essentials should be provided at a comfortable level by employing high standards of design and maintenance, and without detracting from a homely appearance.

1.69. Regulation 7(1) requires sufficient provision of lavatories, wash basins, baths and showers, fitted with a hot and cold water supply, for the use of resident children. It is important to recognise that the most personal aspects of daily life such as using the lavatory or taking a shower or bath should be respected as essentially private activities. Doors should be lockable, with the facility for staff to open them from outside if necessary. The siting of toilet and bathroom and closeness to each child's bedroom should take account of the child's needs and be planned on a domestic scale. Communal facilities are institutional in character and can create opportunities for abuse; they should therefore be avoided wherever possible. Even where some bathing facilities are communal, there should always be the opportunity for any child to bathe in privacy.

1.70. Wherever practicable, children should have a choice as to whether they take a bath or a shower. These should be equipped with effective thermostatic controls. Consideration should also be given to installing baths, showers and toilets in such a way that they are accessible to children with physical disabilities. (See paragraph 1.78 et seq below.)

Decoration and Furnishing

1.71. Regulation 6 requires the provision of suitable space, furniture, bedding and furnishings – this includes curtains, floor covering and, where necessary, equipment. When considering practical arrangements within a home, items such as decor and furnishings should emphasise comfort and informality. Furniture and equipment should be appropriate to the age of the child and should enable the needs and wishes of individual children, including children with disability, to be met sensibly rather than be standard and uniform. The siting of items such as dustbins, meters and larger items such as heating equipment or fuel storage is important and should not detract from a homely appearance nor create health or hygiene hazards.

1.72. Children should be able to personalise areas of the home that are regarded as their own. They should for example be able to display posters or pictures on their bedroom walls if they wish to do so. Facilities should also be available for children to store personal possessions in their own cupboards and/or chest of drawers.

1.73. Regulation 7(2)(b) requires the home to be maintained in a good state of structural repair, clean and reasonably decorated and maintained. The general state of repair and decoration of a home are important factors in maintaining the standards of comfort and promoting a positive feeling by the child for its surroundings. Children resident in the home should have a say in the decor and upkeep of the home if they wish to, and particularly in the decoration and personalisation of their own rooms.

1.74. As well as internal decoration, the exterior of the home should be maintained in sound structural and decorative order. Where the home has any gardens or grassed or hard play areas, these should be kept in good order. They should be made secure by fencing appropriate to the nature of the home. This is particularly important where the home accommodates younger children.

Laundry

1.75. There should be arrangements within the home which ensure that linen and clothing are regularly laundered. There are two needs. A child should always have clean and well laundered bedding, bathroom linen and clothes to wear. In addition, as part of learning self-care, children should have the opportunity, and should be encouraged, to undertake some, or, for older children, all, their own washing. However, first priority should always be given to ensuring the availability of clean linen and clothes. If a child, for whatever reason, cannot do his own washing, the alternative should not be the wearing of dirty or unkempt clothes.

1.76. A children's home must therefore be equipped to manage both eventualities. In smaller homes a utility room equipped with a domestic washing machine and drier may be adequate for both purposes. In larger homes it may be desirable to have heavy duty machines, and in addition domestic machines, suitable for use by resident children, preferably located separately. Centralised or external facilities may sometimes be appropriate. Consideration needs to be given to the demand for heavy washing loads when, for example, bed wetting and soiling is anticipated.

1.77. It should be part of the role of care staff in homes to teach children how to do their own laundering, and indeed how to look after their clothing generally. How and when this is done is a matter for professional judgement in relation to individual children.

Accommodation for children with disability

1.78. Homes governed by the Children's Homes Regulations which accommodate disabled children (see paragraph 1.9(iv)) are required to provide the necessary equipment, facilities and adaptations for children with disability.

1.79. Given the wide ranging variety of physical, mental and sensory impairments and disabilities, and the variety of needs that will arise from them, the extent and type of adaptations and equipment that have to be provided will be a matter for individual professional assessment and judgement, based on the particular needs of the individual child concerned.

1.80. An important principle that should be continually borne in mind however when assessing the adaptations and facilities that may be required is that a child with disabilities is first and foremost a child, and all the general principles in caring for the childs' needs apply and should continue to be applied.

1.81. It may for example be necessary to adapt the physical environment of the home to meet the needs of a child or children accommodated there, in order to permit their integration into the home. This may involve the provision of access for wheelchairs, ground-floor level sleeping accommodation, hand rails on stairways and/or corridors, suitably adapted bathing and washing facilities, and specific lighting or decoration schemes. It may also be necessary to provide specialised equipment, such as visual or hearing aids. The aim should be to integrate the child in every aspect of life in the home, not merely the physical aspects.

Good Order and Discipline

1.82. Different homes will have different philosophies of care. It is vital that staff have a sound understanding of the principles and procedures employed in the home for the care and discipline of the children and the treatment methods used so that they can respond to a child with confidence. Difficulties in control will arise where the objectives of the home are not well defined and consequently not well understood by staff or where the children do not understand the reason for their placement. Systems of control and discipline cannot be divorced from systems of management and systems of care practice and planning within the home. It is important that staff should set standards by their behaviour.

1.83. Physical restraint should be used rarely and only to prevent a child harming himself or others or from damaging property. Force should not be used for any other purpose, nor simply to secure compliance with staff instructions. Homes should have a particularly clear policy on how and when restraint may be used. Training should be provided and managers should regularly and formally monitor staff awareness of the rules governing this aspect of their duties. Where children in homes have suffered particularly damaging experiences and have difficulty developing the self control or good personal relationships which diminish the need for physical restraint it is important that sufficient, able staff are employed to ensure that the children are dealt with sensitively and with dignity.

1.84. The successful conduct of any home is dependent on a combination of sound management, high standards of professional practice and care planning and upon caring relationships. It is for the responsible body, having regard to the role and purpose of each home and to the nature and characteristics of the children accommodated therein, to develop written policies for each home and for the officer in charge of the home to implement these in the day to day management of the home.

1.85. A major determinant of good behaviour and positive ethos of the home is the quality of the relationships between the staff and the children. Relationships between the staff and the children need to be based on honesty, mutual respect and recognised good professional practice. Many children in homes need to experience care which compensates for the loss of the attention and security they would otherwise receive through the direct care of their parents.

1.86. Good order is unlikely to be achieved unless there is an established framework of general routines and individual boundaries of behaviour are well defined. Children need to be aware of what is expected of them and how the arrangements for their care actually work. There must be proper provision for the social, physical, emotional and intellectual needs of the children. It is important that there should be a structure to the child's day and that the correct balance should be achieved between free and controlled time. There should be ample opportunity for children to participate in a range of appropriate leisure time activities. This will aid the maintenance of control.

1.87. Problems will occur where expectations of behaviour are unrealistic or inconsistent or insensitive methods of control are used. Good professional practice would recognise that often misbehaviour by young people stems from a failure by adults to be sufficiently receptive to the needs and problems of the young people rather than from a wilful defiance of authority. The need to avoid labelling children as disruptive or seeking to resolve misbehaviour by moves to new placements without the original behaviour being properly addressed must be recognised. One of the principal purposes of control and discipline is to enable individual children to develop inner controls so that in time they learn self control, establish feelings of worth and self respect and are motivated towards improved behaviour and enabled to live in harmony within a group. They should be encouraged to develop a proper awareness of their rights and responsibilities and those of others.

1.88. It is essential that children should be consulted and their wishes and feelings ascertained in matters concerning them. Good order is much more likely to be achieved in homes where children are routinely involved in decision making about their care. They should be encouraged to accept responsibility for their own care, appropriate to their age and understanding.

Disciplinary Measures – General

1.89. Except in so far as the Secretary of State may direct otherwise in accordance with section 53 of the Children and Young Persons Act 1933 or section 22(7) of the Children Act 1989, Regulation 8 prohibits the use of various measures, including corporal punishment, deprivation of food or sleep, inappropriate clothing and restriction of visits, etc. The Regulation permits only disciplinary measures approved by the responsible body. The listed measures are equally prohibited in boarding schools which are also children's homes (see paragraph 1.10). Prohibited measures are discussed at paragraph 1.91 below.

Permitted Disciplinary Measures

1.90. It is recognised that some form of sanction will be necessary where there are instances of behaviour which would in any family or group environment reasonably be regarded as unacceptable. Often such unacceptable behaviour can be prevented by the use of mild or more severe verbal reprimand. The imposition of formal disciplinary measures should be used sparingly and in most cases only after repeated use of informal measures has proved ineffective. For example there is no intention to reduce the authority of staff in applying reasonable mealtime discipline or in the discretionary use of special treats. There should be a system of rewards (commendations, extension of privileges etc) as well as sanctions. In normal circumstances children should be encouraged to behave well by the frequent expression of approval by staff and by the generous use of rewards rather than by the extensive imposition of disciplinary measures. Where sanctions are felt to be necessary, good professional practice indicates that these should be contemporaneous, relevant, and, above all, just. Children in homes are likely, because of the system, to be confronted as to the consequences of their actions by numerous adults; this often serves merely to compound misbehaviour and undermine the child's self esteem. Staff should appreciate when a misdemeanour is finished and the subject should be dropped. The responsible body should detail in writing the disciplinary measures which it approves for use in the home: other measures may not be used. The measures approved for use in the home should be appropriate to the age and circumstances of the individual child accommodated. Appropriate measures could be reparation, restitution, curtailment of leisure extras, additional house chores, and use of increased supervision. The responsible body must ensure that all staff are aware of the measures which are acceptable, the extent of their discretion in administering them and the requirement to record their use on each occasion. The record of sanctions administered should be kept in a log book (but separately from the home's daily log and should include in each entry the name of the child, details of the inappropriate behaviour, names of staff present, and date and nature of the sanction. Each entry should be signed by a person authorised to sign on behalf of the responsible authority (see Regulation 8(4)). All entries should be written in appropriate language, and all names, including that of the signatory, should be clearly identified. The responsible authority should keep under annual review the appropriateness of the disciplinary measures approved. Responsible authorities should regularly monitor the use of sanctions and other measures of control in their homes, which should also be scrutinised by the inspecting body. Authorities should seek legal advice about the measures to be approved and their use and should ensure that staff responsible for monitoring, managing or inspecting homes also have access to legal advice.

Prohibited Measures

1.91. Prohibited measures are listed below and guidance is provided in respect of each of them.

   i Corporal punishment – Regulation 8(2)(a)
   The use of corporal punishment is not permitted in residential child care establishments. The term "corporal punishment" should be taken to cover any intentional application of force as punishment including slapping, throwing missiles and rough handling. It would also include punching or pushing in the heat of the moment in response to violence from young people. It does not prevent a person taking necessary physical action, where any other course of action would be likely to fail, to avert an immediate danger of personal injury to the child or another person, or to avoid immediate danger to property. The use of "holding" which is a commonly used, and often helpful, containing experience for a distressed child is not excluded.

   ii. Deprivation of food and drink – Regulation 8(2)(b)
   It is well established that the enjoyment of eating and drinking is fundamental to a child's healthy physical and emotional development. Meal times are an important social occasion in the life of a child and it would be quite inappropriate for a child to be refused meals. Deprivation of food and drink should be taken to include the denial of access to the

amounts and range of foods and drink normally available to children in the home but would not include instances where specific food or drinks have to be withheld from a child on medical advice. Equally, it would be inappropriate to force a child to eat foods which he disliked. It would be right however to encourage a child to try a wide range of foods.

iii. Restriction or Refusal of Visits/Communications – Regulation 8(2)(c) & (3)(d).

The value for most children of maintaining contact with their families and friends cannot be overstated. The restriction or refusal of contact as a punishment is not permitted but it is recognised that in some circumstances as part of the management and planning of his care some restrictions may have to be placed on contact with certain individuals or on the facility to receive, or – especially – make, visits. (See Regulation 8(3)(d)). Children sometimes need to be protected from visits. The home must be guided in its approach to contact by the planning decisions of those with parental responsibilities. Where contact is restricted in accordance with these plans it should be recorded on each occasion in the child's personal records. Where parents insist on visiting a child despite this being contrary to the care plan which has been drawn up it will be necessary for staff to find tactful ways of dealing with this and to counsel the child.

In the case of children in secure accommodation the facility to make visits will be less appropriate than in other cases. In general, arrangements for making and receiving visits and for other contacts will have to be compatible with the reasonable requirements of the efficient managment of the home. It will continue to be legitimate to control unplanned visits.

iv. Requiring a Child to Wear Distinctive or Inappropriate Clothing – Regulation 8(2)(d).

Some children in homes will already have a very negative perception of themselves. Requiring them to wear distinctive or inappropriate clothing would serve only to further undermine their self esteem and to damage their self confidence. Distinctive or inappropriate clothes should be taken to include not only any recognisable punishment uniform or badge, for example, but also clothes which are inappropriate to the time of day and/ or the activity being undertaken. This applies also to footwear and hairstyles. However, in some circumstances, uniform or distinctive clothing such as sports kit is not inappropriate and can help to promote a positive self-image. Regulation 8(3)(c) makes plain that wearing distinctive clothing for purposes connected with education or any uniformed organisation (such as Scouts or Guides) is of course not excluded.

v. The Use or the Withholding of Medication or Medical or Dental Treatment – Regulation 8(2)(e).

This would be a dangerous and utterly unacceptable practice and is accordingly totally forbidden in all circumstances, whether as a disciplinary measure or otherwise to control the child. See also paragraphs 1.102 and 1.196.

vi. The use of Accommodation to Physically Restrict the Liberty of Any Child.

This is totally prohibited in community homes except in premises approved by the Secretary of State for use as secure accommodation and under criteria set down in section 25 of the Children Act 1989 and the Children (Secure Accommodation) Regulations 1991 (see chapter 8 and Annex G). However, locking external doors and windows at night time, in line with normal domestic security, is not excluded. Responsible authorities should give clear, written guidance to staff about the extent to which the home, or any part of it, may be locked as a security measure. Similarly, refusal of permission to go out (eg "gating" in schools) short of measures which would constitute restriction of liberty, is not forbidden. Where there is any doubt as to what is permissible, reference should be made to the guidance in Chapter 8, including the definition of "restriction of liberty" in paragraph 8.10.

vii. Intentional Deprivation of Sleep – Regulation 8(2)(f).
Apart from the grave psychological damage deprivation of sleep could inflict, it could also seriously affect the physical health of the young person.

viii. Imposition of Fines – Regulation 8(2)(g)
Fines imposed by courts must, of course, be paid but it is not considered appropriate for those carrying on homes to impose such sanctions. In cases of wilful damage or of misappropriation of monies or goods belonging to others, however, it would be perfectly proper for the perpetrator to be required to pay for or at least to make a contribution towards the costs of repairs or replacement of misappropriated monies or goods. Withholding part of pocket money for misdemeanours is not an inappropriate sanction, but its use is best restricted to cases of wilful damage etc. In any case no more than a maximum of two-thirds of a child's pocket money should be withheld.

ix. Intimate Physical Searches – Regulation 8(2)(h)
Intimate physical searches of children are totally unacceptable. Occasionally, and not as a punishment, a search of a child's clothing may be necessary – eg for weapons – but where this does not allay anxieties about the child's safety or that of others he will have to be kept apart from the group and closely supervised by a member of staff.
If it is suspected that a child has secreted drugs on his person, then the police should be notified.

Health

1.92. All the provisions in the Arrangements for Placement of Children (General) Regulations 1991 (Annex B) and the Review of Children's Cases Regulations 1991, (Annex C) and the guidance on both these sets of regulations, apply to those responsible for all placements of children in homes. This will be either:

local authorities – where the local authority has placed the child in a community home or a voluntary home or a registered children's home.

voluntary organisations – where a child is in a voluntary home and has not been placed there by a local authority.

persons carrying on registered (ie private) children's homes – where the child is in a registered children's home and has not been placed there by a local authority or voluntary organisation.

1.93. Thus either a placing local authority or a voluntary organisation or a person carrying on a registered children's home is required under Regulation 7 of the Arrangements Regulations and Regulation 6 of the Review Regulations to arrange for medical examinations and written health assessments of every child in a home within the periods prescribed in these Regulations and they are required to have consideration to the health issues set out in Schedules 2 and 3 respectively to these Regulations.

1.94. The guidance on health in Chapter 2 of this Volume (paragraphs 2.23 to 2.32) in relation to the Arrangements Regulations applies to children in homes as well as to all the children looked after by local authorities in non-residential care situations and it is most important that those responsible pay close attention to this guidance and comply with it. The health of children in homes is likely to be even more in need of attention than that of other children looked after by local authorities and the following additional guidance is offered in respect of children in homes.

1.95. Children in homes are particularly vulnerable as they frequently have not received continuity of health care because they have been subject to a sequence of moves often within a fairly short time scale. Staff should play an active role in promoting all aspects of a child's health. Health care should include education about alcohol and other substance abuse, sexual matters, and HIV/AIDS and should not be restricted to treatment of illness and accidents. In boarding schools such education should form part of the curriculum. Another example of promoting the child's health would be to ensure that pocket money jobs such as paper-rounds are appropriate to the child's age and strength.

1.96. If a child's stay in a home is likely to be short, or if the home is near to his own home, it is preferable for the child to continue with his own GP. If at all possible there should be scope for the child to have some choice of GP. In particular children should be able to have a doctor of their own sex if they so wish. In boarding schools it will need to be borne in mind that pupils will often be registered with a GP and dentist in the neighbourhood of the family home and that parents may regard it as preferable for medical or dental check-ups to be carried out during the school holidays. In these circumstances the school should still ensure that such check-ups have, in fact, taken place.

1.97. It is often found that children who have had frequent disruption and disturbance in their life have health care needs which are treatable but which over a long period either have not been detected or have been ignored. In order that deficiencies in past medical care may be remedied, care staff need to adopt a very vigilant attitude towards the health of children in homes. Their health should be carefully and continuously monitored and medical advice should be sought promptly when causes for concern are identified. Regrettably there is sometimes a poverty of expectation about the standard of health children in homes should enjoy. The health of a child in a home should be promoted with the same assiduity as would be the case for a child living with caring parents. To ensure this happens care staff will have to pursue a very pro-active approach on health issues. In boarding schools most parents will wish to retain the prime responsibility for their child's health. The parents and the school will therefore need to act in partnership.

1.98. There is a need for close co-operation and effective communication between those with parental responsibilities, the staff in the home, the GP, the health visitor, the school health service and any specialist services which may be required if proper health care is to be provided for a child. Some children will have conditions such as diabetes, epilepsy or haemophilia which will require special medication, or coeliac disease where a special diet is required. Staff in the home need to be fully informed about such conditions. Different races are susceptible to different medical conditions. Staff in homes need to be alert to the possibility of conditions such as thalassaemia and sickle cell anaemia and to have an understanding of them and their treatment. Other children may have mental or physical disabilities and have special needs which require to be met. Advice should be obtained from medical professionals on the appropriate pattern of medical care for all such children and care staff should take responsibility for ensuring that these children receive proper daily health care and for the safe storage of medicines. This should then be recorded in the child's individual health record so that the information is available to care staff when they need it. In boarding schools house staff will need to work closely and as appropriate with those staff in the school who carry a responsibility for health education and other health related matters.

1.99. A health record must be kept at the home in respect of each child. It should build on earlier records. If these are not available, efforts should be made to obtain them. The records should be kept up to date with information about health needs and development, illnesses, operations, immunisations, allergies, medications administered, dates of appointments with GPs and specialists. When the child leaves the home the records should be made available to whoever is to have the subsequent care of the child. Records should not record the antibody status of a child who is HIV positive. This information should be held on a need to know basis only, and authorities should ensure that staff in homes are aware of issues surrounding HIV and

AIDS and take precautions in all cases to avoid situations which could result in the transmission of HIV infection. Detailed guidance on children and HIV will be issued in due course.

1.100. In order that the well being of the children in the home may be safeguarded, all medications including those which can be obtained without prescription should be stored and handled safely. Boarding schools, however, often make arrangements for all medicines to be kept and administered by the matron or similar person. Children of 16 and over should in general be entrusted with the retention and administration of their own medication and be provided with a secure place to keep medication, where necessary. With this exception, all medications should be kept in a secure place (Regulation 9(1)), eg suitable locked cabinet. The administration of medicinal products should be recorded in writing on each occasion in a central register and on the child's individual record. The home should have laid down procedures for the administration of medications. These will vary from home to home depending on the characteristics of the children accommodated. Advice should be sought from the Community Pharmacist who will be able to advise on the safe storage and administration of medications and appropriate methods for recording their use.

1.101. Regulation 9(2) provides that where a medicinal product may not be safely self-administered by a child in a home it may only be administered by a member of the staff of the home or by a doctor or nurse.

1.102. Local authorities and voluntary organisations should have clear policies and procedures in relation to consent to medical treatment for children who are being accommodated by them or on their behalf. These policies and procedures should be included in the care plan for the child. The health authority should be informed of them and the staff in the home should have a clear understanding of them. Guidance on consent to treatment has been issued to health authorities in Circular HC(90)22. Where the child is of sufficient understanding medical treatment may only be given with his consent. Where the child is not of sufficient understanding the consent of the parent including a person who has parental responsibility is required. This would include the local authority if the child is in care. Doctors can of course administer treatment or medication in emergencies without consent if this is medically necessary but firm guidelines should be laid down by responsible authorities about the procedure which should operate for emergency medication. (See also paragraphs 1.91(v), 1.196 and 2.30.)

1.103. It is vital that staff in the home are able to obtain, or ensure through parental action, medical or dental treatment for a child without delay or confusion. In general, it is most convenient if the parent or those with parental responsibilities agree that the staff in home may arrange for routine treatment or minor procedures but that in the case of major procedures or operations parental consent will first be sought except in the case of emergency where any delay would be dangerous. Arrangements should be made to ensure that parents, or those with parental responsibilities, are routinely kept informed of their child's state of health.

1.104. Children of 16 and over can give their own consent to medical treatment. Children under 16 may also be able to give consent depending on their capacity to understand the nature of the treatment. It is for the doctor to decide whether the child is capable of giving informed consent. Children who are capable of giving consent cannot be medically examined and treated without their consent. It is, however, undoubtedly the responsibility of those carrying on the home to help and encourage young people both to understand the importance of health care and to take responsibility for their own health.

Education

1.105. In precisely the same way as provisions about health in the Arrangements and Reviews Regulations apply to all children in homes so do the provisions relating to education. In the case of education the particular relevant regulations are Regulation 4(1) of (and Schedule 3 to) the Arrangements Regulations and Regulation 5 of (and Schedule 2 (paragraph 7) to) the Reviews Regulations. Guidance is given in Chapter 2 (paragraphs 2.33 to 2.39).

1.106. Young people accommodated in homes can be specially disadvantaged educationally. The following additional advice is accordingly offered. Children in homes will often have suffered from a lack of continuity in their education due to frequent changes of placement. Children's homes therefore need to give special prominence to promoting education. The children may, because of difficulties and disruptions earlier in their life, be damaged and vulnerable. They may suffer from low self-esteem and may have under-achieved in the past. It is essential therefore that they be given every opportunity to take full advantage of educational opportunities. They will often need particular help and encouragement to achieve their full educational potential and to equip themselves as well as possible for adult life.

1.107. Encouragement and support from parents improves any child's performance. In instances where such support has previously been lacking it is all the more important for care staff in homes to compensate by giving a young person every assistance to catch up with his peers. While education is primarily the responsibility of teaching staff either in the home or elsewhere, the care staff in the home have a vital contribution to make. In boarding schools which are homes staff often have both teaching and care duties: this can be a positive benefit. Where it is not possible for the child's own parents to fulfil the role of interested and supportive parents the care staff should assume the role. They should observe the child carefully so that they have a sound understanding of his strengths and also those areas in which he has difficulties. They should recognise and applaud a young person's achievements and encourage him to take pride in his successes. Similarly, when a young person encounters disappointments staff need to provide sympathetic support and encouragement to persevere. They should be alive to the possibility of the child being bullied or otherwise discriminated against at school and be prepared in conjunction with the school to deal with it.

1.108. Care or boarding staff should enter into regular dialogue with teachers to ensure that any learning or other difficulties a child is experiencing are identified at an early stage and that plans are made for dealing with them. Similarly, where it has been recognised that a child has a particular talent, measures will need to be taken to ensure that the talent is appropriately fostered. Children with learning difficulties such as dyslexia will need particular assistance. Care staff should work together as appropriate with teachers to ensure that where necessary the young person with special educational needs has access to specialist services within the local authority's education provision. In the case of young people for whom English is not their first language staff should ensure that the language tuition the young person receives at school is supplemented by appropriate support in the home through help with reading and writing and opportunities to practise conversation.

1.109. In homes which are not themselves schools it is most important that care staff should forge good relations with schools and colleges of further education and maintain close contact. Staff should attend such social events as schools fairs, sports days and concerts. Unless parents do so themselves a member of staff should always attend parents' evenings to discuss the progress of each child with teaching staff and should report back the outcome to the young person.

1.110. Young people need to be provided with an appropriate setting for, and oversight of, homework and to be encouraged to do it. They cannot reasonably be expected to study effectively in a room where the television is on or where other people are talking or playing. They will need at a minimum a table and chair and a quiet environment. Provision of study time and appropriate facilities such as access to reference books should be increased when children are taking public examinations.

1.111. Those carrying on homes should ensure that an appropriate selection of books and other reading material is available in the home. Staff should encourage young people to join their local library.

1.112. It is sometimes too readily accepted that further education is not appropriate for young people in homes. This belief needs to be countered forcefully. Young people who have the ability should be encouraged most strongly to continue their education beyond compulsory school age. Young people in homes are frequently considerably disadvantaged. Obtaining a good education can be the key to vastly improving their chances in life. Staff in homes need to emphasise the value of education and to promote the merits of making the most of all opportunities for further education and training. Every encouragement should be given to young people to undertake higher education when they have demonstrated ability to benefit from it.

1.113. If the language or form of language that a child has commonly spoken with his parents or those caring for him is different to the language commonly spoken in the home, those carrying on the home should make suitable arrangements to ensure that the child has the opportunity as far as is practicable to retain and develop this language or form of language in accordance with his wishes.

1.114. The guidance in this Volume applies to Community Homes with Education on the Premises just as to all children's homes. Separate guidance will be issued in due course on factors specific to Community Homes with Education on the Premises. In the meantime regard should continue to be had to the guidance in DH Circular 42/73 dated 31 August 1973 (Children and Young Persons Act 1969 – Arrangements for Education in Community Homes).

Employment and Training

1.115. Regulation 10 requires those responsible for homes to assist with the making of, and give effect to, arrangements made with respect to the continued education, training and employment of young people over statutory school age accommodated in the homes. Staff in homes have a very important role to play in preparing young people for working life and in assisting them to obtain and remain in suitable training or employment. As young people approach school leaving age arrangements concerning further education, training and employment will figure increasingly in their care plans. It will be the task of staff in the home to help to make, and give effect to, these arrangements. They should be concerned to ensure that any employment or training or work experience placement provides a working environment which meets Health and Safety requirements and is legal.

1.116. Young people in homes which are not schools may be expected to experience more than usual difficulties in finding employment or training and may often need support and encouragement beyond that which might normally be given by a caring parent. The task of helping young people to obtain suitable training, education or employment may be one of the most difficult and time consuming undertaken by staff. They will need to make rigorous efforts to counter the low self esteem and lack of self confidence which is often found in young people in such homes. The young people will frequently feel insecure and very anxious about their work prospects. They will require reassurance that finding a job or training is not something they have to tackle alone but that they will receive assistance and support from the staff in the home in their efforts.

1.117. Young people will not necessarily know what they want to do when they reach school leaving age. It is one of the responsibilities of staff to explore ideas with them and to give them help in obtaining information about as wide a range of education, training or work opportunities as possible.

Discussions between staff, school and young people, and, where possible, parents about finding employment need to have started well before school leaving age is attained. Staff will need to ensure that they are well acquainted with the young person's interests and aptitudes if they are to be able to guide them effectively in their consideration of the various options open to them. In boarding schools careers education and guidance should be the joint concern of boarding staff and teachers with special responsibility for this area of the school curriculum.

1.118. For those young people who choose to enter work rather than further education, it is important for staff in homes to have good links with careers advisers, Job Centres and employment agencies, the major local employers and to have accurate, up to date knowledge about local employment prospects. Staff should be ready and willing to provide help with the completion of application forms and to assist with preparation for interviews so that young people are able to present themselves to advantage. Care needs to be taken to ensure that they are enabled to arrive in good time for interviews, that they are appropriately dressed and groomed and that they are sent off with words of encouragement. In boarding schools, staff should be aware of a broad range of career opportunities and any qualifications needed.

1.119. Not all young people will achieve the position of their choice on leaving school. However, all are required to be engaged in work, education or training (or a combination of them) full time. Staff need to be aware of the range of options available and be prepared to help young people to see the desirability of acquiring the appropriate skills, attitudes and qualifications, including the NVQ, so as to increase the likelihood of their obtaining full time employment in the future. Some young people will need sympathy and caring support to cope with initial disappointment and to adjust their original aims should these prove to be unrealistic. Many will also need help to adapt to and cope with a new lifestyle as student or worker.

1.120. Staff will need to familiarise themselves with current procedures for registering for employment and for making claims for benefit. They should respond to requests to accompany young people to interviews with Government agencies and offer assistance with completion of forms where this would be helpful.

Religious Observance

1.121. Regulation 11 requires that each child is, as far as is practicable, to have an opportunity to attend such religious services and receive such instructions as are appropriate to the religious persuasion to which the child may belong. The regulation also requires that the child be provided with facilities for religious observance for example special diets and clothing.

1.122. Persons in charge of children's homes should ensure that enquiries are made into the religious and cultural background of each child as part of planning the child's admission and settling in. Special efforts must be made to ensure that important aspects of a child's cultural and religious heritage are not lost at this crucial stage of his life. Enquiries should be made of the parents, those who looked after the child previously, persons in contact with the child and the Local Authority responsible for arranging accommodation. This information should be recorded in the child case record.

1.123. Positive steps should then be made to provide facilities to allow the child to practise his religion in a manner appropriate to his age. The extent to which care staff can do this directly will of course depend upon their own religious persuasion. It may be necessary to help a child make contact with a local church or group of adherents to the child's religion. Great sensitivity may be needed and the child's own family should be asked to assist. If the child is in close contact with his own family it is possible that he could join his family for religious services. A number of homes which are schools have been founded by particular religious groups. It is important that full details of the nature of religious observance are given in the school's prospectus so that parents and children are fully aware of the religious background and practices of the school. It is also important that SSDs have such information so that they may be made aware of particular matters concerning religious observance and practice before visits are made.

1.124. It may be necessary to allow a child special privacy in order to pray during the course of the day, or to build a small shrine somewhere within the home. Obviously such requirements may impact on other children and will therefore need to be given careful consideration. The ideal may not be possible but it is essential that the need is recognised and the child feels that every possible consideration is being given to respect for his religion.

Catering Arrangements

1.125. Regulation 12 requires that children in homes should be provided with food in adequate quantities properly prepared, wholesome and nutritious and for some reasonable choice to be provided so far as is practicable. Special dietary needs due to health, religious persuasion, racial origin or cultural background must be met.

1.126. Appropriate equipment, crockery, cutlery and storage facilities etc must be provided.

1.127. It is vital to ensure that a varied diet is provided to include all the essential nutrients required for normal growth and development, and that sufficient food is provided to allow children to attain or maintain an appropriate height or weight ratio for their age. Diets should therefore contain a mixture of many different foods.

1.128. Food preferences are established in childhood and may be difficult to change later in life. It is therefore important that children are encouraged to try a wide variety of foods and to be prepared to try unfamiliar food.

1.129. The menus provided should incorporate a reasonable choice, within the limits of the budget available to the home, to allow account to be taken of the individual preferences of children in the home. Each child in the home will have his own individual needs, which may relate to his racial, cultural or religious background, physical or other disability, or special dietary needs because of conditions such as diabetes. Account should therefore be taken of the particular needs of each child in the home, whatever they may be, and appropriate arrangements made.

1.130. In many family homes the kitchen finds itself the focal point of the home. Likewise, in a children's home, meals, cooking and the preparation of food are important parts of a child's day, whether this is a shared activity or not. In homes which are not schools the part of the home where this is done should as far as possible be like an ordinary domestic kitchen. Where appropriate, young children should be encouraged to help out with the preparation of a meal, or to prepare their own snacks and beverages, although such activities should take place under the close supervision of a member of staff. Children in the home should also be involved in the planning of menus for the home where possible, and account taken of their wishes and preferences.

1.131. In homes which are schools the kitchen facilities will need to reflect the size and nature of the school. For example, where large numbers of day pupils as well as boarders receive a mid-day meal large-scale catering facilities will be needed and contract caterers may be employed.

1.132. The person responsible for providing meals in the home will not, in the majority of homes, be the head of the home or boarding house. It is therefore important that the person with overall responsibility for the management and delivery of meals in the home takes account of the operational guidance in the following paragraphs.

1.133. Meal times are a chance for social contact, as is the shared preparation of food, although care should be taken not to limit this to a fixed ritual. Generally staff should eat with the children. Depending on the size and nature of the home, there should be some flexibility over meal times and patterns. It may for example, be appropriate for the times and content of meals to be varied according to schools times, weekends and holidays. It should also be possible for children to be allowed to have visiting friends or relatives stay for meals where this is considered to be appropriate.

1.134. However small the home, it is important to plan and outline a week's menu in advance and to record it in the menu book. If any dishes are altered, for instance to take advantage of bargains, the changes must also be noted in the menu book. Larger homes may find it more convenient to plan menus on a three or four week cycle. Compiling a menu in advance will help ensure that a balanced variety of dishes is available, provide a sound basis for the ordering of provisions, maintain a record of the food served and assist with the control of costing and budgeting.

1.135. When considering the content of the menu, it will be equally important to ensure that proper recipes are available for the dishes involved, especially where more than 10 people are being catered for. In this connection, the Department has issued a document entitled "Catering for Health: The Recipe File" which may be of assistance in the preparation of menus. A copy of the document is available from local District Health Authorities, or from the Department (EHF 4(A)), Hannibal House, Elephant and Castle, London SE1.

1.136. Shopping for food is an important life skill, and wherever possible the children in the home should be involved in the food purchasing process, particularly where this would for example help them to prepare for independent living. In larger homes, where much of the purchasing for general use is by contract or through wholesale suppliers, it may not of course be practicable to include the children in this part of the process. Where this is so however particular attention should be given to assisting the children concerned to attain the necessary skills involved at a relevant level.

1.137. Dependent on the size and structure of the home, there will be certain limitations and practicalities to be taken into account when operating a large scale kitchen in effectively a domestic environment. In particular, the criteria involved in the timing and temperature of food alter significantly when more than 10 people are being catered for at any one time. In such circumstances it is difficult to sustain domestic catering practices, since the quantities of food involved will be larger, and the "cook to customer" ratio greatly increased. In addition, the length of time that food is lying about, either in a prepared or cooked state, will be longer, as well the time required to cook through or to cool down the larger quantities of food involved. There will also be greater quantities of food debris to be disposed of, and a greater risk of contamination.

1.138. This is not to say however that factors such as attention to detail in preparation and cooking practices, the creation of interesting tastes and textures and attention to the appearance of the finished dish should necessarily suffer when catering for larger numbers. Indeed, it is these skills that can add the domestic touch in such circumstances.

1.139. As indicated earlier the shared preparation of food is a chance for social contact. In smaller homes, where the kitchen layout is more of a domestic nature, it should be possible for children to participate in the preparation of a meal. In large homes however, particularly where there is a central main kitchen, this may not be possible since the kitchen may well contain large items of catering and light industrial equipment which children would not be permitted to use under Health and Safety at Work legislation. In such circumstances small kitchen areas, equipped with ordinary domestic cookers and washing up facilities should be provided near to a dining or sitting area, to allow children to be able to prepare their own food, snacks and beverages, under the close supervision of care staff where appropriate.

1.140. It is important that all staff involved in the preparation and service of food within the home should undergo periodic training in safe hygienic practices and good food handling techniques, and that such training is regularly reviewed and monitored.

1.141. The person carrying on the home must ensure that adequate practices and procedures are identified to minimise the risk of illness, whether food or non food related, and accidents. Any outbreak of illness, in particular food related illness, should be notified to the person carrying on the home by any person in charge as soon as is practicable. Depending on the particular circumstances, it may also be appropriate to notify the local Environmental Health Officer. Food samples should be saved. Adequate procedures should also be identified by the person carrying on the home for the containment and eventual termination of any outbreak of illness, particularly where this is, or is thought to be, food related.

1.142. The design, layout, equipment, working practices and procedures of kitchens and meal service areas must be of sufficient standard to satisfy Food Hygiene and Food Safety legislation as well as conforming to the Health and Safety at Work Act 1974 and any other statutory requirements. The person in charge of the home should ensure that all staff and, where appropriate children, in the home are aware of the requirements of the legislation and the procedures to be followed.

Provision of Clothing and Personal Requisites

1.143. Children should be well clothed. Regulation 13 requires that clothes should be purchased for children in homes, preferably by the children being enabled to purchase them themselves. This should be done on an individual basis through normal shopping arrangements. Going shopping is an essential part of life, and this experience should be a regular occurrence for children being looked after in children's homes. It is an occasion when a child should learn to make choices. There is no place generally for bulk buying or special purchasing arrangements. Children should have access to the ordinary range of toiletries, cosmetics and sanitary protection and should be entitled to exercise their own preferences. In some boarding schools the choice of clothing for leisure purposes will be mainly undertaken by children and parents in school holidays. Bulk buying by the school may reduce the cost of school uniform or other items such as sports kit which are needed by all children.

1.144. Younger children should be taken shopping, preferably either singly or in pairs, so that the child can receive the fullest possible attention from the care staff in guiding the child to make his choices. This may be difficult but should never be avoided by imposing a predetermined selection upon the child.

1.145. Older children may prefer to do their own shopping without care staff but where appropriate they should be offered the opportunity to be accompanied. It is desirable that care staff facilitate prior discussion of the proposed purchases in order to help the child clarify his or her ideas and to be aware of limits on spending.

1.146. Those in charge of children's homes should take steps to ensure that the significance of a child's religious, cultural and racial background for his choice of clothing and other personal requisites is fully understood by care staff. For example, a muslim girl may be expected to cover her legs with leggings or trousers. This may mean making specific enquiries of parents, previous care givers or, if necessary some other source of knowledge.

1.147. Care staff should be aware of the special needs of black (Afro Caribbean) children in relation to their hair and skin care, and these children should be assisted to purchase the necessary preparations.

1.148. Children should be allowed to enjoy making spontaneous purchases out of their pocket money. Normal everyday ways of making payment in shops should be used, ie cash, cheques, credit or debit card. Order books should not be used because they stigmatize the child and restrict choice to specific shops. However, some boarding schools provide thrift or tuck shops where purchases may be put on pupils' accounts. There are obvious dangers in large sums of cash being carried about, and where major items are being purchased it may be preferable for a staff member to accompany an older child in order to write a cheque than to take unnecessary risk.

1.149. Where appropriate, consideration should be given to arranging for clothing allowances to be paid into individual post office accounts from which children can make withdrawals under the supervision judged to be appropriate in each case.

1.150. Girls should be allowed to keep their own supply of sanitary requisites. It is not acceptable for such items to be handed out singly when needed. Girls should not have to approach male care workers to request sanitary provision.

Fire Precautions

1.151. Regulation 14 makes various requirements of responsible authorities in relation to fire precautions. Responsible authorities have to notify certain particulars to their local fire authority. Responsible authorities must provide adequate fire precautions, prevention, equipment, fire drill arrangements. Staff and residents in homes must be made aware of fire procedures. Where a fire causes the evacuation of a home or part of a home the person in charge is required to notify the responsible authority. In boarding schools DES requirements on fire safety also apply.

Records on Children

1.152. Under Regulation 8 of the Arrangements for Placement of Children (General) Regulations 1991 (Annex B) a written case record on each child must be established by the authority responsible for the placement of the child. This applies in respect of every child accommodated in any home governed by the Children's Homes Regulations. Guidance on this requirement is given in Chapter 2 (paragraphs 2.78 et seq). In addition Regulation 15 of the Children's Homes Regulations requires that the responsible authority should arrange that an individual case record is maintained in each children's home on each child in the home. Boarding schools are also required under Education legislation to maintain individual records for all pupils, including boarding pupils and conform with regulations concerning admissions and attendance which apply to registered schools. (The Pupils Registration Regulations 1956 as amended by the Pupils Registration (Amendment) Regulations 1988 prescribe the current requirements.)

1.153. The papers constituting the case record should be held in a good quality file capable of being divided into sections to hold different categories of information. The file should be able to hold certificates, photographs, school reports and other important papers which a child will accumulate during his life. The case file should be held in a steel lockable cabinet and access to the records controlled in such a way as to ensure confidentiality and security against loss or theft.

1.154. The case record in the home is of primary importance to the child because it will contain information about his or her life at a time when family relationships are strained, disrupted or even destroyed. It becomes the child's "memory" in lieu of parents' recollections. Details, which at the time might appear trivial, may become very significant as the child grows up and needs to look back to piece together and make sense of a disrupted childhood.

1.155. The child should be aware of the existence of his case file, have access to it, and be encouraged to contribute to the record. Unlike family based care, it is not possible for a children's home to do a professional job without records of this sort. It is therefore desirable to make a virtue out of a necessity, and make the case record a significant and positive feature of the child's life. Boarding schools should consider encouraging pupil self-assessment as part of a record of achievement held in the pupil file.

1.156. The case record is essential for those responsible for making plans for the child as a tool for assembling information and setting out proposals. The file should be read prior to reviews or planning meetings and information extracted and presented to the meeting, so that this contribution to decision making is based on sound documented information, and not insubstantial impressions or opinion.

1.157. Regulation 15 requires that the record should so far as practicable include the information specified in Schedule 2 to the Regulations.

1.158. Much of the information in a child's children's home file will be a duplication of that held as required under the Arrangements Regulations. Homes are required to maintain a register under the Arrangement Regulations – Regulation 10(2). The information collected in the children's home file will be more detailed and personal to the child. It is vitally important that this information is kept safe and is passed on with the child when he moves on from the home. How this is done will depend on the child's destination, and different components of the file may be passed on to different locations for safe keeping. For example, if a child moves into a long term foster home, it will probably be appropriate for the child's personal papers, such as school reports, certificates etc, and medical information to go with him to the foster home, whilst the continuous record of salient information may best be kept in the local authority, voluntary or private agency's central records or kept with the social worker's file. If a child goes into the penal system it will be best for the care authority to hold the whole file on the child's behalf until he is released.

1.159. When a child leaves a children's home, and his case record is passed on, the person in charge of the children's home should ensure that precise information is recorded as to where the file, or components of the record, have been transferred.

1.160. Written entries in the case record should be signed and dated and the name of the signatory clearly identified. Those making entries must adhere to professional standards. Information should be factual, accurate and clear. The record should not include gratuitous value judgements; colloquialisms should, when thought to be the most apt description in the circumstances, be either reported speech or clearly indicated by inverted commas. Records should separate fact from opinion, but it is helpful for staffs' judgement to be recorded. It is particularly vital that a child's case record does not include stigmatising descriptive terms such as "delinquent", "maladjusted" or "uncontrollable" which carry the risk of "labelling" that child.

1.161. A child of sufficient understanding should be allowed regular access to the file consistent with its safe keeping and the best interests of the child. He should read or be told what has been recorded unless knowledge of the material will cause harm to the child or to a third party. A child should be encouraged to record his own observations on the case record including when there is disagreement about an entry in the file. If the children's home needs to hold information to which a child cannot have access, this must be held in a separate part of the file and clearly marked as confidential to staff. When such material is of a highly sensitive nature consideration should be given as to whether it should be held on the children's home file at all.

1.162. The Regulation requires that these records should be retained for at least seventy-five years from the birth of the child or, if less, for fifteen years after the child's death.

1.163. Regulation 16 requires the provision by those responsible for homes to the guardian ad litem for a child accommodated in the home of records and information about the child.

Records on homes

1.164. Regulation 17 requires responsible authorities to maintain in each home the records specified in Schedule 3 to the Regulations and to ensure they are kept up-to-date. The records must be retained for at least fifteen years except for menus which are to be kept for only one year. Entries in records should be signed and dated and the name of the signatory clearly identified. They should be couched in appropriate language and should record the actions of staff in the events described as well as those of the children.

Regulations and Guidance

1.165. Under Regulation 18 a copy of the Children's Homes Regulations and associated guidance (including that in this Volume) is required to be kept in each home and made available to staff, children, parents etc. In the case of poor readers the main features of the regulations may be explained to them as appropriate in language appropriate to their age and understanding.

Notification of Significant Events

1.166. Regulation 19 requires that certain significant events must be notified by the responsible authority to children's parents et al and those paying for the placement (frequently a local authority) and in certain circumstances to the district health authority, the 'local' local authority, the registration authority, the Secretary of State and the police. The events that require to be notified are detailed in Regulation 19(2).

1.167. These provisions include the requirement that the responsible authority must notify the Secretary of State of

(a) the death of a child other than one placed by a local authority (these should be notified under paragraph 20(1) of Schedule 2 to the Act to the Secretary of State). (Notification should be sent to CS3A, Room 233, Wellington House, 133–155 Waterloo Road, London SE1 8UG).

(b) inappropriate conduct by a staff member such that he or she might not be a suitable person for work involving children. (This is the DH "consultancy" service – notification in these cases should be made to CS2B, Room 213, Wellington House, 133–155 Waterloo Road, London SE1 8UG). (Homes which are also schools are required also to notify the Department of Education and Science where staff are dismissed for misconduct or resign in circumstances where they might have been dismissed).

(c) serious harm. This would include where the responsible body believes that abuse of a child has occurred. Guidance about child abuse is given in paragraphs 1.179–1.192 of this Chapter. (Notification should be sent to CS2C, Room 216, Wellington House, 133–155 Waterloo Road, London SE1 8UG).

Absence of a Child without Authority

1.168. Under Regulation 20 the responsible authority must provide to all staff and children written procedures to be followed when a child is absent without permission. In the case of very young children and poor readers the main features of the procedure should be explained to them in language appropriate to their age and understanding. (Schools are reminded that in the case of persistent truancy or abscondences they have an obligation to give details to the LEA in which the school is located.)

Absence of Person in Charge

1.169. Regulation 21 requires the registration authority to be notified four weeks in advance of absences of four weeks or more of the person in charge of a voluntary or registered home. Shorter periods of notice may be accepted by the responsible authority if they think it reasonable in the circumstances. The Regulation details particulars to be notified. These need not be provided where no children are accommodated during the absence of the person in charge but must be if any child is in fact admitted during such a period. The Regulation also provides for what is required when the person in charge returns.

Accountability and Visiting on Behalf of Responsible Authority

1.170. Regulation 22 requires monthly visits to all homes by those responsible, or by their representatives (not being someone employed at the home). Written reports of such visits are to be made to those responsible for the homes. The visits should not be made by anyone employed at the home and a written report of such visits should be made to those responsible for the homes. An important purpose of these visits is to ensure that the day to day conduct of the home is seen by someone not involved in its operation and who can provide an independent report to the responsible authority. The visits should be unannounced and reports of visits should be seen by the responsible authority without amendment or deletion. In the case of a local authority home this will usually mean that the report should be presented to an appropriate committee of members of the authority. In the case of homes managed by voluntary organisations, trustees or corporate bodies the report should be presented to the responsible body or a sub-committee of its members. In the case of a registered home the report should be seen by the proprietor personally. Before each visit the responsible authority should provide the visitor with copies of reports of visits made in the preceding 6 months. The responsible authority should also provide the visitor with guidance as to the purpose of visiting and the items to be covered. These should always include a check of the records of sanctions imposed on children, the home's daily log and the physical condition of the premises. But visitors must always be given opportunity for private conversation with any child, other family member, or staff member who requests it; and should always report on their observations of the children.

Community Homes – Secretary of State's Directions

1.171. The Secretary of State is empowered by Regulation 23 to direct that a child being looked after by a local authority should be accommodated in a controlled or assisted community home when no places in the home are available to the authority looking after the child. Directions may specify action to be taken in respect of the child by the local authority or voluntary organisation responsible for the community home. These provisions simply continue provisions in the Child Care Act 1980.

Registration of Voluntary Homes

1.172. Regulation 24 and Schedule 4 set out what is required in applications for registration of voluntary homes. The registering authority remains the Secretary of State. (Applications should be addressed to CS2C, Room 216, Wellington House, 133–155 Waterloo Road, London SE1 8UG.)

Notification of Particulars with Respect to Voluntary Homes

1.173. Regulation 31 makes provisions regarding particulars to be notified on establishment of a voluntary home (listed in Schedule 7 to the Regulations) and annual returns.

Application for Registration as Registered Children's Homes

1.174. Regulations 25 to 30 govern application for registration, (including particulars required under Schedule 5 to the Regulations), limits on numbers of children that may be accommodated in such homes, particulars to be provided on annual review, inspection, cancellation of registration and change of person in charge. Registration continues until it is removed, and local authorities must inspect the homes at specified intervals, – before registration and then at annual review and on one other occasion in the year. These latter visits must not be notified. There is no requirement that other visits should be notified. Local authorities have the power to charge a reasonable fee for registration under Schedule 6 of the Act, paragraph 1(2)(b). (The intention is that local authorities may recoup, through fees, the cost to the authorities of administering the registration of registered children's homes but they should not provide the local authority with a profit or take account of the costs of appeals.) Local authorities may, under paragraph 4 of Schedule 6 to the Act, cancel registration where a home ceases to meet the requirements for registration. It is an offence to carry on an unregistered children's home without reasonable excuse (section 63(10) of the Act). Schedule 14 paragraph 32(2) provides a three month period after the coming into force of section 63 for application to be made in respect of homes accommodating children placed by local authorities. For homes accommodating other children a similar three month period would, in the Department's view, seem to be reasonable.

Local Authority Visits

1.175. Regulations 32 to 34 govern the duties of local authorities under section 62 and section 64(4) to satisfy themselves as to the welfare of children in voluntary and registered (ie private) children's homes in their areas. Placements are also covered by the Arrangements for Placement of Children (General) Regulations 1991. (See Chapter 2 and Annex B.) Regulations 32 and 33 specify the periods within which the local authority must make first, and subsequent, visits according to the circumstances.

1.176. Regulation 34 imposes requirements for visits including a requirement that an officer of the local authority should see the child during the visit unless exceptionally this is unnecessary. Relevant case papers and records must be read and signed and dated by the visiting officer, who must also make a written report and make it available to those specified in Regulation 34(1)(c).

1.177. The duties imposed by sections 61 and 62 of the Act will apply in respect of *non-maintained special schools.* These are all provided by voluntary orgainsations and are governed by the Education Act 1944 section 9(5). They are not approved under section 11(3)(a) of the Education Act 1981. They are not independent schools and are therefore not governed by section 87 of the Children Act. However LASSDs are advised, in undertaking their duties under section 62 in relation to non-maintained special schools, to follow the general guidance in Volume 5 in this series regarding the welfare of children in boarding schools. Attention is also drawn to the last sentence of paragraph 1.10.

Revocation of Former Regulations

1.178.Regulations 35 revokes the previous child care regulations governing local authority and voluntary childrens homes.

CHILD ABUSE IN CHILDREN'S HOMES

1.179. All those concerned with children's homes must be aware of the possibility that a child may be abused during the period he is in a home. Staff in homes have key roles in identifying abuse when it occurs and in bringing it to the immediate attention of the responsible authorities. Responsible authorities must ensure that the home has clear policies and written procedures for responding to abuse which are integrated with local procedures agreed by the Area Child Protection Committee. They must also ensure that staff have adequate training in recognising abuse and in the home's procedures. Staff in homes should have routine links with other agencies concerned with child protection; the SSD, schools, hospitals, GPs etc and should not work in isolation from them. Abuse always constitutes serious harm to the child and formal notification of it must be given as required by Regulation 19 (see also para 1.167(c)).

1.180. Whenever staff in a children's home receive evidence that a child is suffering or has suffered abuse, they have no choice other than to pass that information on to a person with the authority to investigate and evaluate the information. Normally this means informing the local social services department who will in turn involve other agencies, including the police or NSPCC who may become involved with the investigation according to the circumstances and local arrangements. The home's written guidance to staff should describe the sort of circumstances in which referral could and should be made and should identify exactly to whom referral should be made. There may be unusual circumstances in which it is best to inform the police first, for example when there is direct evidence that a serious crime has been committed or the child is in such immediate danger that the protective powers or the police are needed. In such circumstances the SSD should always be informed immediately as well. Guidance on the duties of agencies in investigating child abuse was given in the booklet "Working Together. A guide to arrangements for inter-agency co-operation for the protection of children from abuse", published by HMSO (ISBN 0 11 321154 6). This is currently being revised and will include guidance specific to abuse in homes. A copy of "Working Together" should be kept in every children's home.

1.181. Those responsible for running the home should produce a written statement which gives procedural guidance to all staff on what to do when they receive possible evidence of child abuse. This document will need to be written in consultation with the Area Child Protection Committee. The Social Services Department, through its Child Protection Coordinator, should play an active part in promoting the development of child protection policies in residential settings, in ensuring that there is adequate continuing training for residential staff and in ensuring that they are aware of the specialists they can turn to for advice or as a first contact in times of crisis. Abuse occurs in a range of circumstances. The child may have suffered abuse whilst away from the children's home, for example at the family home, or at a friends or at school. The child may also have been abused within the children's home by another child or a member of staff or by a visitor. Whatever the circumstances, it is essential that first priority is given to protecting the child and then setting in motion the investigation through making the reports described above.

1.182. Some children may seek to tell staff, in confidence, that they have been abused. Staff must understand that it is not possible to give children absolute guarantees of confidentiality because that could put staff in the untenable position of being in possession of information that a crime has been committed without the necessary freedom to report it, and it may make it impossible for the child to be protected from further abuse. It is good general child care practice to resist being drawn into secretive and collusive relationships with children. It is essential that a relationship is built up between children and staff such that children feel that they can trust staff to do the best thing with a disclosure of abuse. This means that the child feels his or her wishes about what should happen are taken into account and that the consequences of disclosure do not make matters worse for the child.

1.183. To make it possible for staff to feel confident about the reassurances that they can give to children, those in charge of children's homes should ensure that they are fully abreast of local practice and procedures and those of the placing Authorities of the children they care for. Heads of homes should make known to the SSD Child Protection Coordinator and the Area Child Protection Committee their need to be able to be very clear with children about what they can expect to be involved in following a disclosure of abuse. It is also important for staff to know what to do if they believe insufficient action has been taken in relation to a suspicion or allegation of abuse.

1.184. When a child in a children's home abuses another child, a very clear distinction will need to be made between, on the one hand, behaviour which amounts to serious physical assault, intimidation and sexual assault which requires external child protection intervention and possibly criminal investigation and, on the other hand, normal childhood behaviour or sexual exploration which should be dealt with by care staff. Abuse will need to be reported and investigated as with any other abuse. A child in a children's home has the same rights to protection by the police and care agencies as any child. It is important that training and written guidance addresses the boundaries between behaviour which can be regarded as "normal", and behaviour which cannot. Bullying or intimidation also need to be taken into account in training and guidance. There needs to be continuing professional discussion between staff, with appropriate managerial or supervisory support, to re-affirm what is normal behaviour.

1.185. This has implications for all the children in the home. Other children might have been abused by the same child but not told staff or have known about the abuse but felt too afraid or guilty to tell anybody. Care authorities and those with parental responsibility for all children affected by the incident should be informed and involved in discussions about handling the situation. It is important that staff in the children's home co-operate fully with external investigators in order that the full extent of abuse is discovered and that the children caught up in the problem receive proper counselling and the implications of the incident(s) for the future plans of each child are considered methodically. Staff need supervisory or managerial support to deal effectively with this process and avoid defensiveness. In this way the precipitate removal of children, which may not be in their long term interests, is most likely to be avoided.

1.186. It has also to be recognised that children in children's homes can be abused by a member of staff. What has been said above applies equally well to this situation. The immediate local authority, the care authorities using the home, the police and those with parental responsibility for children in the home must all be informed. It is obviously in the best interests of the children and the home for there to be the fullest possible co-operation with the investigating authorities. There is a need for advice to junior staff to encourage them, when necessary, to share with the SSD their concerns about senior staff. This is very difficult for them to do and they need to be reassured that it is the right thing to do. Procedures which ensure this should be set out in the written guidance to staff and be dealt with in training and supervision.

1.187. Those managing the home will also need to consider what steps are required within their disciplinary procedures with respect to the staff member concerned. It would normally be appropriate for the staff member to be suspended from duty either on the grounds of the possibility of the alleged abuse recurring or concern that his presence might interfere with the investigation. It is also important to ensure that a member of staff in this situation is advised of the need to seek his own advice on protecting his interests in relation to both criminal and disciplinary investigations and proceedings.

1.188. It is important for those managing homes, in situations where a member of staff is alleged to have abused a child in the home, to appreciate that each of three strands of investigation has to be followed through to a positive conclusion:

i. The inter-departmental and inter-agency child protection investigation which should proceed to a case conference where decisions will be made on the action necessary to ensure the continuing protection of the child. Decisions will be based on professional judgements of the information presented to the conference. Any court proceedings to protect the child will be based on the balance of probabilities.

ii The police investigation of whether a crime has been committed. In order to prosecute, there must be sufficient evidence to support a case that an offence has been committed beyond reasonable doubt. It is most important to understand that if there is insufficient evidence to support a prosecution, it does not mean that there is no need to take steps to protect the child, including care proceedings, or that the member of staff concerned should not face disciplinary proceedings by his employers.

iii The employer's disciplinary procedure should discover whether the staff member has been guilty of misconduct or gross misconduct in the course of his duties as an employee. In addition to the facts concerning what the staff member is alleged to have done to the child, employers will need to consider his performance in such matters as carrying out procedures, making proper records, and reporting incidents to others. These factors may be secondary to the alleged abuse but nontheless vitally important to good practice and management which is designed to support good child care in the home. The employer should also review the recruitment and supervision of the staff member and undertake any further checks that may be appropriate.

1.189. It is essential that the common facts of the alleged abuse are applied independently to each of the three strands of investigation. The fact that a prosecution is not possible, does not mean that action in relation to child protection or employee discipline is not feasible or necessary. The outcome of one strand of investigation may have a bearing on another. The important thing is that a definite conclusion is reached in each case.

1.190. It is essential that all staff in children's homes, including agency staff, receive induction and initial training in the recongnition of child abuse and the home's procedures for reporting it. Staff should also receive follow up training which is appropriate to the aims and objectives of the home and is closely linked in with the training initiatives of the Area Child Protection Committee. They may need some separate training but on many occasions this should be undertaken jointly with others engaged in this work.

1.191. It is essential that staff caring for children who have been abused receive specific training and supportive professional supervision. Staff should be made aware of how the experience of being sexually abused affects the way a child relates to adults, so that they can take full account of this in the way they respond. Those responsible for children's homes should also give consideration to the need for external consultancy when staff are caring for children who have been abused or in cases of particular seriousness and complexity.

1.192. A copy of the Area Child Protection Committee's Child Protection Procedures and the procedures prepared by the responsible SSD, should be available to all staff in the home and steps should be taken to ensure they read and understand these and are able to act on them.

OTHER GUIDANCE

Health and Safety

1.193. Health and Safety legislation must be complied with in children's homes as appropriate. The home should have a written statement of its safety policy.

Checks on Registration etc

1.194. Local authorities should, when placing children in voluntary and registered homes check that the homes are registered ie with the Secretary of State (DH CS2C, Room 216, Wellington House, 133–155 Waterloo Road, London SE1 8UG) if a voluntary home, and with the local authority (their own authority or another authority if an 'out of county' placement) if a registered children's home. The SSD should take all appropriate steps to ensure that it is well informed about the practice of the home before making the placement including consulting any published report about it. Similar considerations should apply to residential placements in schools, nursing homes and residential care homes. In these cases, it would be good practice to consider the views of both the "home" and "local" Local Education Authority in the case of schools and of the Health Authority in the case of nursing homes. In relation to schools published reports would include any produced by the "local" Social Services Department as a result of their duties under Section 87 and in some cases HMI reports.

1.195. These sections deal with children accommodated:

(a) by health and education authorities;

(b) in residential care, nursing or mental nursing homes (ie homes governed by the Registered Homes Act 1984).

1.196. The purpose of these sections is to ensure that the welfare of children being provided with accommodation by any health authority or local education authority (section 85), or in any residential care home, nursing home or mental nursing home (section 86) is being adequately safeguarded and promoted. These sections are an important part of the intention of the Act to ensure that children who are, for example, mentally handicapped or disabled and therefore may be particularly vulnerable are brought into the mainstream of child care legislation. (But see paragraph 1.9(iv) above re registration under Registered Homes Act 1984). Its intention is to make sure children are not placed in schools, hospital facilities, nursing homes and so on for more than three months without the local authority social services department being notified so that they can assess whether any form of intervention to promote or safeguard the child's welfare is necessary. School holidays will not count towards the three months. This means that this section will not generally be expected to apply to children accommodated by local education authorities. Section 85 is also not expected to apply to children who go home at the weekend. Where LASSDs are considering placing children in a psychiatric unit, hospital or registered mental nursing home on a Children Act secure order it is particularly important to ensure that consent by the children to any treatment, including the administration of drugs is given following agreement by, and with the full understanding of, the child. Treatment and consent to treatment may then only be given in line with Part IV of the Mental Health Act and staff practice informed by the Code of Practice of the Mental Health Act. Unless treatment with sedative drugs is clearly needed for a child's medical condition SSDs should take into account an establishment's practice in this respect when making placements. SSDs should be cautious about exposing a child to a regime where sedation is used to control behaviour in any case and should be very cautious where major tranquillisers (eg Largactil) are involved. In such cases it may be appropriate to consider whether formal admission under the Mental Health Act would be a more appropriate way of protecting the child's interests. This would require the strict criteria laid down in the Mental Health Act to be met. (See also paragraphs 1.91(v) and 1.102.)

1.197. Sections 85(1) and 86(1) require the accommodating authority or the person carrying on the home, as appropriate, to notify the responsible authority if a child is provided with accommodation for a consecutive period of at least three months, or if it is intended to do so. In so far as health and local education authorities are concerned, the responsible authority is defined for this purpose as being the local social services authority within whose area the child was resident immediately before being accommodated or, if the child was apparently not resident in any local authority area, the local social services authority within whose area the accommodation being provided is situated. Persons carrying on residential care homes, nursing homes or mental nursing homes are required to notify the local social services authority within whose area the home is being carried on. Notification is also required under section 85(2) and 86(2) when a child ceases to be so accommodated.

1.198. Once a local authority have been notified under the terms of these sections that a child is being accommodated, the authority are required by section 85(4) or 86(3), as appropriate, to take such steps as are reasonably practicable to enable them to determine whether the child's welfare is being adequately safeguarded and promoted.

1.199. In order to fulfil this requirement, it will first be necessary for the local authority to ascertain the circumstances of the particular case, to enable them to assess what steps may need to be taken. The local authority should therefore make enquiries of the education or health authority accommodating the child, or the person carring on the home in which the child is accommodated, in order to determine the circumstances of the child being cared for.

1.200. Such enquiries should be indertaken within 14 days of the authority being notified that the child is being accommodated. Initially, it may not be necessary for the enquiries to be by means of visiting the premises where the child is being accommodated, and in the first instance it may be considered reasonable to contact the authority or person carrying on the home by letter or telephone.

1.201. The authority should seek to assure themselves that contact between the child and its parents or persons with parental responsibility is adequate, having regard to the circumstances of the case. It should at least obtain written assurances from the authority or person carrying on the home that proper parental contact and responsibility is established or is being maintained. If the authority think it appropriate in the circumstances it may also consider writing to, or otherwise contacting, the parents or persons with parental responsibility directly to confirm that parental contact is being maintained and that parental responsibility is being exercised adequately to safeguard and promote the welfare of the child.

1.202. If however, the local authority become aware that parental contact with the child concerned has ceased, or other concerns come to their attention which suggest that the welfare of the child may not be adequately safeguarded or promoted, the authority should consider what steps need to be taken, having regarded to the circumstances of the case. In any event, where it appears that proper parental contact has not been maintained, or the authority have other concerns over the welfare of the child, arrangements should be made for the child to be visited as soon as possible and not later than 14 days from the date the concerns first came to the authority's attention.

1.203. Having established the circumstances of the case, the authority are also required by sections 85(4)(b) or 86(3)(b), as appropriate, to consider the extent to which (if at all) they should exercise any of their functions under the Act in respect of the particular child.

1.204. Under section 86(5) persons authorised by a local authority may enter any residential care home, nursing home or mental nursing home within the authority's area to establish whether the requirements of the section are being complied with. Thus an authority that had reason to believe for example that the home was accommodating a child without notification under section 86(1) could if the circumstances required it enter the home to ascertain whether the child was in fact being accommodated and his welfare was being adequately safeguarded and promoted. It is an offence to intentionally obstruct a person authorised by a local authority in exercise of his powers of entry.

1.205. Such powers do not exist however in respect of local health and education authority establishments. Authorities may nevertheless, wish to make suitable arrangements with such establishments in their area to be given access to the premises in order to determine that the requirements of section 85 are being complied with.

CHAPTER 2   <u>ARRANGEMENTS FOR</u>
<u>PLACEMENT OF CHILDREN</u>

2.1. This Chapter gives guidance on arrangements for placement and planning to safeguard and promote the welfare of children looked after by the local authority or accommodated by a voluntary organisation or registered children's home without the involvement of the local authority. The agency looking after or accommodating the child is henceforward referred to in this Chapter as *the responsible authority* unless otherwise indicated. The Arrangements for Placement of Children (General) Regulations and guidance reflect the emphasis in the Children Act on partnership between parents, children and the responsible authority and between the responsible authority and other agencies, as being the most effective means of meeting the needs of the individual child. These regulations and guidance together with the regulations and guidance relating to specific types of placements provide a statutory framework within which responsible authorities should work with children and families and act as good parents.

CHILDREN WHO ARE LOOKED AFTER BY THE LOCAL AUTHORITY

2.2. A child is looked after by a local authority if he is in their care by reason of a court order or is being provided with accommodation for more than 24 hours by agreement with the parents or with the child if he is aged 16 or over (section 22(1) and (2)).

2.3. Under voluntary arrangements the local authority does not obtain parental responsibility for a child looked after, but is obliged to comply with the appropriate regulations. Although a care order gives the local authority parental responsibility for the child, any person who is a parent or guardian retains their parental responsibility and may continue to exercise it to the extent that their actions are not incompatible with the care order (see section 2(8) and section 33(3)(b) of the Act). This reflects the intention underpinning the Children Act that parents should be encouraged to exercise their responsibility for their child's welfare in a constructive way and that where compulsory intervention in the family is used it should where possible enhance rather than undermine the parental role.

2.4. Children who are kept away from home under an emergency protection order (EPO) where they are accommodated by or on behalf of the local authority are "looked after" children (under an EPO the applicant has parental responsibility for the child). So too are those children on remand or under supervision with a residence requirement requiring them to live in local authority accommodation and those children in police protection or arrested and at the police's request accommodated by the local authority. These children are not in care.

Welfare

2.5. The primary duty of the local authority is to safeguard and promote the welfare of a child who is looked after and to make such use of services available for children cared for by their own parents as appears to the authority reasonable in the case of a particular child (section 22(3)(b)). Although the Child Care Act 1980 requirement in respect of promotion of a child's welfare, "throughout his childhood" is not reproduced the intention is still that both the immediate and long-term needs of the child should be considered and provided for in the local authority's planning for the child. In undertaking that planning for a child in care the local authority is required to give the same attention to the wishes and feelings of the child, parents and others as they must when providing accommodation under voluntary arrangements. The local authority should also take into account and consider fully the child's religious persuasion, racial origin and cultural and linguistic background. Children with physical and/or sensory disability or mental handicap will require particular consideration and the accommodation provided for them should not be unsuitable to the needs of the child (section 23(8)).

Family Links

2.6. When a child is being looked after by the local authority, the local authority is required to make arrangements for that child to live with a member of his family unless to do so would be impractical or inconsistent with the child's welfare (section 23(6)). "Family" in the context is any person falling within the scope of section 23(4) of the Act or a relative, friend or other significant person in the child's life (such as, where a child is in care, a person in whose favour a residence order was in force immediately before the care order was made). This requirement is intended to ensure that the Act's emphasis on the promotion of the upbringing of children within or by their families is applied equally to looked after children. The accommodation provided should be near the child's home so far as is reasonably practicable and consistent with the child's welfare (section 23(7)(a)). The provisions of paragraph 8 of Schedule 2 (provision for children living with their families) and paragraph 10 (maintenance of the family home) can be used together to achieve reunification of a family when the child is living apart from some or all of his family but is not looked after by the local authority. This would be a matter for consideration also when a local authority is notified of a child accommodated by a health or local education authority or others (sections 85 and 86 – See also Chapter 1 paragraphs 1.195 to 1.205.)

2.7. The same emphasis on the importance of family links is found in the requirements that a child be accommodated near his family home (section 23(7)(a)) and that siblings be accommodated together as long as this is practicable and consistent with each child's welfare (section 23(7)(b)).

Protection of the Public

2.8. If it appears necessary in the public interest to protect members of the public from serious injury from the actions or behaviour of a child, the local authority may exercise its powers in a manner which is not necessarily consistent with its duties under section 22. This reservation is set out in section 22(6). A further limitation on the welfare duty is contained in sections 22(7) and (8) which states that the Secretary of State may, if it is considered necessary to protect members of the public from serious injury, give directions to a local authority and, that where such directions are given the local authority shall comply with them even though to do so is inconsistent with their duties under section 22.

Arrangements for Placement of Children (General) and Review of Children's Cases Regulations

2.9. The Arrangements for Placement of Children Regulations place a new duty on local authorities, voluntary organisations and registered children's homes in making arrangements to place a child to draw up and record an individual plan for the child. (The Review of Children's Cases Regulations require that the plan is reviewed and amended as necessary on a regular basis—see Chapter 8). In these Regulations, the expression "*arrangements*" is used (see Regulation 3). This is referred to in the guidance by the social work term "*plan*". The primary purpose of planning and review is to safeguard and promote the welfare of a child living away from his family. Planning is required from the earliest possible time after recognition of need or referral where the provision of accommodation (whether under voluntary arrangements or on a compulsory basis) is likely to be necessary. Thereafter, the plan should be reviewed on an ongoing basis. All the necessary considerations for the child's welfare, including the child's wishes and feelings and the wishes and feelings of the parents and others the responsible authority are required to seek and take into account, must be given due attention.

PARTNERSHIP AND PARTICIPATION

2.10. One of the key principles of the Children Act is that responsible authorities should work in partnership with the parents of a child who is being looked after and also with the child himself, where he is of sufficient understanding, provided that this approach will not jeopardise his welfare. A second, closely related principle is that parents and children should participate actively in the decision-making process. Partnership will only be achieved if parents are advised about and given explanations of the local authority's power and duties and the actions the local authority may need to take, for example exchanges of information between relevant agencies. The general duties of responsible authorities in sections 22, 61 and 64 of the Children Act are primarily based on these principles. These duties require responsible authorities to consult parents and others and the child (where he is of sufficient understanding) before any decision is made affecting a child who is about to be or is already being looked after by a local authority, or who is accommodated in a voluntary home or registered children's home. This new approach reflects the fact that parents always retain their parental responsibility. A local authority may limit parents' exercise of that responsibility when a child is looked after by a local authority as a result of a court order, but only if it is necessary to do so to safeguard and promote the child's welfare (section 33(3)(b) and (4)).

2.11. Planning and review of a child's case with the involvement of parents will provide the basis of partnership between the responsible authorities and parents and child. The development of a successful working partnership between the responsible authorities and the parents and the child, where he is of sufficient understanding, should enable the placement to proceed positively so that the child's welfare is safeguarded and promoted.

2.12. The successful development of partnership with parents should in most cases avoid the need for care proceedings or emergency action. Although genuine partnership will be easier to achieve in the absence of compulsory measures, the same kind of approach should be taken in cases where a child is in the care of the local authority as a result of a court order. This will be achieved by:

(a) consulting and notifying the parents about decisions affecting the child;

(b) promoting contact between the child and his parents and family where it is reasonably practicable and consistent with the child's welfare; and

(c) by seeking to work with the parents to achieve a safe and stable environment for the child to return to (where this is judged feasible) or by finding a satisfactory alternative placement for the child.

PROVISION OF ACCOMMODATION BY VOLUNTARY AGREEMENT

2.13. The provision of accommodation for a child by the local authority under voluntary agreement with the parents will occur when the parents suggest that kind of arrangement to the local authority, specifically request such provision or accept proposals made by the local authority. The parents contribute their experience and knowledge of the child to the decision. The local authority brings a capacity to provide services, to co-ordinate the contribution of other agencies and to plan for and review the child's needs. Such placements fall within the scope of the Arrangements for Placement of Children Regulations which require the local authority to agree a plan with the parents for the placement of the child. The plan should take into account the wishes and feelings of the child where he is of sufficient understanding. The Review of Children's Cases Regulations require a review of that plan on a regular basis. Accommodation may also be provided to a child aged 16 or over, despite parental objection if the child agrees (section 20(5) and (11) of the Act). In these cases, the local authority will be working closely with the child to agree the plan for providing accommodation.

2.14. Agreements between parents and the responsible authority should reflect the fact that parents retain their parental responsibility. The responsible authority's responsibilities under these Regulations should not detract in any way from the parents' continuing parental responsibility. Their continuing involvement with the child and exercise of their responsiblity should be the basis of the agreed arrangements; all concerned in the arrangements should be aware of this. One agreement may cover several short-term placements such as a respite care arrangement if the conditions of Regulation 13 are satisfied (see paragraph 2.16 below and guidance on agreements in paragraphs 2.63–2.67).

CHILDREN LOOKED AFTER WHO ARE SUBJECT TO A COURT ORDER

2.15. The Arrangements for Placement of Children Regulations apply to all cases where a child subject to a court order is looked after by a local authority on a compulsory basis.

SHORT-TERM PLACEMENTS

2.16. Regulation 13 allows for a defined series of short pre-planned placements (eg for respite care, phased care and family link schemes) to be treated as a *single placement* for the application of these regulations. A plan for the child is required and all the requirements of the Regulations apply, but need not be repeated for each episode of accommodation so long as the conditions in Regulation 13 are met. The conditions in Regulation 13 are:

"(a) all the placements occur within a period which does not exceed one year;

(b) no single placement is for a duration of more than four weeks; and

(c) the total duration of the placements does not exceed 90 days."

All the placements should take place with the same carer for a family placement and at the same establishment for a residential placement ("at the same place").

MAKING THE PLAN

2.17. The Arrangements for Placement of Children Regulations place a statutory duty on responsible authorities to draw up a plan in writing for a child whom they are proposing to look after or accommodate in consultation with the child, his parents and other important individuals and agencies in the child's life (Regulation 3). Planning for the child should begin prior to placement. After placement, the plan should be scrutinised and adjusted (if necessary) at the first review four weeks after the date the child was first looked after and at subsequent reviews.

2.18. In some cases, such as an emergency or immediate placement, it may not be possible to draw up a long term plan prior to placement. However, a provisional outline plan should always exist. The firm plan should then be drawn up as soon as possible after the child has been looked after or accommodated. Once a plan has been drawn up it should be notified to the child and his parents. Persons who have been consulted and other relevant individuals should be notified on a need to know basis. This notification should normally take place prior to placement. Where this is not possible, notification should be given as soon as possible after placement. Any amendments made to the plan at the first or subsequent reviews should be recorded in writing and notified to those consulted or involved in the reviews as required by the Review Regulations.

2.19. Where a child is provided with accommodation under agreed voluntary arrangements the plan for the child will have been agreed with the parents. It will form the basis of a written agreement between the responsible authority and the parents. However, where the accommodation is being provided as the result of a self-referral for assistance to a local authority by a child aged 16 years or over the agreement should be between that child and the local authority (see paragraphs 2.63–2.67 re agreements). Where a child is looked after subject to a court order, the local authority should still seek to work in partnership and reach agreement with the parents, wherever possible. The arrangements made must be recorded in writing and a copy given to the parents (see paragraph 2.68 on provision of information to others).

THE PURPOSE OF PLANNING

2.20. The purpose of planning is to safeguard and promote the child's welfare as required by the general welfare duties in sections 17(1) and 22(3) and 61 and 64 of the Act. The drawing up of an individual plan for each child looked after will prevent drift and help to focus work with the family and child. This will be achieved in broad terms by:

(a) assessing the child's needs;

(b) determining what objectives have to be met to safeguard and promote the child's welfare;

(c) consulting with parents, the child and others whom the local authority consider are relevant;

(d) appraising fully the available options to meet those objectives;

(e) making decisions only after full consultation with the child, his parents and other agencies and individuals with a legitimate interest;

(f) identifying which individuals are to undertake which tasks; and

(g) setting a timescale in which tasks must be achieved or reassessed.

WELFARE OF THE CHILD

2.21. Regulation 4 and Schedules 1–3 of the Arrangements for Placement of Children Regulations list matters to be considered by the responsible authority, so far as is reasonably practicable, when drawing up a plan for a child who is to be looked after or accommodated. This list covers different aspects of the child's welfare, but is not intended to be exclusive and does not repeat matters already covered in the Act. There may well also be other matters for consideration in individual cases. The Act and the Regulations indicate the need to cover the following aspects in relation to the child's welfare:

- the child's needs;
- the ability of the parent to adhere to an agreed plan (relevant except in cases where a child is looked after subject to a court order);
- parental responsibilities and the parents' capacity to provide for the child's needs;
- the wishes and views of the child having regard to his understanding;
- the provision of services under Part III of the Act in respect of children looked after by a local authority;
- what is necessary to fulfil the responsible authority's duty under the Act to safeguard and promote the child's welfare;
- the type of placement best suited to the child's needs (taking into account the duty in relation to children looked after by a local authority to place the child near his home and with siblings if applicable);

- what is necessary to make the appropriate provision for the child's religious persuasion, racial origin and cultural and linguistic background;

- any needs the child may have because of disability. This may include a consideration of the type of accommodation to be provided, the suitability of the carer, the need to arrange any specific assessments (for example, under the Education Act 1981) and for any physical and/or sensory disability or learning difficulty;

- the local authority's duty under section 23(6) to enable the child to live with a parent, other person with parental responsibility for the child, relative or friend. Where the child is in care, a person in whose favour a residence order was in force immediately before the care order was made, or other person with a legitimate interest in the child;

- Reunification issues not covered above;

- the arrangements proposed for contact with regard to the duty on the local authority in paragraph 15 of Schedule 2, to promote and maintain contact between the child and his family or contact under directions from the court;

- the requirement in Regulation 6 that a voluntary organisation or the person carrying on a registered children's home should endeavour to promote contact between the child and his parents, other persons with parental responsibility or a relative, friend or person connected with him; and

- the arrangements to be made for the child's health and education. (Health and education are dealt with more fully below).

2.22. All factors relevant to the welfare of the individual child must be taken into account in assessing the child's needs and making decisions about the child's welfare. None of the separate factors involved should be abstracted and converted into a general pre-condition which overrides the others or causes any of them to be less than fully considered. The only general policy that is acceptable in making decisions about placing children is that all relevant factors should be considered. Different factors will obviously vary in importance in relation to different children or in relation to the same child at different times. It will be right in those circumstances to weigh different factors differently. But it is not right to define any factor as of such general significance or primacy that it overrides or qualifies the duty to consider together all factors bearing on the welfare of the child as an individual.

Health Care

2.23. Responsible authorities should act as good parents in relation to the health of children looked after or accommodated by them. Health care implies a positive approach to the child's health and should be taken to include general surveillance and care for health and developmental progress as well as treatment for illness and accidents. The health care of all children looked after by local authorities or accommodated by voluntary organisations or in registered children's homes should be provided in the context of the child health surveillance programmes in the area which are designed to provide child health surveillance and promote the physical, social and emotional health and development of all children. (**Health circular HC(F)(89)20/ HC(89)(32) Health Services Development – Promoting Better Health**: Management of General Medical Services (7.11.89) (paragraphs 34/35) advises on joint development and implementation by DHAs and FHSAs of agreed child health surveillance programmes).

2.24. Regulation 7 requires responsible authorities, when drawing up a plan for a child, to ensure that the child is provided with health care, including any specifically recommended and necessary immunisation and any necessary medical and dental attention. This will include registering the child with a registered general medical practitioner and entering into a contract with a general dental practitioner to enable the child to be offered the full range of NHS dental treatment. (This contract will need to be renewed annually). In the case of children with disabilities and those with special needs, consideration must be given to continuity of specialist care. Use of NHS provision and school health services should be the same for the child being looked after or accommodated as it is for any other child. An informed and sensitive approach is especially necessary for these children since they will often have suffered early disadvantage and may be at risk because they have not received continuity of care.

2.25. The responsible authority's plan for the child should include health care arrangements which should be kept under review (see Regulation 6 and Schedule 2 of the Review of Children's Cases Regulations). Responsible authorities and district health authorities should make arrangements for professional advice to be available to responsible authorities to interpret health reports and information, assist in preparing and reviewing the arrangements for health care and assist in decisions relating to the child's care. One way of providing for this would be to agree that a designated doctor should undertake this work.

2.26. Responsible authorities should be alert to the health care needs of children from ethnic minority groups and make sure that they receive appropriate health care. Social workers should put carers in touch with a named health professional who can provide carers with an understanding of particular health conditions such as sickle cell disease and thalassaemia and help them to respond appropriately to such conditions.

2.27. Responsible authorities are required by Regulation 7 to arrange for a medical examination and written health assessment of a child before placement if reasonably practicable unless an assessment has been carried out within the last three months (but see also paragraphs 2.30–2.32). In the case of an immediate placement, the authority should arrange for a health assessment as soon a possible thereafter. The health assessment may be an initial assessment when a child is first placed or may be a reassessment in the case of a child who has been placed for some time or who has been placed again after an interval. The aim of this requirement is to provide a comprehensive health profile of the child and provide a basis for monitoring the child's development whilst he is being looked after or accommodated.

2.28. There is a requirement in Regulation 6 of the Review of Children's Cases Regulations for medical examination and written health assessment of children during placement to take place at least once in every period of six months before the child's second birthday, and at least once in every period of twelve months thereafter. Up to school age, it is recommended that medical examination and written health assessment should take place and should follow, and use wherever possible, information gained from the schedule of development surveillance prescribed by the district health authority in which the child is placed. It is also recommended that medical examination and written health assessment should take place prior to each change of school or at intervals specified in the plan for the child.

2.29. These requirements provide only a basic framework for practice. Arrangements for ensuring that children receive proper health care during placement will involve the responsible authority, parents, the child, other carer, GP, community child health doctor, health visitor, the school health service and, depending on the child's needs, specialist and domiciliary services. Regulation 5 of the Arrangements for the Placement of Children Regulations requires health authorities to be notified of each placement. Responsible authorities and health authorities should together aim to develop effective arrangements for the communication of information relating to a child's health to all the health professionals who are involved with the child.

Consent to Examination or Treatment

2.30. Responsible authorities should have clear policies and procedures in relation to consent to the medical examination and treatment of children who are placed by them and should make these known to the health authority and the child's carers. The arrangements for this should be clearly set out in each plan or agreement. These will vary according to whether a responsible authority does or does not have parental responsibility for the child. The arrangements should enable carers to seek and obtain any specifically recommended immunisations and medical and dental treatment for a child, without delay or confusion. There may be occasions when parents refuse consent to a medical examination or treatment and the child is not of sufficient understanding to make the decision. In such cases where a child is in care and the local authority has not acted to restrict the parents' exercise of parental responsibility under section 33(3)(b) in this respect then they must do so to comply with these Regulations and to ensure that necessary medical examinations and treatment are made available to the child. When a child is not in care and the parents refuse consent, the local authority may have to resort to obtaining an appropriate court order (including for example, a section 8 specific issue order or an emergency protection order or child assessment order) (see also paragraph 1.102).

2.31. The relevant individual health professionals should be aware of and co-operate with the arrangements which are made. The most convenient arrangement is likely to be where a carer has delegated authority from the parent or the local authority for routine treatment and minor procedures. If the parent holds the child's health record, it may be appropriate for it to be given to the carer for the duration of the placement. The need for operations and major treatment should be discussed with parents, and their consent obtained subject to the exercise by a local authority of its powers in section 33(3)(b) in respect of a child in care. Parents should be kept informed of their child's state of health and it should be agreed in each case whether this should be done by the carer or the authority.

2.32. Children of sixteen and over give their own consent to medical treatment (**see also HC(90)22 Health Service Management: Patient Consent to Treatment or Examination**). Children under sixteen may also be able to give or refuse consent depending on their capacity to understand the nature of the treatment; it is for the doctor to decide this. Children who are judged able to give consent cannot be medically examined or treated without their consent. The responsible authority should draw the child's attention to his rights to give or refuse consent to examination or treatment if he is 16 or over or if he is under 16 and the doctor considers him of sufficient understanding to understand the consequences of consent or refusal. There is no prohibition on placement if it is impossible to persuade a child to be medically examined. But it is a responsibility of the authority, and part of the carer's task, to help and encourage young people to understand the importance of health care and to take responsibility for their own health.

Education

2.33. Schedule 3 to the Regulations sets out the considerations about a child's educational needs which form part of the planning process. Children who are looked after or accommodated have the same rights as all children to education, including further and higher education and to other opportunities for development. Some children's perception of their ability may have been undermined and their true potential may not be immediately evident. As children who may be damaged and vulnerable, they often need extra help and encouragement and opportunities to compensate for early deprivation and for educational disadvantage arising from changes of placement while in care. In planning for a child, responsible authorities should have regard to the importance of continuity of education and of taking a long term view of a child's education; providing educational opportunities and support; and promoting educational achievement. It is also important to recognise the value of peer group relationships made in educational settings. The aim should be to help all children to achieve their full potential and equip themselves as well as possible for adult life. However expectations must be realistic. Responsible authorities have the responsiblity of acting as a good parent in relation to the child's education.

2.34. Regulation 5 requires responsible authorities to notify the local education authority of placement. Arrangements for liaison and coordination should aim to ensure that information reaches those who need it in good time, especially the school. Special care and support is needed where a change of school cannot be avoided. Responsible authorities should ensure that the carer's role and responsibility towards the child are understood by the school. In many cases carers will exercise the parental role in relation to the school in day to day matters but there will be cases where parents continue to play that part. It will be up to the social worker to clarify such arrangements with the school if any confusion seems likely to arise, in order to avoid loss of confidence and cooperation.

2.35. Carers have an important contribution to make to a child's educational progress and development. They are in a good position to observe and to help identify and assess both the child's real capabilities and any difficulties, fears and development deficits. Carers will need to be supported in this role. With the help of the carer and through school reports and direct contacts with the school, the child's educational progress must be kept under review along with other aspects of the child's welfare. Difficulties should be explored and help provided, including where appropriate, arrangements for access to specailist services within the local authority's educational provision.

2.36. Social services departments and education authorities should collaborate to safeguard the interests of children with statements of special educational needs under the Education Act 1981 and in accordance with sections 5 and 6 of the Disabled Persons (Services, Consultation and Representation Act 1986). Local authorities should see that the parent's rights are exercised in respect of requests for assessment, monitoring and reviews. Whether or not the local authority has parental responsibility they should act in consultation with parent and foster parent.

2.37. Children should be encouraged and given opportunities to develop and pursue leisure interests and any special gifts they may have, and to share in the activities of their peers. Even where a child is looked after or accommodated for a relatively short period, the aim should be to provide opportunities for development so that the child can benefit as far as possible from the placement; and to identify the help the child may need to sustain new interests on return home.

2.38. Where a local authority propose to place a child in an establishment at which education is provided for children accommodated there, there is a duty in section 28 of the Children Act 1989 for the local authority to consult the appropriate education authority before doing so and inform them of the arrangements that have been made for the child's accommodation. When the child ceases to be accommodated the local authority is required to inform the appropriate local education authority. The aim of this provision is to ensure that appropriate educational facilities are available for the child. (See also paragraph 1.114 regarding Community Homes with Education on the premises.)

2.39. The appropriate local education authority means:

(a) the local education authority within whose area the local authority's area falls; or,

(b) where the child has special educational needs and a statement of his needs is maintained under the Education Act 1981, the local education authority who maintain the statement.

Race, Culture, Religion and Linguistic Background

2.40. A child's ethnic origin, cultural background and religion are important factors for consideration. It may be taken as a guiding principle of good practice that, other things being equal and in the great majority of cases, placement with a family of similar ethnic origin and religion is most likely to meet a child's needs as fully as possible and to safeguard his or her welfare most effectively. Such a family is most likely to be able to provide a child with continuity in life and care and an environment which the child will find familiar and sympathetic and in which opportunities will naturally arise to share fully in the culture and way of life of the ethnic group to which he belongs. Where the aim of a placement is to reunite the child with his or her own family, contact and work with the family will in most cases be more comfortable for all and carry a greater chance of success if the foster parents are of similar ethnic origin. Families of similar ethnic origin are also usually best placed to prepare children for life as members of an ethnic minority group in a multi-racial society, where they may meet with racial prejudice and discrimination, and to help them with their development towards independent living and adult life.

2.41. These principles should be applied with proper consideration for the circumstances of the individual case. There may be circumstances in which placement with a family of different ethnic origin is the best choice for a particular child. In other cases such a placement may be the best available choice. For example, a child may have formed strong links with prospective foster parents or be related to them. Siblings or step siblings who are not all of the same ethnic origin may need placement together. A child may prefer and need to remain close to school, friends and family even though foster parents of the same ethnic origin cannot be found in the locality. A child with special needs may require carers with particular qualities or abilities, so that choice is limited. The importance of religion as an element of culture should never be overlooked: to some children and families it may be the dominant factor, so that the religion of foster parents, for example, may in some cases be more important than their ethnic origin.

2.42. For a child whose parents are of different ethnic groups, placement in a family which reflects as nearly as possible the child's ethnic origins is likely to be the best choice in most cases. But choice will be influenced by the child's previous family experience and, as with all placement decisions, by the child's wishes and feelings. In discussing and exploring these with a child, responsible authorities should be ready to help the child with any confusion or misunderstandings about people of different ethnic groups which may have arisen through previous family or placement experience. Children of mixed ethnic origin should be helped to understand and take a pride in both or all elements in their cultural heritage and to feel comfortable about their origins. Carers must be able to provide this, with the help and support of others where necessary. This applies equally whether a child is placed with a minority ethnic family or with a white family or a family including members of differing ethnic origins. Where it has not proved possible to make a placement which entirely reflects the child's race and culture, an independent visitor could provide a link with the child's racial and cultural background (if the criteria for appointing an independent visitor apply).

THE PLANNING PROCESS

2.43. A plan to meet the child's needs may exist before a specific placement is considered; either because of the degree of service provision to the child living in his family home, or because the child is moving from one planned placement to another. Where no plan exists the planning process must begin once a child in need has been identified as being likely to require accommodation. Contingency planning for the possible accommodation of a child while efforts continue to support the family and keep the child at home may achieve a more successful and less disturbing transition for the child. Chronologically, the planning process should comprise the following typical stages: *inquiry*, *consultation*, *assessment* and *decision-making*. These are described in the following paragraphs.

Inquiry

2.44. Inquiry consists of:

(a) Working with the child and his parents, other members of the family (and other involved adults) to obtain their wishes and views. It is at this stage that work to develop partnership with parents, to encourage continuance of the parental role and to help the child and parents share in decision-making must start. Patterns of working and attitudes established now will in most cases influence all future work.

(b) Collecting information about the child and his family. The level of consultation will depend on the circumstances of the individual case. This will involve approaching other involved professionals (eg GP, community child health doctor, school teacher, health visitor, police, child psychologist etc) and other individuals (eg relatives, family friends etc) as necessary.

Consultation

2.45. It is essential when planning a placement to consult all those concerned with the child from the outset. The need for consultation should be explained to the parents and the child. The responsible authority should co-ordinate the involvement of all relevant agencies, and all the individuals who are significant in the child's life and the child so that a plan is drawn up which meets the child's individual needs.

2.46. Sections 22(4), 61 and 64 of the Children Act 1989 state that before making any decision with respect to a child whom they are looking after or propose to look after or accommodate, the responsible authority should obtain and take account of the wishes and feelings of—

(a) the child;

(b) his parents;

(c) any person who is not a parent of his but who has parental responsibility for him; and

(d) any other person whose wishes and feelings the authority consider to be relevant (see paragraphs 2.51–2.52 for guidance).

The Child

2.47. The child's views should be sought in discussion with the child, subject to the child's understanding (see sections 22(4)(a) and (5), 61 and 64 of the Children Act). It will always be necessary for the child's views as expressed to be discussed, recorded and given due consideration before a placement decision is made and at every review meeting and at case conferences. The implications and options in the plan should be explained, discussed and if necessary, reassessed in the light of the child's views. The social worker should be aware and acknowledge that there may be good reasons why the child's views are different from those of his parents or the responsible authority. The more mature the child, the more fully he will be able to enter into discussion about plans and proposals and participate in the decision-making process. When older children are involved, and particularly in a case of self-referral, there may well be a different perception of the child's needs and interests as seen by the child and his parents. With young children, the social worker should make efforts to communicate with the child and discover his real feelings. All children need to be given information and appropriate explanations so that they are in a position to develop views and make choices.

2.48. Providing children with reassurance and helping them with their anxieties about a placement is essential to the success of a placement. Children should feel that they have been properly consulted, that their views have been properly considered and that they have participated as partners in the decision-making process. However, they should not be made to feel that the burden of decision-making has fallen totally upon them, nor should they be forced to attend meetings if they choose not to do so. The reasons for this choice should be explored so that they are given real opportunities to understand the good reasons for taking part in meetings. The possibility of the child being accompanied to a meeting by a person who is able to provide friendly support should be considered. Where the child has communication difficulties appropriate specialist provision will need to be made so that it is possible for the child to express his views and for those views to be considered. Such provision could include someone with the appropiate communication skills such as a sign language interpreter. In the case of a child whose first language is not English, an interpreter should be provided if necessary.

The Family

2.49. The child's family, parents, grandparents and other relatives involved with the child should be invited to participate actively in planning and to make their views known. The Children Act 1989 requires that parents (including the unmarried father who may not have parental responsibility) should generally be involved in all planning for the child, and should be kept informed of significant changes and developments in the plan for the child. Similarly, members of the child's family or others who play a significant part in the child's life should be involved in the making of arrangements for the child. Such sharing of information and participation in decision-making should be the norm subject only to the overriding best interests of the child.

2.50. In drawing up a plan, therefore, responsible authorities should ensure that the parents of the child, the child himself and other significant persons are given the opportunity and appropriately helped to express their views on the objectives of the plan and on how the responsible authority proposes that the objectives should be achieved. How far their views influence outcomes will depend on the circumstances of the individual case. Where the child is to be provided with accommodation by voluntary agreement, the responsible authority will be working with the parents in the child's best interests on the proposed plan and arrangements to implement it. In child protection cases, parents' views about the proposed plan should not be allowed to prevent the local authority from carrying out its duty to protect the child. If agreement cannot be reached with the parents on a voluntary basis, and lack of agreement makes it impossible to implement a suitable plan, it may be appropriate to apply for an order under Parts IV or V of the Act.

Others

2.51. To meet the requirements of the Act (section 22(4)(d)), responsible authorities will need to use their discretion to consult all the relevant statutory agencies which are and have been previously involved with the child and his family and other relevant agencies and persons before a child is looked after or accommodated. The responsible authority should explain and make sure that parents and children understand why there is a need to consult and what the consultation process involves and obtain the relevant consent. It is essential that other agencies involved with the child are consulted about the needs of the child and his family so that the proposed plan is based on as complete an assessment as possible. People to be consulted in addition to the child, his parents and any person with parental responsibility may include:

(a) the district health authority;

(b) the child's general medical practitioner;

(c) the appropriate local authority, where it is proposed that the child (who is not looked after by that authority) will be placed in their area;

(d) the local education authority (and school);

(e) any other person whose views the responsible authority consider should be sought. For example; child's extended family, a guardian ad litem, a worker in a voluntary agency involved with the child and his family, a former foster parent, the officer in charge of a home where the child had previously been placed, a teacher who has been significantly involved with the child or a community leader.

2.52. Responsible authorities should seek to identify and make contact with specific officers in other agencies who will be contacted when pre-placement enquiries are made and who will consult colleagues in the field involved with the child and report back. The parents and the child, if he is of sufficient understanding should be informed of who is to be consulted and that the information gathered will be properly safeguarded. Existing carers, including foster parents, a head of community home, etc should already be involved in day to day planning for the child but a specific opportunity to contribute to formal planning or review considerations should be arranged.

Recording Consultation

2.53. It is important that the information obtained during consultation is clearly recorded in writing on the child's case record so that it will be easy for someone unfamiliar with the case to see:

(a) what the considerations in arriving at decisions were;

(b) how the objectives of the plan have been decided upon; and

(c) how proposals for achieving these objectives have been reached.

In this way the decision-making process will be clear for the record. This discipline will assist the responsible social worker to ensure that all the necessary factors in relation to the child's welfare are considered fully. (It will also inform the line management supervision process).

Assessment

2.54. Using the information gathered together in the inquiry process it will be possible to make a full assessment of the child's needs in relation to safeguarding or promoting his welfare, taking into account any services the responsible authority or other agencies may already be providing. The assessment should link in to other assessment processes. The Act provides that a local authority may assess a child's needs for the purposes of the Children Act at the same time as any assessment under:

(a) the Chronically Sick and Disabled Persons Act 1970;

(b) the Education Act 1981;

(c) the Disabled Persons (Services, Consultation and Representation) Act 1986; or

(d) any other enactment.

2.55. Joint assessment in appropriate cases will help to ensure that the child's needs are not addressed in isolation and that the child is looked at 'in the round'. Working in collaboration with other agencies will help to identify how the responsible authority and other agencies can best meet the child's needs.

2.56. In assessing the need for local authority provision of services due account needs to be taken of the particular needs of the child ie health, disability, education, religious persuasion, racial origin, cultural and linguistic background, the degree, (if any) to which these needs are being met by existing services to the family or child and which agencies' services are best suited to the child's needs.

2.57. Assessment must identify a child's ethnic origins, religion, special needs and family experience to provide as comprehensive a guide as possible to the child's needs. Necessary experience and expertise should be provided for in staffing of services and through relationships with other professions and services and with the community. In some areas the local community may include too great a variey of ethnic groups to be reflected fully in composition of staff. In others, local authorities may be called on only rarely to provide a service for a child or family from a minority ethnic group. In both these circumstances, local authorities will need to identify sources of advice and help so that the necessary experience, expertise and resources are available when needed. Care is needed so that the terms 'black' and 'black family' are not used in isolation in such a way as to obscure characteristics and needs. In assessing the needs of a child with communication difficulties or a child with a parent with communication difficulties, it is important that local authorities are aware that a sign language interpreter, large print, tape and braille may need to be provided if communication is to be effective.

2.58. The Department's publication **Protecting Children: A Guide for Social Workers undertaking a Comprehensive Assessment (HMSO 1988)** contains much useful guidance which is applicable to all assessments of children by social workers.

Decision-making

2.59. During the process the social worker will be deciding on the best approach to the case by identifying the child's needs, obtaining and taking into account the wishes and feelings of the child, his parents and others involved with the child, seeking the advice of other professionals in the consultation process and will be considering:

- is the best approach the provision of services (including if appropriate) accommodation by voluntary agreement;
- whether or not child protection action is needed (which may often include provision of accommodation for the child by voluntary agreement); or
- is it compulsory care subject to a court order that is required.

2.60. Decision-making will entail:

- translating the assessed needs into aims and general objectives;
- listing and appraising the specific options available (or which may need to be created) for achieving these objectives;
- deciding on the preferred option, setting out the reasons for the decision.

2.61. The proposed plan will explain in detail how the objectives can be achieved ie if and what sort of accommodation is needed; what other services for the child and services for parents or other members of family or the child's carer need to be provided; services which might be provided by other agencies such as the health authority or a voluntary organisation; likely duration of the placement; and arrangements for sustaining family links, promoting contact and reunification of the family.

Contents Of The Plan For The Child

2.62. There is no prescribed format for a child care plan (but see the considerations in Regulation 4 and Schedules 1–4). The plan should be recorded in writing and contain the child's and his family's social history and the following key elements:

- the child's identified needs (including needs arising from race, culture, religion or language, special educational or health needs);
- how those needs might be met;
- aim of plan and timescale;
- proposed placement (type and details);
- other services to be provided to child and or family either by the local authority or other agencies;
- arrangements for contact and reunification;
- support in the placement;
- likely duration of placement in the accommodation;
- contingency plan, if placement breaks down;
- arrangements for ending the placement (if made under voluntary arrangements);

- who is to be responsible for implementing the plan (specific tasks and overall plan);
- specific detail of the parents' role in day to day arrangements;
- the extent to which the wishes and views of the child, his parents and anyone else with a sufficient interest in the child (including representatives of other agencies) have been obtained and acted upon and the reasons supporting this or explanations of why wishes/views have been discounted;
- arrangements for input by parents, the child and others into the ongoing decision-making process;
- arrangements for notifying the responsible authority of disagreements or making representations;
- arrangements for health care (including consent to examination and treatment);
- arrangement for education; and
- dates of reviews.

Agreements

2.63. Regulation 3 which governs the making of arrangements (the plan) requires that a responsible authority should draw up a plan in writing. Where a child is not in care the responsible authority should reach agreement on the plan with the parents, other person with parental responsibility, or if there is no such person, the person caring for the child. Regulation 4, governs the considerations on making and contents of arrangements and requires at 4(2) that where practicable the plan should include details of the matters specified in Schedule 4 to the Regulations. Where a child is provided with accommodation by voluntary agreement the plan should form the basis of a written agreement between the responsible authority and the parents or if there is no such person, the person caring for the child prior to the provision of accommodation. The agreement must set out the role for the parent in the day to day life of the child. This will have been discussed and agreed in negotiations between the responsible authority and the parents with the involvement of the carer.

2.64. Regulation 5(3) requires the responsible authority to produce a written copy of the agreement which incorporates the detail of the plan for the child and the arrangements made. There is no requirement for the agreement to be signed, but in cases where the parent, although consenting to the plan does not wish to sign the agreement, the responsible authority will wish to sign the document to indicate their commitment to the plan for the child. A copy of the agreement should be sent to the person with whom it is made. The child should also receive a copy in a form appropriate to his understanding. The older child of 16 or over should be encouraged to sign the agreement when he has referred himself to the local authority and is to be provided with accommodation by the local authority by virtue of their powers under section 20 (3), (4) and (11). Again, there is no requirement that the agreement should be signed.

2.65. Where agreement is reached with one person with parental responsibility, the responsible authority is entitled to act on that if that parent has a residence order in his favour (section 20(9)). In other cases, the local authority can act unless another person with parental responsibility is willing and able to provide accommodation for the child or arrange for accommodation to be provided for him and objects to the proposed arrangement (section 20(7)). If accommodation is being provided in accordance with an agreement and the other person subsequently objects and can provide accommodation or arrange for accommodation to be provided, again the local authority would have to comply with their request. This advice would not apply in respect of arrangements concerning a child aged 16 or over (section 20(11)).

2.66. An agreement should include arrangements for the child leaving accommodation, such as a period of notice to allow time for preparation of the child for this event and to ensure that the child's wishes and feelings are taken into account. Where a child is provided with accommodation by voluntary agreement for a substantial period and has become attached to the carer, this will be important if the child and the carer are to have a sense of stability and security. An agreement should also include a statement of the steps each party should take if another party decided to change the agreement. For example, if the local authority was unable to provide a service it had agreed to provide or proposed to move the child to another carer, the agreement might state that the parent would withdraw the child from accommodation. Or if the parent decided to take action which was harmful to the child the agreement might state that the local authority would consider applying for an emergency protection order.

2.67. Although the Regulations do not require a local authority to reach agreement on the planned arrangements for a child in their care, it is the intention, so far as is practicable, and in the child's best interests that arrangements should be made in partnership with parents. Where the interests of the child or the non co-operation of the parents require that initial arrangements are made without agreement, part of the planned work should be to try to establish a working relationship for the future. A child's interests are likely to be served best if the parents are encouraged to keep in touch and take an active role in planning for the child. This will be the case even where the long-term plan for the child is that he remains in care.

Notification

2.68. It is essential that those involved in the decision-making process are notified of the decision (Regulation 5) so that they may have an opportunity to make any necessary arrangements for their involvement in the placement or to make their views on the placement decision known. Careful note should be taken of the provision in regulation 5(3) about the notification of information to third parties. Such notification should only contain the amount of information it is necessary to divulge. The responsible authority will need to identify others who were not involved in the decision-making process but who will be involved with the child and have a need to know of the placement arrangements. Consideration should be given, in the light of circumstances of an individual case, of the need to notify people who have been involved in the child's life but who are not specified in Regulation 5.

2.69. All responsible authorities should notify the local authority in whose area the child is placed, providing sufficient information for the local authority to fulfil their duties in respect of registration of placements. Responsible authorities should notify the specific officer in other agencies already identified and consulted about these placements (see paragraph 2.52). These officers should be asked to disseminate the information as appropriate to their colleagues in the field who are or will be involved with the child including, in those cases where a child protection case conference has been consulted, the members of the case conference.

2.70. Once the plan has been decided upon, it should be notified in writing to the parents, the child, other carers, representatives of other agencies involved with the child and others with a sufficient interest in the child. Good practice requires that the responsible authority's social worker explains personally to the parents and the child what the plan entails and the reason for reaching the decisions therein. This should be done in addition to any explanations given during the assessment and planning process.

2.71. Where a child's or parent's first language is not English, an interpreter may be required. Sensorily impaired children and adults may need a specific format of any formal written notification. For blind or visually impaired people it could be braille, on tape or in large print. Deaf or hard of hearing impaired people have a range of communication needs depending on the type of deafness and the age of onset. Appropriate provision should be made for a child or parent with such communication difficulties. This may range from making available someone who is a clear speaker with understanding and knowledge of the speech and language difficulties of hearing impaired people, to an accredited sign language interpreter. Interpretation resources will also be required for a child who uses the Makaton system.

Format of Notification

2.72. The written notification of the agreement (or of the plan if no agreement has been reached) should include:

- a summary of the proposed arrangements and the objectives covering details of the placement and its likely duration;
- arrangements for contact;
- who is responsible for implementing the plan;
- the role of the child's parent on a day to day basis;
- arrangements for or issues of reunification; and
- contingency plans if the placement is unsuccessful.

Where a child is provided with accommodation by voluntary agreement, the notification should also set out the arrangements for the ending of the placement. The oral explanation given by the responsible social worker to the parents and the child will supplement this. In exceptional circumstances where a child is in care or subject to an emergency protection order, the carer's name and address may be omitted from the notice; this would be when the local authority has reasonable cause to believe that informing a person would prejudice the child's welfare (paragraph 15(4) of Schedule 2). Where it is necessary to take this exceptional decision to safeguard a child's interests, the circumstances and reasons should be recorded on the child's case record and notified to the parent in writing. The letter of notification should also refer to the representations procedure which each local authority is required to set up under the Children Act (see Chapter 5). It will be helpful to enclose an information leaflet so that the parents, the child and others notified of the arrangements are aware of the channel open to them for making representations or complaints.

IMPLEMENTATION OF DECISIONS ARISING FROM THE PLAN

2.73. One of the most important aspects of planning is to ensure that the decisions arising from the plan are implemented. This is best done by ensuring that all those involved in the planning and subsequent review process know clearly who is responsible for implementing which decisions and when. The value of the plan will rapidly diminish if objectives are not met in part or in whole because there has been poor communication, lack of clarity about who is responsible for what and the relevant timescales. Therefore the letter notifying the proposed plan should make it clear who is responsible for the implementation of different components of the plan.

MONITORING THE SUPPORT AND SUPERVISION OF THE PLACEMENT

2.74. The regulations relating to specific placements provide for support and supervision of the placements. Arrangements must also provide for line management supervision and monitoring of the social worker's performance in supporting and supervising the placement. Good records will play a key part in this appraisal of the worker's performance in relation to the placement's aims and objectives. The examination by the line manager of records should precede as well as accompany periodic discussions about the placement.

INTER-AGENCY ARRANGEMENTS IN ENGLAND AND WALES

2.75. Where a child is placed by a local authority (the local authority) under these Regulations in the area of another local authority (the area authority) the local authority should inform the area authority of the placement and provide sufficient information for the area authority to be able to complete their register in accordance with Regulation 10 (see paragraphs 2.79 and 2.80). The local authority should notify also the other relevant authorities, the district health authority, the local education authority etc of the placement and arrangements for supervision.

2.76. A local authority with responsibility for the care of a child may arrange for any or all of their functions in relation to the child to be performed by another local (area) authority (section 101 of the Local Government Act 1972). In such cases the local authority should provide the area authority with all the information which is needed to discharge the local authority's duties in accordance with these Regulations and the other Regulations relating to specific placements. Regulation 12 requires the area authority to keep the local authority informed of the progress of the child and, in particular, make reports to the local authority following each visit to the placement and each occasion on which the child is seen (in accordance with sections 17(5) and 27 of the Children Act 1989) and following each review. The authorities are required to consider together as necessary and at least after each review what action, if any, is needed.

PLACEMENT OUTSIDE ENGLAND AND WALES

2.77. A local authority may arrange (or assist in arranging) for a child for whom they are providing accommodation by voluntary agreement to live outside England and Wales with the approval of every person who has parental responsibility for the child (paragraph 19(2) of Schedule 2). In the case of a child who is in care, the court's approval must be sought (paragraph 19(1) of Schedule 2). This may only be given in certain circumstances, namely where: every person with parental responsibility for the child consents or his consent is dispensed with under paragraph 19(5), the child himself consents (if he has sufficient understanding), suitable arrangements have been made for the reception and welfare of the child in the new country and living there would be in the child's best interests (paragraph 19(3) and (4) of Schedule 2). Where the child is moving to another jurisdiction within the British Islands (ie the United Kingdom, the Channel Islands and the Isle of Man) the effect of the care order may be transferred to the relevant public authority in the receiving jurisdiction under regulations to be made by virtue of section 101 of the Act.

RECORDS

2.78. Accurate, comprehensive and well organised records are essential to good practice. They are the basis, as social workers and carers change, for a clear and common understanding of the plan for the child, the arrangements made, agreements which have been reached and decisions which have been made and the reasons for them. Careful recording of agreements and decisions relating to the plan for the child, the aim of the placement and of the child's progress in the placement enables the implementation of planning decisions to be monitored effectively and kept under review. The responsible authority's records will be one important source of information for the child who is permanently placed away from his birth family.

2.79. Regulations 8 and 10 require responsible authorities to keep two sets of records:

(a) a case record for every child placed by the responsible authority; and

(b) a register of all children in the local authority's area who are placed under these Regulations whether by the local authority or another responsible authority, and of all children placed by the local authority outside their area.

Different requirements in respect of registers apply to voluntary organisations and registered children's homes. The detail of Regulations 10(2), 10(4) and 10(5)–(7) should be studied.

Registers

2.80. The register provides a record of the identity and whereabouts of every child placed by a responsible authority. The local authority's register will provide a means of immediate reference to basic information about any child placed in an area as local authorities have to register children placed by them and other responsible authorities in their area. They also have to register children placed by them (the local authority) outside their area.

Case Records

2.81. A child's case record should include all the information about family history, involvement with the authority and progress which is relevant to the child being looked after or accommodated. The case record will be an integrated case record for all purposes. Regulation 8(2) in respect of the material to be kept in the record requires that the case record contains:

(a) a copy of the arrangements made for the child (the plan);

(b) copies of any written reports in the responsible authority's possession concerning the welfare of the child; this will include family history and home study reports, reports made at the request of a court, reports made of visits to the child, his family or his carer, health reports etc;

(c) copies of all the documents used to seek information, provide information or record views given to the authority in the course of planning and reviewing the child's case and review reports (see also Regulation 10 of the Review of Children's Cases Regulations);

(d) details of arrangements for contact and contact orders and any other court orders relating to the child; and

(e) details of any arrangements made for another authority, agency or person to act on behalf of a local authority or organisation which placed a child.

It is also recommended that any contribution the child may wish to make such as written material, photographs, school certificates etc. should also be included.

2.82. The record should be kept in such a fashion that it is easy to trace the process of decision-making and in particular so that the views of the child and his parents can be easily found and related to the sequence of decisions taken and arrangements made. In addition, any papers temporarily placed in the record which are the property of the child should be identified as such and marked for return at the appropriate time.

2.83. The child's record should be separate from management records, records relating to a foster parent or residential care matters which are not solely concerned with the individual child. Where some information on one of these other records is relevant to the child a duplicate entry should appear in the child's record. Records should not be amalgamated even in the case of siblings although a degree of cross-reference and duplicate entry will be necessary.

Safekeeping of records

2.84. Regulation 9 and good practice require that authorities should take steps to ensure the safekeeping of records. This requires not only arrangements for the physical security of the records but effective procedures to restrict access to the records to those who are properly authorised and need access because of their duties in relation to a case.

Access to Records

2.85. The Children Act requires authorities to give access to records to persons duly authorised by the Secretary of State (such as the Social Services Inspectorate) and to guardians ad litem appointed by the court. Access by the Local Commissioner is provided for in the Local Government Act 1974. Other legislation affecting social work records is the Data Protection Act 1984 and the Access to Personal Files Act 1987, which give individuals rights of access to certain information about themselves. The Data Protection Act applies only to computerised records, and the Data Protection (Subject Access Modification) (Social Work) Order 1987 (SI 1987/1904) under the Act provides for certain information to be exempted in prescribed circumstances from the right of access as does the Data Protection (Miscellaneous Subject Access Exemptions) Order 1981 (SI 1987/1906) which maintains existing restrictions, including in relation to adoption records.

2.86. The Access to Personal Files Act 1987 and the Access to Personal Files (Social Services) Regulations 1989 similarly provide for subject access to information which is kept manually by local authorities (not voluntary organisations or persons who carry on a registered children's home) and the circumstances in which information is exempt from the right of access. The Department of Health issued a circular (LAC(88)17) in September 1988 containing guidance on the safeguarding of personal information held in local authorities records for the purposes of their Social Services functions and on the disclosure of that information to others within the authority and to other organisations. The Department has issued two circulars on the Data Protection Act and Social Work Order (LAC(87)10 and LAC(88)16) and a circular on the Access to Personal Files Act and the Access to Personal Files (Social Services) Regulations 1989 (SI 1989/206) (LAC(89)2) which relate to the client's own access to his records. The latter also includes an amendment to LAC(88)16 and its own detailed guidance on the handling of requests for information made by or on behalf of children.

2.87. Responsible authorities should act in accordance with the above guidance and with their own legal advice in matters relating to the disclosure of information held in the records. It is good practice that information held about an individual should be shared with him unless there are special reasons for withholding it covered by the legislation and guidance mentioned.

Retention of Records

2.88. Regulations 9 and 10 specify the length of time for which records are to be kept. These should in some cases be regarded as minimum periods rather than an inflexible rule. Responsible authorities should consider their policies on retention in relation to their records as a whole and to individual records, bearing in mind the purpose and value of retention of the different records.

2.89. Entries in the register must be kept until the child to whom the entry applies reaches the age of 23 or for five years after the death of the child before reaching that age.

2.90. The child's case record must be kept until the seventy-fifth anniversary of his date of birth or fifteen years from the date of death in the case of a child who dies before reaching the age of eighteen.

CHAPTER 3   REVIEW OF CHILDREN'S CASES

INTRODUCTION

3.1. Chapter 2 dealt with planning of arrangements for children who are looked after by a local authority or accommodated by a voluntary organisation or a registered children's home. This chapter deals with the review of children who are looked after by a local authority or accommodated by a voluntary organisation or a registered children's home. Reviews form part of a continuous planning process – reviewing decisions to date and planning future work. The purpose of the review is to ensure that the child's welfare is safeguarded and promoted in the most effective way throughout the period he is looked after or accommodated. Progress in safeguarding and providing for the child's welfare should be examined and monitored at every review and the plan for the child amended as necessary to reflect any significant change.

3.2. The Review of Children's Cases Regulations (like the Arrangements for Placement of Children (General) Regulations) apply to local authorities which are looking after children and to voluntary organisations and registered children's homes which accommodate children not looked after by the local authority. For the purpose of this guidance, 'review' means review under the Review of Children's Cases Regulations. 'Responsible authority' in this Chapter means local authority, voluntary organisation or person carrying on a registered children's home. Where guidance deals with a matter which is not equally applicable to all groups, this is made clear.

WHAT IS A REVIEW?

3.3. The concept of review as governed by the Reviews of Children's Cases Regulations and discussed in this guidance is a continuous process of planning and reconsideration of the plan for the child. Review will include a number of components leading to meetings held to discuss the plan which has been drawn up for a child who is being looked after or accommodated by a responsible authority. This will require consultation and the gathering of information on an ongoing basis, discussing that information and making decisions to amend the plan as necessary. The agenda for meetings should include consideration of progress in implementing the plan, need for changes in approach on service provision, a possible reallocation of tasks or a change in the status of the child (need for care proceedings or discharge of a care order, for example). Any meeting which is convened for the purpose of considering the child's case in connection with any aspect of the review of that case falls within the scope of these Regulations. Whether such a meeting is called a planning meeting or a review or review meeting will not determine whether it is in fact part of a review. This will depend on the purpose for which the meeting is convened.

3.4. A review is not a reconsideration after a complaint or a part of line management supervision of a decision although either could indicate the need for a review of the child's circumstances. Neither is it a case review as described in "Working Together". A review is different from a case conference, although case conferences could well provide information to be considered in a review (a case conference is a multi-disciplinary meeting usually called to formulate advice on a specific issue). But where the discussion at a case conference combines consideration of wider issues affecting the plan for the child, it constitutes part of a review and falls within these Regulations. It also differs from a case discussion as part of line management as that is an exercise whereby managers, amongst other matters, review the performance of their staff. Guidance on a review of a decision in the light of a complaint is dealt with in Chapter 10 on representations procedures. See also **Working Together** Part 7 re case conferences and case reviews. A review of an individual child's case is held solely to make plans in the interests of safeguarding and promoting that child's welfare.

REQUIREMENT TO REVIEW AND FREQUENCY

3.5. Regulation 2 places a specific statutory duty on the responsible authority to review the case of a child who is looked after or accommodated, in accordance with these Regulations. Regulation 3 sets out the maximum intervals that may separate reviews. The first review should take place no later than four weeks after the date on which the child begins to be looked after or is provided with accommodation. In the case of a child looked after by a local authority this will bring together the assessment and planning that has been taking place since the child was indentified as being in need of the local authority's services. The second review should take place not more than three months after the date of the first review. Thereafter, subsequent reviews should take place at intervals of not more than six months after the date of the previous review.

3.6. The frequency of reviews required by the Regulations is the minimum standard and a review of the child's case should take place as often as the circumstances of the individual case requires. If the need arises for substantial changes to the plan, then the date of the next review should be brought forward. Parents and children should be consulted about the need for additional reviews on a regular basis. Any request for an additional review from a parent or a child should be given serious consideration.

SHORT-TERM PLACEMENTS

3.7. Regulation 11 allows for a defined series of short pre-planned placements (eg for respite care or staying contact) to be treated as a *single placement* for the application of these Regulations and those relating to specific placements. All the requirements of the Review Regulations apply, but need not be repeated for each episode of accommodation so as long as the conditions in Regulation 11 are met. The conditions in Regulation 11 are:

"(a) all the periods are included within a period which does not exceed one year;

(b) no single period is for a duration of more than four weeks; and

(c) the total duration of the periods does not exceed 90 days."

All the placements should take place with the same carer for a family placement and at the same establishment for a residential placement ("at the same place"). Similar provision is made for short-term placements in the Regulations relating to specific placements.

A SYSTEM FOR REVIEWS

3.8. Each responsible authority will wish to revise their present arrangements to ensure that they provide a system for review of children's cases which will satisfy the requirements of the Children Act and Regulations 4, 8, 9 and 10 as described below. In revising existing arrangements or establishing new procedures responsible authorities should ensure that their review system provides for:

● the full participation of both children and parents in the decision-making process;

● a structured, coordinated approach to the planning of child care work in individual cases; and

● a monitoring system for checking the operation of the review process.

3.9. Regulation 4 sets out the manner in which cases are to be reviewed and requires that the arrangements should be in writing and made known to children, parents, other persons with parental responsibility, other persons whose views the responsible authority consider relevant and those involved in conducting reviews of children's cases (Regulation 4(1)). The responsible authority is required by Regulation 4(2) to co-ordinate review action and by Regulation 4(3) to appoint an officer to achieve that coordination. The responsible authority need not make a special appointment to deal with these duties. For example in the case of local authorities, it is suggested that senior officers should be designated to fulfil this role in each management area of the authority. These officers could combine this role with their other duties.

Preparations for the Review

3.10. Before the review is arranged the field social worker responsible for the case, in discussion with his line manager, should identify who should be invited. Only in exceptional cases should a parent or a child not be invited to a review meeting. The first review meeting is the occasion on which the planning process is most clearly illustrated as being inseparable from the review process. It is the first opportunity to confirm formally that the plan is meeting the child's needs. Those to be invited should include those who have been consulted (including the child and his parents) in drawing up the initial plan and who may need to contribute to the review.

Consultation

3.11. As with planning, it is essential that there is full consultation with all the relevant individuals before the review meeting is held. There should also be a written record kept on the child's case record of the results of the consultation exercise before each review meeting. Appropriate provision should be made for children and parents with communication difficulties or whose first language is not English. Sections 22(4), 61 and 64 of the Children Act state that before making any decision with respect to a child looked after or accommodated by a responsible authority, the responsible authority should obtain and take account of the wishes and feelings of:

(a) The child (subject to his age and understanding and so far as this is in his best interests);

(b) His parents;

(c) Any person who is not a parent of his but who has parental responsibility for him;

(d) Any other person whom they consider ought to be notified.

'Any other person' may include:

(i)   His current carer (foster parent or residential social worker);

(ii)   The independent visitor (if one has been appointed);

(iii) The relevant health care professionals of the district health authority;

(iv) The child's general medical practitioner (GP);

(v)   The appropriate local authority where it is proposed (or it is the case already) that the child will be looked after in their area;

(vi) The local education authority;

(vii) The child's teacher (in relevant cases);

(viii) Any other person whose views the responsible authority consider should be sought (for example, a representative from a voluntary agency, police child protection liaison officer, housing officer or community leader).

(See paragraphs 2.45–2.53 which contain guidance on consultation in relation to the Arrangements for Placement of Children (General) Regulations which is equally applicable to the Review of Children's Cases Regulations.)

3.12. Where it is considered that written views or reports will be adequate these should be sought and obtained in time for the review. Any relevant information which needs to be circulated before the meeting should be sent out with the agenda (see paragraph 3.14 below). A process should already be in place to ensure the continuous collection of information as part of the planning system rather than as a separate one-off exercise for a review. Consultation about the initial plan for the child, amendments to that plan as time passes and subsequent reviews will inform the planning process and will be relevant material for discussion at all review meetings.

Who Chairs a Review?

3.13. A meeting to review a child's case should be chaired by an officer of the responsible authority at a more senior level than the case social worker. The field social worker responsible for the child's case and that person's supervisor should be in attendance. The intention is that the role of the chairperson will bring a degree of oversight and objectivity to the monitoring of the responsible authority's practice and decision-making in relation to the plan for the child.

Agenda

3.14. It will be useful to have a checklist or agenda of the issues for discussion at a review meeting which is circulated in advance to those attending including the parent and the child. Items for the agenda will arise out of the considerations for discussion in paragraphs 3.19–3.20 below. This will help to ensure that no issues are overlooked and that the people attending the meeting are prepared to discuss and consider the relevant issues. Use of such a list or agenda should not become exclusive or inhibiting; those present should be free to raise issues they consider to be important.

Who Should Attend?

3.15. Regulation 7(2) requires that the responsible authority, where they consider it appropriate, should involve the child and his parents in review meetings. The involvement of the child will be subject to his understanding and welfare. The possibility of a child being accompanied to a review meeting by a person who is able to provide friendly support should be considered. Where a child's welfare would be prejudiced by his parent's attendance at the same time as the child, separate attendance may be arranged. The attendance of the child and his parents at meetings to review the child's case will be the norm rather than the exception (subject to the reservations already expressed). It is expected that the parents and the child (if he is of sufficient understanding) will be present at the whole of the review, but this will depend on the circumstances of each individual case. The involvement of the parents and the child in review meetings is in line with the basic philosophy of the Children Act in relation to the participation and wishes and feelings of the child and his parents, and the spirit of partnership between the local authority and parents.

3.16. The flexibility given to responsible authorities in the Regulations regarding the attendance of the child and parents at review meetings recognises the fact that in a few cases their attendance will not be appropriate or practicable. This may be the case if there is a clear conflict of interests which might militate against the attendance of either the child or the parents or both. However, the fears or inhibitions of professionals should not be the reason for excluding a child or his parent from a review. Alternative arrangements should be considered. Any decision to exclude the child or the parents from a meeting (or part of a meeting) should be discussed and agreed with the chairperson. If a parent or child is excluded from a review, a written explanation should be given with a copy placed on the child's case record on other arrangements made for their involvement in the review.

3.17. In addition to the parent and child, the child's carer should be invited. Other people with a legitimate interest in the child should also be invited if they have a contribution to make which indicates that they should take part in the discussions at the review meeting. This may apply, for example, to the child's GP, the child's community health doctor, health visitor, child psychologist, school teacher, residential care social worker, independent visitor (if appointed) or ethnic minority representative. The attendance of such people should always be discussed with the child before invitations are made and his views on their attendance obtained. It may be appropriate where the contribution from such people is strictly factual for the information to be provided in writing. Where a long-term plan has been set in place, a small group (those consistently and constantly involved with the child) should be identified as essential attenders at the next and subsequent review meetings. In the majority of cases, the group will consist of the social worker, the child, parents, the chairperson and the carer (if different from the parent). This will vary according to the circumstances of the individual case.

Venue for A Review Meeting

3.18. Separate, but equally important considerations apply in deciding where to hold a meeting to review a child's case. The child should always be asked for his views about the venue. Meetings should be arranged at a place (and time) which will be the most likely to provide a setting and atmosphere conducive to the relaxed participation of all those attending. Particular regard should be paid to the needs of the child. Arrangements should be made to secure the attendance of those identified as necessary to the particular review and allow serious discussion and planning to take place. Consideration should be given to assisting parents with travelling costs or the provision of other support, such as a child-minder, if there would otherwise be difficulty for a parent in attending a review (paragraph 16 of Schedule 2 to the Act may be relevant).

Matters for consideration in the the Review

3.19. The primary matter for consideration at the review is the plan for the welfare of the child (under the general welfare duties placed on authorities by sections 22, 61 and 64 of the Children Act). At the first review this will be done by examining and confirming the plan, with or without amendments. Subsequent reviews will be occasions for monitoring the progress of the plan and making decisions to amend the plan as necessary in the light of changed knowledge and circumstances. As the reason for planning and review is to safeguard and promote the welfare of the child the matters for consideration when planning and reviewing a case are nearly identical. After the first review, a review should always include consideration of progress made since the previous review – whether the goals and tasks set have been achieved; and if not, why not and what action is needed.

3.20. Schedule 2 provides a checklist of matters for consideration at the review which is not comprehensive or exclusive but sets the minimum requirements. In addition, the review must consider matters specified in the Act relating to the welfare of the child. Other matters will arise in individual cases which it is not possible to cover in a list of general application. The matters covered by Schedule 2 and the relevant statutory provisions are:

(a) an examination of the responsible authority's plan for the child in relation to the wishes and feelings of the child and having regard to his understanding;

(b) an examination of the responsible authority's plan for the child in relation to the wishes and feelings of the parents;

(c) whether the plan fulfils the responsible authority's duty under sections 22(3), 61(1) or 64(1) of the Act to safeguard and promote the child's welfare.

Paragraph (c) above includes the following:

● where the child is in the care of a local authority, whether or not the care order can be discharged or varied to a lesser order;

● whether the placement continues to be appropriate;

● the views of the child's carer;

- whether the plan makes necessary provision for the child's religious persuasion, racial origin and cultural and linguistic background;

- where a child is looked after, whether the plan takes account of the duty under section 23(6) to enable the child to live with a parent, other person with parental responsibility, relative, friend; and where the child is in care, a person in whose favour a residence order was in force immediately before the care order was made, or other person with a legitimate interest in the child;

- the arrangements made for contact and where the child is looked after by a local authority with regard to the duty on the local authority in paragraph 15 of Schedule 2 to the Act to promote and maintain contact between the child and his family;

- where a child is looked after, the views of an independent visitor if one has been appointed, and if not whether to appoint one;

- whether the plan takes account of any particular needs the child may have, eg if the child has a disability;

- the arrangements made for the child's health (including consent to examination or treatment);

- the arrangements made for the child's education;

- the arrangements, if any, for financial support of the placement;

- where the child is provided with accommodation by voluntary agreement, whether or not the arrangements for the involvement of the parents in the child's life are appropriate; whether the social worker needs to encourage greater exercise of the parents continuing responsibility to the child; whether or not there is still a need for accommodation or whether another sort of service would be more appropriate, or whether, in the case of a local authority there is a need to take care proceedings;

- reunification of the child with his parents and family;

- where a child has been in an agreed placement (not in care) for some time, whether the existing plan ensures that the child and the carer have an adequate sense of stability. Whether the carer should seek a residence order, for example; and

- where appropriate, arrangements for aftercare.

Report of Review

3.21. Regulation 10 requires that a written record of each review is drawn up and put on the child's case record for further reference. The record of the review should have attached to it the results of the consultation exercise, including any written reports submitted. It should also include the agenda with a note of the discussion under each item, what was decided and who is responsible for implementing particular decisions. It should be clearly noted whether the child and his parents were invited to the review, if they were not, the reason why not, whether they attended and what views they expressed on each of the agenda items. Any dissenting opinion should be recorded with an explanation of the rationale of decisions taken. The chairperson should check the record of the review to ensure that an accurate, comprehensive record is placed on file and, in particular, that any necessary action has been correctly identified and tasks allocated.

Notification

3.22. Regulation 7(3) requires that the child, his parent, others with parental responsibility and other persons considered appropriate are notified of the result of the review and decisions taken in consequence of the review. It may be necessary to notify third parties of the result of the review, because they need to know about a decision. Care should be taken to provide only that information which the third party needs to know.

3.23. The notification of the result of each review meeting should be a written summary of the main points of the written report of the review which makes clear who is responsible for implementing decisions arising from the review and the relevant time-scales. The field social worker responsible for the case should supplement this written notification by explaining in advance wherever possible to the parents and the child the decisions taken at the review meeting and the reasons for these decisions, even if the parents and child were present for all or part of the meeting. Where they were not present, it will be particularly important to do this. It is recommended that this notification is sent no later than 14 days after the review has been held. The notification should indicate whom the child or parent should contact if there is disagreement about any of the decisions taken.

Implementing Decisions

3.24. As part of the review system each responsible authority will need to set in place arrangements for implementing decisions made in the course of a review of a child's case (Regulation 8). Health authorities, local education authorities, local housing authorities and other social services departments have a duty under section 27 of the Children Act to comply with a request from a social services department for help in the exercise of their functions under Part III of the Act. Consultation in child protection work is provided for in Section 47(9) and (11) of the Act. Section 28 imposes new duties on local authorities to consult the appropriate local education authority before they accommodate a child in an establishment which provides education. All responsible authorities will need to make specific arrangements to secure the cooperation of all others who have a role to play in implementing the plan for the child.

Disagreements

3.25. Where disagreements arise in the course of the review process between the child and parents, the child and the responsible authority or the parents and the responsible authority, the responsible authority should make every effort to resolve these by explaining fully the reasons for their decisions. When a disagreement cannot be resolved, the responsible authority should ensure that the child (where he is of sufficient understanding), parents, carers and others involved with the child are aware of the representations procedure required by section 26(3) of the Children Act 1989 and are given advice and assistance as necessary (see Chapter 5).

MONITORING THE SYSTEM

3.26. Responsible authorities are required by Regulation 9 to set in place a system for monitoring of the operation of the review system. While the review of an individual case and the implementation of decisions will involve sharing information and action with others the monitoring of responsible authority's review system will be a matter for that responsible authority alone. The purpose of the monitoring exercise will be to assess how far the system has achieved the objective of ensuring good management of individual cases, to provide an indication of the quality of practice, how far practice reflects the authority's policies and service priorities and to afford an overview of effectiveness in decision making and social work practice. In some local authorities an officer with a title like Principal Assistant (Child Care) is appointed to be concerned with policy rather than line management and to concentrate on deployment of resources and service monitoring. Where such posts exist it would be appropriate for such a person to conduct the oversight of the review system. Local authorities may wish to consider this in connection with other quality assurance measures being set in place.

CHAPTER 4   <u>CONTACT</u>

INTRODUCTION

4.1. The new legislative framework of the Children Act remedies the acknowledged defects in previous legislation which prevented parents and others from seeking the court's view in disputes about contact. The Children Act imposes a new duty to promote contact between a child who is being looked after and those connected with him. This applies whether a child is accommodated by voluntary arrangement or as a result of a court order. The Children Act empowers the courts to make orders regarding contact in all circumstances where a child is in care. This is unlike the previous legislation which provided for the courts to make orders in respect of a child in care only when access by specific persons had been refused or terminated.

LEGISLATIVE FRAMEWORK AND GENERAL PRINCIPLES

4.2. Section 34 of the Children Act 1989 requires the court to consider the proposed arrangements for contact between a child who is the subject of care proceedings and the child's parents and other involved relatives. The court may make directions about the kind or amount of contact which should be allowed. When preparing an application for a care order, an outline of the proposed contact arrangements should be drawn up, so that the court can give consideration to the local authority's proposals and the submissions of others about the proposals. Local authorities will be expected to provide details of the proposals for contact when applying for an interim or full care order.

4.3. The Contact with Children Regulations, made under section 34(8) of the Act, impose requirements on local authorities in relation to refusal of contact, departure from the terms of an order made under section 34 and notification of variation or supervision of contact arrangements made otherwise than under a section 34 order (see Annex D).

4.4. The guidance that follows builds upon that provided by the **Code of Practice – Access to Children in Care** which it replaces. This guidance, unlike the code, covers all children looked after (the code did not apply in most respects to children received into care). Policies, procedures and practice will need revision to take account of that and of the new legal position of parents upon the making of a court order; that is the sharing of their parental responsibility with the local authority rather than loss of that responsibility. Equally the emphasis on participation in local authority decision-making by children and parents will require changes in approach, where this has not been the policy and practice prior to the implementation of the Children Act. For instance, many foster parents have played a crucial part in promoting contact with the child's family, and this needs to be reflected in the involvement of foster parents in the decision-making process. Others will need more training and support to enable them to work under the new approach.

CONTACT WITH CHILDREN IN CARE

4.5. Where a child is in care, the local authority must allow reasonable contact with a child's parents, any guardian and any other person with whom he was living under a court order immediately before the care order was made (section 34(1)). The court order may be a residence order or an order under the inherent jurisdiction of the High Court. The power to make orders concerning contact are set out in section 34(2), (4), (5), (6) and (7). In the event of a dispute about contact when a child is not in care, a section 8 order may be made on the application of the child, a parent or other person, if the matter cannot be resolved by agreement, or the representations procedure has not provided a solution. The Contact with Children Regulations require local authorities to notify those affected about proposals to change arrangements for contact in relation to a child in care. If those arrangements are defined in a court order, Regulation 3 provides for the terms of the order to be departed from with the agreement of the person named in the order in specified circumstances. In these cases, notification should also be given to the child's parents (if not the person with whom the agreement has been made), a guardian, a person in whose favour a residence order was in force immediately before the care order was made; and if the child is in care, any person who had care of the child by virtue of a wardship order and any other person whose wishes and feelings the authority consider to be relevant (Regulation 2).

4.6. Subject to any order of the court, it is for the local authority to make decisions about contact arrangements in an individual case where a child is in care. As stated already, the Children Act imposes a new duty to promote contact between a child who is being looked after (whether or not the child is in compulsory care) and those who are connected with him (paragraph 15(1) of Schedule 2). These people include the child's parents, any one else with parental responsibility for him and any relative or friend of the child, unless it is not reasonably practicable or consistent with the child's welfare to do so. To support the new duty, the local authority are required to take reasonable steps to inform the child's parents and any other person who has parental responsibility for the child of the child's address (paragraph 15(2) of Schedule 2). However, information need not be given if the child is subject to a care order and it would prejudice the child's welfare to give it (paragraph 15(4) of Schedule 2). Equally, a parent or other person with parental responsibility for the child in care must inform the local authority of his address (paragraph 15(2)(b) of Schedule 2).

CONTACT WITH CHILDREN LOOKED AFTER BY VOLUNTARY AGREEMENT

4.7. Arrangements for contact with children looked after by voluntary agreement are a matter for negotiation and agreement between the local authority, the older child, parents and others seeking contact. The local authority should ensure that parents and others know where to seek advice about negotiations over contact.

PROMOTION OF CONTACT WITH CHILDREN NOT LOOKED AFTER

4.8. Where a child in the area of the local authority and in need is living apart from his family, but is not looked after by that local authority, paragraph 10(b) of Schedule 2 requires the local authority to promote contact between the child and his family. For example, in the case of a child living in a long-stay health authority establishment, the local authority could decide to provide services to the child or family under Part III of the Act to promote contact.

IMPORTANCE OF CONTACT

4.9. For the majority of children there will be no doubt that their interests will be best served by efforts to sustain or create links with their natural families. Contact in the sense of personal meetings and visits will generally be the most common and, for both families and children, the most satisfactory way of maintaining their relationship. But other means which can help to keep family bonds alive should be borne in mind: letters, telephone calls, exchange of photographs. Contacts, however occasional, may continue to have a value for the child even when there is no question of returning to his family. These contacts can keep alive for a child a sense of his origins and may keep open options for family relationships in later life.

4.10. The first weeks, during which the child is looked after by the local authority, are likely to be particularly crucial to the success of the relationship between the parent, the social worker and the child's carers and to the level of future contact between parent and child. It is at this time that patterns are set which it may be difficult to change, whether the child is looked after by a voluntary arrangement or as a result of a care order. Parents should be involved in the assessment and planning prior to placement wherever possible. Emergency admissions require special care if parents are to be reassured from the outset that they have a continuing role in their child's life and to minimise distress for the child. Early visits and meetings should be encouraged, even though parents may need help to enable them to cope with the child's distress and their own. These considerations, subject to whatever safeguards are necessary for the child's protection, are equally important where children are subject to emergency protection orders.

CONTACT AND CHILD PROTECTION ORDERS

Child Assessment Order

4.11. If in making a child assessment order, the court directs that the child may be kept away from home, it must also give directions as it thinks fit about contact between the child and other persons during this period. A temporary overnight stay cannot be equated with being placed in care, but the court may well be guided on contact by the presumption of reasonable contact between a child in care and his parents, guardian and certain other persons established by section 34. The court would also want to consider requests to be allowed contact from other persons who have to be notified of the hearing. As for all questions affecting the child that arise under the Act, the court must give paramount consideration to the child's welfare when considering contact (section 1(1)).

Emergency Protection Order

4.12. Where the court makes an emergency protection order (EPO) it has the discretion to give directions as appropriate with regard to contact which is or is not to be allowed between the child and any named person (section 44(6)(a)). The court direction may impose conditions (section 44(8)). However, subject to any of these directions, there is a general duty on the applicant to allow the child reasonable contact with a range of persons. These are his parents, any person who is not a parent but has parental responsibility, any person with whom he was living before the order was made, any person in whose favour a contact order (a section 8 order) is in force with respect to the child, any person who is allowed contact by virtue of an order under section 34 (see guidance in volume 1 in this series) or anyone acting on behalf of any of these people. The court may give directions regarding contact not only when the EPO is made, but also at any time while it is in force. The court may also vary the directions at any time.

Contact with a Child in Police Protection

4.13. While a child is in police protection under section 46, the designated officer must allow such contact (if any) as he considers is reasonable and in the child's best interests with the following categories of persons:

(a) the child's parents;

(b) any person who is not a parent of the child but who has parental responsibility for him;

(c) any person with whom the child was living immediately before he was taken into police protection;

(d) any person in whose favour a section 8 contact order is in force with respect to the child;

(e) any person who is allowed to have contact with the child by virtue of a section 8 order;

(f) any person acting on behalf of any of those persons.

If the child in police protection is accommodated by the local authority for the area in which the child usually lives, the local authority are required by section 46(11) to afford such contact to these people.

PLANNING AND CONTACT

4.14. The responsible authority must make plans for the child (see guidance on planning contained in Chapter 2 – Arrangements for Placement). Consideration of contact is an essential element in the planning process. So far as is reasonably practicable, the views of the child, if he is old enough, the parents and the child's carers must be ascertained before a decision about contact arrangements is made (section 22(4), 61(2) and 64(2) of the Act). The value and purpose of contact should be clearly understood and agreed so far as possible by all concerned. There should be a clear understanding from the outset about all the arrangements and what is expected of the parents, the responsible authority and the child's carers in connection with the arrangements.

4.15. The contact arrangements should include those made in respect of relatives, siblings, grandparents and unmarried fathers; all those people with whom the child's contact should be preserved. In some cases it may be appropriate to identify relatives, who may include a parent, with whom contact has lapsed and to follow up the prospects of re-establishing contact. Care will clearly be needed where there is family or marital conflict, but responsible authorities should be ready to explore possibilities of preserving, establishing or promoting contact which could be beneficial to the child. In doing so they should not overlook problems which may arise when a child is placed with a person who may be reluctant to provide contact with, for example, an unmarried father, relatives or friends of the child. Carers and the child may need support to cope with these situations.

SECTION 34 ORDERS FOR CONTACT

4.16. When an order for contact under section 34 is in force, the local authority remains responsible for the child's welfare. Subject to the terms of the order in relation to decisions about contact, the local authority must continue to plan and care for the child in accordance with their general duty under section 22(3)(a) of the Children Act. In handling decisions about contact within the terms of the order, local authorities should continue to apply the principles set out in this guidance.

PLACEMENT AND CONTACT

4.17. The implications for contact are among the factors which should be considered when deciding where to place a child. In the case of children looked after by local authorities, section 23(7)(a) of the Children Act specifically requires local authorities to place a child near his home, so far as practicable, subject to his welfare being safeguarded. The effect on parental contact should always be considered when it is proposed to seek the court's consent to the emigration of a child in care (paragraph 19 of Schedule 2 to the Act).

THE SETTING FOR VISITS

4.18. Visits by the parents to the child in his foster home, residential home or in the family home are the most usual forms of contact. They can provide continuity for the child in that setting and opportunities for the parents and carers to meet. If family reunification is the plan, visits should be in the family home at the earliest possible stage. Such visits also have the advantage of maintaining links with the neighbourhood to which the child will be returning. However, other venues may have advantages for some children and in some circumstances. Outings are one example. Whatever the venue, the aim should be to ensure that privacy and a welcoming and congenial setting are available. If possible, parents should be encouraged to participate in some way in the child's daily life, by preparing tea, for example, or shopping for clothes or putting a young child to bed.

4.19.–4.20. Unallocated.*

RESIDENTIAL CARE

4.21. Residential care staff also need training and preparation to make a positive contribution to the success of contact arrangements and to deal with tensions and difficulties which can arise. The potential influence of the establishment's regime should not be overlooked, in particular for children who have been placed in secure accommodation. In every establishment care is needed to ensure that the importance of the contact arrangements is recognised, that the internal organisation and timetable do not make visiting difficult and that arrangements for visiting are sufficiently flexible.

4.22. Regulations preclude the use of sanctions which could affect agreed arrangements for contact between the child and his parents or other relatives as a form of control of the child (see also paragraphs 4.25–4.26 below). More detailed guidance on specific issues in respect of residential placements will be found in the volume on residential care in this series.

TRAVELLING ARRANGEMENTS AND EXPENSES

4.23. Parents and others having contact may need advice and help with travelling arrangements. Local authorities have power under paragraph 16 of Schedule 2 to help with the cost of visiting looked after children where there would otherwise be undue financial hardship. The power is not limited to assistance with travelling expenses, but can be used to meet all reasonable costs associated with visiting. Parents may also need advice about benefits which may be payable during a child's extended visits home.

THE CHILD'S WISHES

4.24. The local authority have a duty to give due consideration to the child's wishes and feelings, having regard to his understanding in relation to decision-making by the authority (section 22(5)(a)). Generally children want to see their parents, other members of their family and family friends. However, sometimes children are openly unwilling to see some or all of their family or have ambivalent feelings about contact which make them reluctant to see their parents or experience persistent distress at the prospect. The social worker, with the help of the carers and any other adults in whom the child may have confided, must attempt to understand the source of these feelings. They may arise from factors which can be changed or which the child can be helped to understand. The social worker and carers should also make real efforts to help the child to understand what is likely to be of greatest benefit to him both for the short and long-term.

4.25. Where the difficulties cannot be resolved the local authority may conclude that a child's reasons for not wanting contact are valid. A child should not be forced to persist unwillingly or unhappily with seeing a parent or other person. In such a case local authorities will need to obtain legal advice.

---

*Footnote: these paragraphs in Volume 3 relate to Foster Care and are therefore not relevant to Volume 4. The paragraph numbers are unallocated in this Volume in order to secure consistency of paragraph numbers between the two Volumes. (Chapter Numbers have, of necessity, to differ.)

A child in care has a right to make an application to the court to authorise the local authority to refuse to allow contact between the child and a named person (section 34(4)). It may be that the local authority will decide that it is in the child's best interest to initiate such proceedings if the child so wishes. The child's feelings may change as he develops and in the future he may be more ready to see his parents. The fact that the child or the local authority has obtained an order ending contact does not preclude the need to reconsider issues of contact.

RESTRICTIONS OF CONTACT WITH CHILDREN IN CARE

4.26. Planning will generally be based on the assumption that contact will be beneficial to the child unless there are clear indications to the contrary. There are sometimes reasons why, to safeguard the child's welfare, contact must be supervised, restricted or suspended. A child may be committed to care in circumstances which call for a decision to refuse contact from the beginning. Where there are special circumstances which mean that no contact arrangements – including short-term arrangements or supervised arrangements – can be offered to a parent while a decision about contact is under consideration, local authorities must bear in mind section 34(1) of the Children Act 1989 and any order under section 34(3). Section 34(6) of the Act provides for local authorities to refuse to allow contact that would otherwise be required under section 34(1) or by a section 34 order if:

"(a) they are satisfied that it is necessary to do so in order to safeguard or promote the child's welfare; and

(b) the refusal –

(i) is decided upon as a matter of urgency; and

(ii) does not last for more than seven days."

4.27. Regulation 2 of the Contact with Children Regulations requires local authorities which have decided to refuse contact under section 34(6) to notify in writing as soon as a decision to refuse contact has been made:

"(a) the child, if he is of sufficient understanding;

(b) the child's parents;

(c) any guardian of his;

(d) where there was a residence order in force with respect to the child immediately before the care order was made, the person in whose favour the order was made;

(e) where immediately before the care order was made, a person had care of the child by virtue of an order made in the exercise of the High Court's inherent jurisdiction with respect to children, that person; and

(f) any other person whose wishes and feelings the authority consider to be relevant."

It will be important to inform the child in a manner appropriate to his understanding and to explain the reasons for the action.

4.28. The notification should contain as much of the information referred to in the Schedule to the Regulations as the local authority decides is necessary. The information referred to in the Schedule includes:

● local authority's decision;

● date of the decision;

● reasons for the decision;

● duration (if applicable);

● remedies in case of dissatisfaction.

4.29. Local authorities must have a clear understanding of what is being considered and why. Local authorities should always obtain legal advice about provisions concerning contact under section 34, which generally require court authority, unless all parties are in agreement. Local authorities should consider making applications to the court for decisions under section 34 in advance of the implementation of the Act on 14 October 1991, if they wish to maintain a restricted contact regime on or after that date, in cases where the presumption under section 34(1) applies.

4.30. Local authorities should also bear in mind that the Act urges that there should be no avoidable delay in decisions relating to children, because of the unintended and generally undesirable effects of delay on the plans for the child's future (sections 1(2) and 32). A child's experience of the passage of time varies according to age and to his general stage of development. Even temporary breaks in contact can have especially damaging effects on the relationship between parents and very young children. Older children will be more able to benefit from help from the social worker and from their carers in understanding the reasons for any necessary limitation or disruption of contact. These considerations apply equally whether decisions are being made when a child begins to be looked after or after he has been in care for a lengthy period. Whatever the decisions made about contact at any stage in a local authority's involvement with a child, it will be necessary to review the decisions in the light of current circumstances at each review.

DEPARTURE FROM TERMS OF COURT ORDER ON CONTACT UNDER SECTION 34

4.31. Regulation 3 of the Contact with Children Regulations provides for a local authority to depart from the terms of any order for contact under section 34. The circumstances in which this may be done are as follows:

- there is agreement between the local authority and the person in relation to whom the order is made;
- the child, if of sufficient understanding, also agrees;
- written notification of the agreement is provided within seven days to all the persons listed in Regulation 2. This notification should be on a need to know basis.

This provision allows for flexibility and partnership in contact arrangements, obviating the need to go back to the court when all concerned agree a new arrangement.

VARIATION OR SUSPENSION OF CONTACT ARRANGEMENTS NOT GOVERNED BY A SECTION 34 ORDER

4.32. When a local authority decide to vary or suspend an arrangement for contact between one person and the child in care with a view to affording another person contact with that child, they are required to notify those persons specified in Regulation 2 of the Contact with Children Regulations. This requirement is set out in Regulation 4 which states that the notification should be given as soon as the decision to vary or suspend contact is made. The information provided in the notification should be on a need to know basis.

COMMUNICATING DECISIONS ABOUT CONTACT

4.33. Subject to what is said in paragraphs 4.27–4.32 above, all decisions about contact should be explained to parents and discussed with them. Local authorities should also confirm in writing to the parents all decisions and agreements about contact arrangements and any changes to the arrangements and the outcome of all formal and informal reviews of contact. Where limitations or control on contact have been imposed, these should be clearly stated. Similarly, any postponement of contact should be confirmed in writing together with the reasons. Unless the child is subject to a court order, limitations, controls and postponements of contact should be agreed by all those involved.

4.34. Simple but informative leaflets about care and the law can be helpful, especially when a child begins to be looked after whether on a voluntary basis or by order of a court. They can help parents to understand their position and that of their child in relation to the authority and can reassure them about their continuing place in their child's life. Similarly, descriptive leaflets produced by community homes with information about visiting and public transport can help and reassure parents. Local authorities may prefer to design their own leaflets or to use publications available from other agencies and organisations. Leaflets should be couched in terms which are simple and clearly understood, avoiding professional terminology and jargon. Local authorities should produce leaflets in languages other than English where there is a local need and produce information in a format accessible to people with communication difficulties. Leaflets should never be used in place of personal letters confirming decisions and agreements about the individual child.

4.35. It is equally important that there should be clear and full communication and understanding of all contact decisions and arrangements among all those who are involved with the child's care, including foster parents and officers in charge of residential homes. Where children are cared for by other agencies, there should be effective liaison and clear agreements with the agency about all matters relating to contact.

DISAGREEMENT WITH PARENTS

4.36. Local authorities should ensure that they have clear arrangements to inform parents and others about how to pursue complaints about contact and ask for decisions to be reviewed. Responsible authorities should ensure that the representations procedure recognises the need to accept complaints from people, other than parents, who have contact with children who are being looked after.

4.37. Arrangements should be made for parents to discuss their anxieties and dissatisfactions with senior officers if they feel they have reached an impasse with their social worker. Those arrangements should not be used to prevent or hinder use of the representations procedure required by the Act. All parents and, where appropriate according to the child's understanding, the child should be informed of these procedures. (See guidance in Chapter 5 on the operation of the representations procedure). When a disagreement persists, parents of a child subject to a care order should be advised to seek a legal opinion on the most appropriate action open to them.

REVIEWING CONTACT

4.38. Contact arrangements, whichever responsible authority is involved, should be kept under review, and not necessarily just as part of reviews. Contact should be monitored to check whether the arrangements are working as intended and to identify any problems which have arisen and any changes which are needed: whether, for example, the arrangements are unnecessarily restrictive. Difficulties should be discussed openly with the parents and with the child's carers so that solutions can be explored and help given. It cannot be in the interests of the child and is no service to parents to allow them to drift to the periphery of a child's life, without reminding them of the possible implications of this course to the plan for their child and his relationship with them.

4.39. Some children will be cared for by other agencies, for example, in voluntary homes, special schools, Youth Treatment Centres or by another local authority. Wherever the child is placed, the statutory responsibility for his welfare lies with the local authority. They should continue, in co-operation with any other agency which is involved, to keep under review the child's contacts with his family and the progress of contact arrangements.

4.40. When an order for contact is made under section 34, the local authority will need to review the plan for the child. Contact should continue to be monitored. The local authority will need to consider whether it would be appropriate to apply to the court for variation of the order, including variation of any of the conditions attached to the order.

RECORD KEEPING

4.41. Full and clear records are essential to the effective monitoring of contact. They will provide a basis for a clear understanding, when social workers or carers change, of the decisions about contact which have been made and the reasons for them. Records about contact should form part of the child's case record required by the Arrangements for Placement Regulations.

CHAPTER 5 <u>REPRESENTATIONS</u> <u>PROCEDURE</u>

5.1. Local authorities, voluntary organisations and registered children's homes (henceforward called 'responsible authorities') are required to have a procedure for considering representations (including complaints) about children's services. This procedure relates to sections 24(13), 26(3)–(8), 59(4), paragraph 10(2)(l) of Schedule 6 and paragraph 6 of Schedule 7 to the Children Act. It should cover all representations about local authorities' actions in meeting their responsibilities to any child in need under Part III of the Act. Voluntary organisations and registered children's homes are also required to set up representations procedures to consider representations – including complaints – made by or on behalf of children accommodated by them but not looked after by the local authority. The primary legislation and the Representations Procedure (Children) Regulations are a common framework on which all the responsible authorities should build to achieve a procedure and approach which best suits their local needs and organisational structure. The Regulations set the minimum standard of provision that responsible authorities should establish to meet the requirements of the Children Act 1989.

5.2. This procedure and that required for other local authority social services functions by the Directions made under section 7B of the Local Authority Social Services Act 1970 (inserted by section 50 of the National Health Service and Community Care Act 1990) are broadly compatible. Both procedures have been designed so that local authorities wishing to do so will be able to use common structures for handling representations, including complaints. The main difference between the two procedures is that the Children Act requires the involvement of an independent person at each stage of consideration of a representation or a complaint. The links between the procedures are discussed at other points in the guidance.

5.3. The Children Act envisages a high degree of co-operation between parents and authorities in negotiating and agreeing what form of action will best meet a child's needs and promote his welfare. It also calls for the informed participation of the child and his parents in decision-making about services for the child. Sometimes the required co-operation will not be achieved or will break down or delays will occur. The Act requires that responsible authorities establish a procedure which provides an accessible and effective means of representation or complaint where problems cannot be otherwise resolved. Definitions of representations and complaints are set out in paragraph 5.5 below. It is envisaged that the procedure will be used primarily for handling complaints rather than representations. Accordingly the guidance concentrates on complaints. The procedure will involve independent persons in responsible authorities' considerations and should ensure that the child, his parents and others significantly involved with the child have confidence in their ability to make their views known and to influence decisions made about the child's welfare.

5.4. The responsible authority should aim to develop a procedure which is understood and accepted by all involved: children, parents and their representatives, as well as the responsible authority's staff and the local authority's elected members. Plans for implementing representation procedures should take account of the need for consultation with community groups, voluntary and other organisations with an interest, carers and with staff at all levels. The responsible authority should seek to involve the community in setting up their representations procedures so that the procedure reflects the needs of those who may need to use it. Adherence to the principles of the Race Relations Act 1976 and other equal opportunities legislation requires consultation with community groups reflecting the racial and cultural diversity of the local community.

DEFINITIONS

5.5. For the purpose of this guidance, the following definitions are used:

(a) A 'responsible authority' is a local authority, voluntary organisation or registered children's home;

(b) 'Representations' will include enquiries and statements about such matters as the availability, delivery and nature of services and will not necessarily be critical;

(c) A 'complaint' is a written or oral expression of dissatisfaction or disquiet in relation to an individual child about the local authority's exercise of its functions under Part III and paragraph 4 of Schedule 7 of the Children Act 1989 and matters in relation to children accommodated by voluntary organisations and registered children's homes. A complaint may arise as a result of an unwelcome or disputed decision, concern about the quality or appropriateness of services, delay in decision-making about services or about their delivery or non-delivery (the precise meaning of complaint is a matter for interpretation by the courts);

(d) A 'complainant' is the child or person making the complaint on his behalf;

(e) An 'independent person' is a person, not a member or officer of the authority handling the child's case who is required by section 26(4) to take part in the authority's consideration of a complaint made to them and not excluded by the provisions of Regulation 1(3). The independent person is not an advocate for the child nor an investigator; his role is to provide an objective element in the authority's considerations (see Regulations 6 and 8);

(f) A 'panel' is a group of 3 persons, at least one of whom is independent (as defined in Regulation 1(3) of these Regulations) appointed by the authority to consider complaints reviewed by the responsible authority under the complaints procedure when the complainant remains dissatisfied and to make a recommendation about further action (see Regulations 8 and 9).

(g) The 'procedure' is the representations and complaints procedure which responsible authorities are required to set up by the Children Act;

(h) The 'designated officer' is the officer which the authority is required to appoint to assist in the co-ordination of all aspects of the consideration of complaints (see Regulation 3(1)).

WHO MAY COMPLAIN

5.6. Section 26(3) requires the responsible authority to establish a procedure for considering any representations (including any complaint) made to it by:

"(a) any child who is being looked after by them or who is not being looked after by them but is in need;

(b) a parent of his;

(c) any person who is not a parent of his but who has parental responsibility for him;

(d) any local authority foster parent;

(e) such other person as the authority consider has a sufficient interest in the child's welfare to warrant his representations being considered by them,

about the discharge by the authority of any of their functions under this Part in relation to the child."

5.7. The first person listed is the child. The responsible authority should always check with a child (subject to his understanding) that a complaint submitted on his behalf reflects his views and that he does wish the person submitting the complaint to act on his behalf. Where it is decided that the person submitting the complaint is not acting on the child's behalf, he may still be eligible to have the complaint considered under the procedure. Regulation 4(4) makes it clear that the local authority have discretion to decide in cases where eligibility is not automatic whether or not an individual has sufficient interest in the child's welfare to justify his own representation being considered by them (section 26(3)(e)). The local authority should have a clear policy on this matter that takes account of the Act's emphasis on participation in decision-making of all those persons who are significant to the child or can make a positive contribution to planning for the child's future. A flexible approach to this issue will ensure that such individuals are not overlooked or obliged to use other means to make their views or complaint known.

WHAT MAY BE COMPLAINED ABOUT

5.8. A local authority's procedures must cater for complaints from the people mentioned above about local authority support for families and their children under Part III of the Act. This will include complaints about day care, services to support children within their family home, accommodation of a child, aftercare and decisions relating to the placement of a child or the handling of a child's case. The processes involved in decision-making or the denial of a service must also be covered by the responsible authority's arrangements. In addition to those matters directly related to the provision of services to children in need, other matters fall within the scope of the Regulations and must be covered by the procedure a local authority sets up to meet the requirements of these Regulations. Regulation 12(2) refers to representations about decisions by a local authority in respect of exemptions to the "usual fostering limit" (paragraphs 4–6 of Schedule 7). Such representations should be dealt with in accordance with these Regulations and the guidance below. Regulations 11(1) and (2) require that voluntary organisations and registered children's homes also set up representations procedures in line with these Regulations to consider representations from children accommodated by them and others eligible to make representations.

5.9. The responsible authority should consider what other matters might be appropriate to the procedure set up to meet the requirements of these Regulations. The responsible authority should allow representations to be made about matters which affect a group of children rather than an individual child to be processed within their Children Act procedure. For example, inappropriate restrictions on the lives of children in residential care such as preventing children's activities for the convenience of staff, fixing meal times to suit staff rather than to fit in with the normal needs of children or preventing children's normal activities outside the home.

5.10. Representations or complaints about child care matters which fall outside Part III of the Act are not covered by this procedure but by the Complaints Procedure Directions. However, dissatisfaction about a local authority's management or handling of a child's case, even where related to a court order, may be appropriate to the procedure. The inclusion of a child's name on a child protection register is an administrative action not carried out under any statutory provision (even where the decision is linked to a recommendation to seek a court order) but it is part of an inter-agency process for which the local authority is in the lead but does not carry full responsibility. While the requirements of section 26 are confined to the local authority's functions under the Act it would be good practice to provide, with the agreement of the Area Child Protection Committee (ACPC), an appropriate procedure to handle complaints about inter-agency case conferences and their recommendations.

OBJECTIVES

5.11. Children and others making representations including complaints should have access to a procedure which provides them with an opportunity to make representations and complaints about and challenge decisions made in relation to services provided to them direct or via an agency. This is particularly important when no other means of redress is open to them but is valuable even when alternative avenues exist. A well publicised statement of commitment to the representations procedure should encourage the identification and speedy resolution of representations and complaints as they arise. A secondary benefit of the system will be to illustrate for the responsible authority how policies translate into practice and to highlight areas where the responsible authority should be more responsive to the needs of individual clients and the community.

5.12. The statutory requirements and the associated guidance seek to achieve an accessible and effective means of making complaints, close to the point at which the problem arose but with an independent element that will inspire confidence in the procedure. That confidence will not develop unless complaints are acted on in the shortest possible time and an opportunity to challenge the outcome of the considerations is available. For that reason the Regulations require that the responsible authority's arrangements should provide a process which satisfies those criteria. It is not intended that all problems that arise in the day to day handling of child care services should automatically be elevated to the status of a complaint. A matter which is promptly resolved to everyone's complete satisfaction when drawn to the attention of an officer of the responsible authority is not something that requires referral to the procedure.

PROBLEM SOLVING

5.13. Where a problem arises, it will usually be possible to resolve the issue satisfactorily before a complaint is made. Efforts to resolve matters will include discussion and reconsideration as well as explanations of decisions made and actions taken. The aim should be to resolve dissatisfaction as near to the point at which it arose as possible. The responsible authority may wish to consider how they can ensure that advice and support is available to persons expressing dissatisfaction at this stage. Some local authorities have appointed an officer with responsibility to support children and their representatives in participation in decision-making and in voicing their concerns. The appointment of such an officer in the authority or the involvement of people and agencies in the community who can provide independent advice would assist problem-solving and may, therefore, prevent dissatisfaction developing into a matter for complaint. Advocacy as a service to the child as part of child care service provision is not ruled out by these Regulations, nor is it ruled out if a responsible authority wish to provide such a service to support the child in this or other procedures. However, attempts at problem-solving should not be used to divert an eligible person from lodging a complaint under the statutory procedure.

5.14. Staff will need advice on the difficult issue of when an unresolved problem becomes a complaint. This will help to ensure that the problem solving stage is not prolonged beyond any positive period of action, thereby delaying or preventing recourse to the representations procedure, and that problems capable of simple resolution do not become complaints. The responsible authority may wish to consider whether it would be helpful to individuals to know that they are expected to resolve a request for a review of a decision within a specified time limit. Attempts at problem-solving should not end once a complaint has been registered. Rather, there should be continued efforts to resolve the dissatisfaction of service users so that the matter complained of is resolved during consideration of the complaint.

PUBLICITY

5.15. Section 26(8) requires local authorities to publicise their representations procedures. It is recommended that the local authority should publicly announce the setting up of the procedure and invite the participation of service users, community groups and others. The publicity should make clear who is entitled to make use of the procedure and how they may do so, what the procedure covers, to whom a representation or complaint should be addressed, who is available to give advice, the stages in consideration of a representation or complaint and the timescale for each stage. The publicity should be framed in terms that make clear that the procedure is a part of the local authority's commitment to partnership and the informed participation of child and parents in the authority's decision-making about provision of services to safeguard and promote the welfare of a child in need.

5.16. Information should be available in the form of leaflets and posters at social services departments, health service clinics, schools, libraries, family centres, doctors' surgeries, residential homes, Citizens Advice Bureaux and other suitable places. Information leaflets and booklets, using plain language and, where relevant, in other appropriate languages, should be freely available to children where they are of sufficient understanding, parents and others who may be eligible to use the procedure. In addition it would be good practice to ensure that the information on the representations procedure forms part of an information pack made available prior to a first review of a child's case. Every child in a home should be provided with an information leaflet that includes the telephone number of someone independent of the home whom the child can contact if he has any problems. The local authority may wish to discuss with voluntary organisations and others how best to provide the information in alternative formats such as in large print, braille, on tape or video. All the material should present a positive view of the use of the procedure and seek to diminish fears that invoking the procedure will cause problems for a complainant in their day to day contact with authorities' staff.

MANAGEMENT ISSUES

5.17. A representations procedure will be effective only if the responsible authority demonstrates commitment to it, ensuring, as required by Regulation 3(2), that their policy and the detail of the procedure are known, understood and accepted by elected members, staff, independent persons and clients. Staff may have concerns about workload, their own ability to operate within the procedure or their vulnerability to unfounded complaints. An unequivocal policy statement on the scope and benefits of the procedure, together with recognition of the need for management structures and staff training which reflect the demands of that policy will help to reassure staff. Discussions with staff and their associations will identify areas of concern and afford opportunities for addressing these concerns. Some responsible authorities will have procedures in place that will require little modification to meet the requirements of the Children Act. Where this is the case staff will still need to know of any changes, including the scope of the procedure and an explanation of the effect on the procedure of the Children Act's requirements. Other responsible authorities will be establishing a formal procedure for the first time. Responsible authorities and their staff are more likely to operate the procedure fairly and properly if it is viewed as an aspect of service provision to promote partnership.

REPRESENTATIONS INVOLVING MORE THAN ONE LOCAL AUTHORITY

5.18. If a representation is made which involves more than one local authority, it should be considered by the local authority which is looking after the child. If the child is not being looked after but provided with other services the local authority in whose area the child normally resides should consider the complaint. In such cases, it is suggested that the designated officers of the local authorities involved work together and maintain good liaison.

LINKS WITH OTHER PROCEDURES

5.19. The responsible authority should be aware of the need in appropriate cases to identify where a complaint is more appropriate to another procedure or where linked issues require joint consideration. A local authority's procedure for dealing with child care matters will have links with their procedure for hearing other representations and complaints described in "Community Care in the Next Decade and Beyond: Policy Guidance" Chapter 6, "Complaints Procedures" (HMSO 1990). How far the two procedures operate separately or come together will be for individual authorities to decide, bearing in mind the need to safeguard the welfare of the child and to provide appropriate child care expertise. The two procedures are administratively similar and in practice the two procedures might operate together at the point at which the panel becomes involved.

5.20. There will be a need for links with other procedures including those within health authorities and other agencies contributing to child care services. For example, NHS staff may be involved in family support and child protection work. Other agencies apart from health authorities who may be involved in child care services include local education authorities, housing authorities, voluntary and private child care organisations, the probation service and the police. It is essential that arrangements cover both the separating out of representations or complaints appropriate to another procedure and cases where some joint action is appropriate.

OTHER AVENUES OF COMPLAINT

5.21. The procedure required by these Regulations is not an appeals procedure. Separate procedures exist under the Children Act for appeals against the "usual fostering limit" exemption. Appeals against court orders will be to the court. Such court procedures need not exclude the processing of a complaint which is eligible for consideration under the representations procedure, but legal advice should be sought in such cases.

The Commissioner for Local Administration

5.22. The existence of a second stage panel within this complaints procedure does not affect any rights an individual might have under Part III of the Local Government Act 1974. This is because the panel is not a decision-making body. A Local Commissioner may therefore investigate a complaint about local authority maladministration where the complainant is not satisfied with the conduct or outcome of the authority's own investigation.

Elected Members

5.23. Similarly, the complaints procedure should not affect in any way the right of an individual or organisation to approach a local councillor for advice or assistance. The procedure should, however, indicate clearly how complaints made to councillors which cannot be resolved on the spot should be handled.

Children with Disabilities

5.24. Complaints about the discharge by the local authority of any of their functions under Part III of the Children Act 1989 including functions in relation to children with disabilities will be dealt with under this procedure, whether the complaint is about services provided or about decisions on what services are or are not to be provided following an assessment of a child's needs.

5.25. Whenever a complaint is made the implications for other procedures should be considered and addressed. Procedural guidance will need to be clear on the distinction to be made between a complaint, a grievance and the reporting of a matter which is a criminal offence. Staff will wish to be reassured that the establishment of a representations procedure will not lead to the by-passing of existing grievance and disciplinary procedures and clients need to know which procedure is deemed appropriate and why.

5.26. The handling of a complaint may be concurrent with action under the disciplinary procedures or child protection action and on occasion a police investigation. Decisions on how to proceed will be made on the basis of individual cases and local guidance will be necessary on how priorities are identified and decisions made in relation to individual cases. The need to protect a child has to be the first priority and where the complaint is made by a child, the need for child protection action should be considered. If child protection action is appropriate, the inter-agency procedure should be brought into action at the earliest possible stage. The fact that a child is accommodated by or on behalf of the local authority makes this more important, not less (see **Working Together, HMSO 1988).**

5.27. Usually a complaint will be a perceived failure of the responsible authority, not the individual and will be clearly a matter for consideration under this procedure. A complaint may be linked to a matter that is being dealt with under the grievance procedure (which concerns staff issues such as conditions of service) or the disciplinary procedure (which applies to actions of staff in relation to failures to comply with instructions, guidance or codes of practice etc. The responsible authority should make clear to staff (and trades unions and professional associations) that consideration of the complaint is separate to any action that may be necesary under the grievance or disciplinary procedures. In such cases staff and trades unions should be kept informed of progress in consideration of the complaint, but they should not be given any details that would breach confidentiality or work against the child's best interests.

SUPPORT OF THOSE USING THE PROCEDURE

5.28. The responsible authority will need to consider what type of support and encouragement it can offer to clients both to make use of the system and to pursue their representation or complaint through the procedure. Information leaflets and open letters to children and parents being provided with services will help to make clients aware of the procedure. However, some parents and most children will need advice and confidential support to make their representation or complaint, to pursue it, to understand the administrative process and to cope with the outcome.

5.29. Regulation 4(1) requires that responsible authorities offer "assistance and guidance on the use of the procedure or give advice . . . " on where this may be obtained. Responsible authorities will wish to consider how this obligation can be fulfilled. Where the responsible authority has made the kind of provision to assist problem-solving outlined in paragraph 5.13, it may wish to extend those arrangements to provide support for complainants. Children accommodated in a residential care setting are likely to need support at every stage if they are to be confident enough to invoke the procedure and to be sure that making a representation will not rebound upon them. This may mean that a person who has no line management or service delivery responsibility or involvement in the child's case should be available to work with the child in the matter of a representation. The responsible authority will wish to consider how this could best be arranged. Where voluntary organisations and registered children's homes are providing accommodation for children in small establishments, they will need to take special care that their arrangements provide the children with appropriate support and the independent element required in the procedure.

5.30. Staff directly involved in a matter complained of or with the child in another context should be informed of a complaint and actions that are taken during the considerations by the authority. Whatever their involvement staff may need increased support and supervision from line managers to help them co-operate with considerations under the procedure and to work positively with the child.

STAFFING

5.31. The Regulations give responsible authorities discretion as to how to decide to use the officer they are required to designate to assist in the co-ordination of all aspects of the consideration of representations. However it is recommended that each responsible authority designate an officer to take day to day responsibility for the co-ordination of the procedure. The post will need to be at a sufficiently senior level to reflect the importance of the task and the responsible authority's commitment to it. The skills required are not specific to any one discipline and it may be that an administrator would best combine the variety of tasks the post will include. The appointment of an administrator, recognisably independent of professional line management, could help demonstrate the separate role of the designated officer. Small responsible authorities such as registered children's homes will need to give careful consideration to how they achieve that objectivity.

5.32. In particular, the designated officer might:

- receive and investigate, or oversee the receipt and investigation of complaints that cannot be resolved informally;
- give advice on the response of the responsible authority to individual complaints;
- ensure the smooth running of the panel arrangements, including the appointment and servicing of panels.

The responsible authority may wish additionally to give responsibility for the overall organisation and effectiveness of the authority's procedure to a senior officer of the authority. This job could include:

- establishing, resourcing and monitoring the procedure;
- directing and overseeing the arrangements made for training and publicity;
- the collation of data on complaints and the dissemination of that data to line managers and to members of the authority.

Either of these posts could combine responsibility for the local authority's Local Authority Social Services Act and Children Act complaints procedures.

INDEPENDENT ELEMENT OF THE PROCEDURE

5.33. The Regulations provide for a two stage procedure with an independent element at each stage. Regulation 5 requires that an independent person be involved from the outset of the considerations and Regulation 8 requires that a panel be convened including at least one independent person where a first stage consideration has not satisfied the complainant. There is nothing in the Regulations which prohibits the independent person involved in the first stage consideration of a case from being a member of the panel, but the responsible authority will wish to consider to what extent the panel can take a fresh look at the case if the same independent person is involved. The responsible authority may wish to draw up a list of independent persons suitable and willing to act as an independent person or to sit on a panel. It would be good practice to consult community groups when drawing up a list. Consortium or reciprocal arrangements between authorities may be one way to facilitate the availablity of independent persons. Local authorities should seek also to draw upon voluntary groups, other agencies and independent professionals to ensure that independence is demonstrably built into their procedure. Responsible authorities will need to look carefully at the independence of a member of a voluntary organisation when contractual arrangements exist between the authority and the organisation.

5.34 Local arrangements will reflect the demand upon the procedure, the different racial and cultural groups in the area and the availability of suitable people willing to serve. In some areas a standing panel appointed for a period (perhaps not exceeding 3 years) might be an effective arrangement. In other areas, it may be more appropriate for a panel to be convened for each occasion. The responsible authority will need to consider what training or other support such as legal advice it might wish to provide for independent persons. This might be appropriately dealt with by joint initiatives to devise appropriate training strategies between responsible authorities.

APPOINTMENT OF INDEPENDENT PERSONS

5.35. The responsible authority will need to appoint independent persons both to consider complaints as individuals at the first stage and as part of a panel at the second stage. Regulation 2(3) states who is excluded from acting as an independent person. In addition, it is recommended that the independent person should not be a spouse of an officer or member of the responsible authority. It is also recommended that co-habitees of those excluded from being independent persons are excluded. The responsible authority will need to make clear to prospective independent persons the nature of the task and the degree of commitment required. The responsible authority will need to be able to identify quickly independent persons with particular skills or knowledge that may be required in a particular case. Independent persons should be given a letter of appointment explaining the duties they will be required to carry out, drawing attention to important issues such as confidentiality, and making clear the working arrangements involved in the consideration of complaints. The letter should also describe the expenses and other payments to which they may be entitled.

SETTING UP THE PROCEDURE

5.36. The complaints procedures established by the responsible authority should be uncomplicated, accessible to those who might wish to use them, understood by all members of staff and should reflect the need for confidentiality at all stages. The responsible authority has discretion to decide how exactly to implement the Regulations and set up the procedure to best suit local needs. However, to meet the minimum requirements of the Regulations and the Act, the responsible authority should:

- designate an officer to assist in the co-ordination of all aspects of the consideration of complaints (Regulation 3(1) and paragraphs 5.31 and 5.32);

- publicise the procedure (section 26(8) and paragraphs 5.15 and 5.16);

- ensure that members of staff of the responsible authority and independent persons are familiar with the procedure (Regulation 3(2) and paragraphs 5.17 and 5.34);

- acknowledge all complaints received by sending the complainant an explanation of the procedure and offer assistance and guidance on it or advice on where assistance and guidance may be obtained (Regulation 4(1) and paragraph 5.37);

- accept and record any oral complaints in writing agreeing them with the complainant (Regulation 4(2) and paragraph 5.38);

- appoint an independent person to consider the complaint with the responsible authority (Regulation 5 and paragraphs 5.33–5.35);

- consider the complaint with the independent person and respond within 28 days of receipt of the complaint (Regulation 6 and paragraph 5.41);

- address their response to the person from whom the complaint was received; and also, where different, to the person on whose behalf the complaint was made and to any other persons who appear to have a sufficient interest or are otherwise involved or affected. The response should advise the complainant what further options are open should he or she remain dissatisfied (Regulation 8 (1) and paragraph 5.42);

- make arrangements so that where a complainant remains dissatisfied and requests (within 28 days) that his complaint be reviewed, a panel is constituted by the responsible authority to meet within 28 days of the responsible authority's receipt of the complainant's request (Regulation 8(2) and (4) and paragraphs 5.42 and 5.43). (The panel is required by Regulation 8(3) to include at least one independent person). The complainant, the local authority and the independent person appointed under Regulation 5 should be allowed to make oral or written submissions to the panel if he is not a panel member (Regulation 8(5) and paragraph 5.45). The complainant may be accompanied at a panel meeting by another person of his choice who may speak on his behalf (Regulation 8(6) and paragraph 5.45);

- ensure that the panel's recommendation is recorded in writing within 24 hours of the completion of their deliberations (Regulation 9(1)), and is sent (formally) to the responsible authority, to the complainant, to the first stage independent person and to anyone acting on the complainant's behalf (Regulation 9(1) and paragraph 5.47);

- decide on their response to the recommendation of a panel after consideration with an independent person from the panel (section 26(7)(a), Regulation 9(4) and paragraph 5.48) and make their decision known in writing to the person who requested that the complaint be considered by the panel, and where different, the person on whose behalf the request was made, the first stage independent person (if different from the independent person on the panel) and any other persons as appear to have a sufficient interest or are otherwise involved or affected. Notification should be given within 28 days of the date of the recommendation. The letter should explain the responsible authority's decision and the reasons for it and any action they have taken or propose to take (section 26(7)(b));

- keep a record of all complaints received and the outcome in each case; and identify separately those cases where the time limits imposed by the directions have been breached (Regulation 10(1) and paragraph 5.52);

- provide an annual report on the operation of the procedure (Regulation 10(3) and paragraphs 5.54 and 5.55).

Receipt of Complaint

5.37. When a responsible authority receives a complaint about the discharge of any of its functions under Part III of the Act in relation to a child by any of the persons eligible to make a complaint (see paragraph 5.6 above and section 26(3)(a)–(d) of the Act), an acknowledgement of the complaint should be sent to the complainant with a leaflet describing how the representations procedure works and giving the name of the designated officer with responsibility for co-ordinating the handling of complaints under the procedure (see Regulation 3 and paragraphs 5.31 and 5.32). The provision of a clear and easy to understand leaflet is an important part of the local authority's duty to publicise the representations procedure (see section 26(8) of the Act and paragraphs 5.15 and 5.16 for guidance on publicity). It will be good practice for the leaflet to inform the complainant of other avenues by which to puruse their complaint including, in the case of a local authority, the option of complaining directly to the Commissioner for Local Administration.

Oral Complaints

5.38. If a complaint is made orally, the responsible authority is required by Regulation 4(2) to arrange for it to be recorded in writing and agreed with the complainant. The authority will need to consider how to meet the varying needs of children in this respect. This will be particularly important in relation to children from ethnic minorities and whose first language is not English and children with communication difficulties. Similar consideration will also apply in relation to adults from these groups who may be making the complaints. Facilities available for people from these groups should be well publicised including to local voluntary organisations and community or self-help groups.

Determination of Eligibility to Complain

5.39. The responsible authority may also receive complaints in relation to a child from persons other than those covered by the categories who are automatically entitled to complain by virtue of section 26(3)(a)–(d) (see paragraph 5.6 above). The complaint could be made by a relative, friend, teacher, GP or any other person. The responsible authority has to consider whether that person has sufficient interest in the child in order to determine their eligibility. The responsible authority should consider the views of the child where he is of sufficient understanding and of the other people mentioned in section 26(3)(b)–(d) to help them decide whether it is necessary to consider the representation in order to promote and safeguard the welfare of the child.

Notification of Determination of Eligibility

5.40. Once the responsible authority has determined whether the complaint is eligible for handling under the procedure, the complainant should be notified in writing and provided with a copy of the responsible authority's leaflet on their representations procedure. The child should also be notified where he is not the complainant if the authority considers he is of sufficient understanding, whether or not the complaint is deemed to be eligible. The date of receipt of a complaint which required consideration for eligibility will be the day on which the authority makes their decision about eligibility. Where it is decided that an individual is not eligible to pursue a complaint on behalf of a child, the authority should consider whether the substance of the complaint needs to be addressed as if the child had complained.

Consideration with Independent Person

5.41. The basis of the representations procedure is that an independent person should be actively involved in considering the complaint (section 26(4) of the Act). Once appointed by the responsible authority the independent person should take part in all discussions the responsible authority may hold about the complaint. He should be allowed to interview the child, the complainant where this is not the child, parents and other involved persons including relevant members of staff if he considers this necessary in order to form an independent view. He should also be given access to relevant parts of the case record. It is recommended that the independent person should provide written comments to the responsible authority.

Notification of Responsible Authority's Decision

5.42. The responsible authority should notify the complainant, the child (if he is of sufficient understanding), the independent person and any other person whom the local authority consider has a sufficient interest in the child of the proposed result of their consideration (Regulation 8(1)). The letter should be clear and simple and give reasons, whether or not it changes an earlier decision which gave rise to the complaint, and proposed action. The letter should also remind the complainant of his right to request that the complaint is considered by a panel with an independent person sitting on it. If the complainant does wish to take advantage of this he should be asked in the letter of notification to make a formal written request which should reach the responsible authority no later than 28 days from the date on which the letter of notification was sent (Regulation 8(2)).

Reference to Panel

5.43. If the complainant is dissatisfied with the responsible authority's proposal, whether or not the independent person is in agreement with that decision, he can request that the complaint be considered by a panel. The panel should meet within 28 days of the responsible authority's receipt of the complainant's request for the matter to be referred to a panel and should consist of three persons at least one of whom should be an independent person. Under these Regulations, the responsible authority is required to appoint a panel and arrange for the panel to meet to consider the complaint within 28 days of receipt of the letter from the complainant requesting the complaint to be considered by the panel. If no such letter is received from the complainant then consideration of the complaint is ended.

Notification of Panel Meeting

5.44. It is recommended as part of the arrangements for the meeting, that the complainant and the independent person who considered the complaint at the previous stage (if he is not a member of the panel) are notified in writing of the date, time and venue of the meeting and invited to attend. It would be good practice to inform the complainant of the name and status of the panel members specifying which members are independent persons and which officers of the responsible authority will be present.

Submissions to the Panel

5.45. The complainant may make written submissions to the panel before the meeting and make oral submissions at the meeting. The authority has a corresponding right to make submissions to the panel (Regulation 8(5)). The first stage independent person also has the right to make written and oral submissions to the panel (if he is not a member of the panel). His letter of appointment will have made this clear (see paragraph 5.35). The complainant should also be informed of his entitlement to be accompanied by another person who shall be entitled to be present at the whole meeting and to speak on his behalf if he so wishes (Regulation 8(6)).

Conduct of the Meeting

5.46. It is suggested that the meeting is conducted in as informal an atmosphere as possible. In arranging a meeting, the responsible authority will have to consider whether any special provision needs to be made for complainants from ethnic minorities whose first language may not be English or for complainants with disabilities who may have mobility problems or communication difficulties.

The Panel's Recommendation

5.47. Regulation 9(1) requires that the panel records the reasons for their recommendation in writing. The panel is also required by Regulation 9(1) to decide on its recommendation within twenty four hours of the meeting and to notify in writing the responsible authority, the complainant, the independent person involved in the first stage consideration (if he is not a member of the panel) and any other person who the responsible authority considers has sufficient interest in the case (Regulation 9(2)). The panel may, if they consider it appropriate, make their decision at the meeting. If the panel do not make their decision at the meeting or immediately after the meeting, they must reconvene within the twenty four hour limit to make their decision. The letter of notification should explain simply and clearly the reasons for the decision. The letter should also advise the complainant that the responsible authority are required to consider and have due regard to the panel's recommendation.

Reconsideration of Decision by the Responsible Authority

5.48. The responsible authority are required to consider what action should be taken in the light of the panel's findings, in conjunction with an independent person from the panel (Regulation 9(3)). The Act requires that the responsible authority should "have due regard to the findings of those considering the representations;" (section 26(7)(a)). Authorities will also wish to take account of the effect of the findings and the outcome of their considerations upon the child (and complainant if not the child). There may be aspects of the complaint which require further enquiry under different procedures.

Notification of Responsible Authority's Consideration of Panel's Recommendation

5.49. The responsible authority should notify the complainant, the child (if he is considered to have sufficient understanding) and such other persons as the responsible authority consider appropriate (section 26(7)(b)). This notification should be given within 28 days of the date of the panel's recommendation. The notification should be clear and simple, explaining the responsible authority's reasons for the decision. Those whom the responsible authority should consider notifying may include the panel, the independent person involved in the first stage consideration (if he is not a panel member), relevant members of staff in the responsible authority and other agencies. The responsible authority may also wish to notify a child's independent visitor or someone in another agency working with the child, particularly where the child will need support to come to terms with the decision. The responsible authority should arrange for explanations to be given in advance of formal notifications wherever possible to the child and to parents and to other complainants if appropriate. In particular, the child may need reassurance and should be given opportunities to discuss his feelings about the outcome of the consideration. This will be the case whether or not the outcome is one that the child or complainant welcomes. Where it is appropriate the responsible authority should advise the complainant of other avenues of complaint or appeal that may be open to him. Informative leaflets could be provided with the notice of decision. Equally, members of a responsible authority's staff who were involved in the matter complained of should receive an explanation of the outcome of the considerations.

Subsequent Action

5.50. The responsible authority should take any action decided upon as a result of the findings in an individual case as soon as possible after the decision has been reached. Delay would undermine confidence in the procedure and might well become the subject of another complaint or cause the complainant to seek another remedy.

5.51. The responsible authority will wish to take note of aspects of the case complained about that require action under other procedures or that have general implications for policies or practice. In the first instance the relevant procedure should be identified and other authorities should be informed and appropriate arrangements made. Where issues of policy and practice arise, the authority will need to consider how best to address the issue and the timescale for action. Serious matters will need immediate attention.

MONITORING

5.52. Regulation 10 sets out requirements for responsible authorities to monitor the operation and effectiveness of their representations procedure. A record should be kept of each complaint received which details the nature of the complaint, the action taken, the outcome of each complaint and whether there was compliance with the time limits specified in Regulations 6, 8(4) and 9(1) (Regulation 10(1)). Local authorities should use this information to provide the Social Services Committee with regular and anonymised information about numbers and types of complaint received, the time taken to deal with them and their outcome. All responsible authorities should devise systems locally to provide for:

● the dissemination of this information to line managers;

● its use as a measure of performance and means of quality control;

● information derived from complaints about services subject to statutory regulation, or where services purchased under contract are concerned, to the person responsible for monitoring the contract.

Information about complaints that are dealt with and resolved at the first stage may be of equal value to information about the smaller number of complaints referred to the panel. Where such (first stage) complaints raise policy, resource management, staffing or other issues, line managers should be informed.

5.53. Information collected during the monitoring process and during consideration of individual complaints will provide feedback on management and operational matters such as how policies are interpreted by staff and service users, how effective communication is within the responsible authority and to the public, where staff training is required and whether resources are targeted correctly.

5.54. An annual report dealing with the operation of the complaints procedure should be compiled and in the case of local authorities be presented to the Social Services Committee. In the case of a voluntary organisation or registered children's home, the report should be available, with a copy of the procedure, at any inspection authorised by the Secretary of State. The report should include:

● a summary of the statistical and other information which may have been supplied at more frequent intervals to the Committee;

● a review of the effectiveness of the procedure.

In preparation for making the annual report, or separately, responsible authorities should consider inviting comment from those consulted during the setting up of the procedure on the question of its effectiveness and on the scope for possible improvements.

5.55. All or part of the periodic reports made to the Council or Social Services Committee by local authorities should be open to inspection by members of the public under the terms of the Local Government (Access to Information) Act 1985. They should be anonymised where necessary to ensure there is no breach of confidentiality.

5.56. The responsible authority should consider inviting comment from those consulted during the setting up of the procedure (community groups, service users etc – see paragraph 5.4) on the effectiveness of the procedure and ask for suggestions for improvement. Regular consultation with such groups and sharing information on the outcome of the monitoring process will help to build confidence in the operation of the procedure.

CHAPTER 6 INDEPENDENT VISITORS

INTRODUCTION

6.1. This Chapter gives guidance on the statutory framework in paragraph 17 of Schedule 2 to the Children Act 1989 governing the appointment, role and function of independent visitors. The categories of persons who are not to be considered as independent are set out in the Definition of Independent Visitors (Children) Regulations 1991.

DUTY TO APPOINT AN INDEPENDENT VISITOR

6.2. Paragraph 17 of Schedule 2 to the Children Act places a duty on a local authority to appoint an independent visitor in respect of any child they are looking after if they believe that it would be in a child's best interest and certain conditions are satisfied. The need for such an appointment arises where communication between the child and his parent or a person who is not a parent but who has parental responsibility has been infrequent, or where he has not visited or been visited by his parents or a person who is not a parent but who has parental responsibility during the preceding 12 months.

6.3. Under the old law the appointment of visitors was restricted to children who were accommodated in community homes which provided education (section 11 of the Child Care Act 1980), and then only in respect of children in compulsory care. The Children Act extends the requirement to include all children who are being looked after by a local authority. A child is being looked after by a local authority if he is in care or if he is not in care but is provided with accommodation by the authority (section 22(1)).

6.4. The appointment of an independent visitor is not a duty falling to a local authority with respect to any child not being looked after by them. The provisions do not extend to children accommodated by health authorities or children accommodated in residential care, nursing or mental nursing homes unless the child is being looked after by a local authority which has placed the child (who may perhaps be disabled) in any of the above type of facility under their general accommodation and maintenance duties (section 23(2)).

DEFINITION OF INDEPENDENT VISITOR

6.5. Paragraph 17(7) of Schedule 2 to the Children Act empowers the Secretary of State to make regulations as to the circumstances in which a person appointed as a visitor is to be regarded as independent of the local authority appointing her.

6.6. The regulations provide that a person is not to be regarded as independent if he is a member of the local authority or of its committees or sub-committees whether elected or co-opted or is an officer of the social services department of the authority or is the spouse of any of these. Additionally, where the child is being accommodated by an organisation other than the local authority, eg in a voluntary or registered children's home, a person who is a member or a patron or trustee of the organisation, or who is employed by the organisation whether paid or not, or who is the spouse of any such person is not to be regarded as independent.

6.7. Local authorities should consider in this connection whether it would be appropriate to treat people who are in a stable cohabitation relationship as spouses.

IDENTIFICATION OF CHILDREN FOR WHOM AN INDEPENDENT VISITOR SHOULD BE APPOINTED

6.8. Regulation 5 of the Review of Children's Cases Regulations 1991 places a duty on a local authority to consider at reviews whether an independent visitor should be appointed in respect of a child looked after by them. It is likely to be at a review that consideration is first given to the appointment of an independent visitor. However, in some cases the question may arise when the local authority first draws up a plan for a child whom they are looking after (Regulation 4 of the Arrangements for Placement of Children (General) Regulations 1991).

6.9. If either of the two following criteria is satisfied the local authority may be required to appoint an independent visitor:

(i) where it appears to a local authority in relation to any child whom they are looking after that communication between the child and a parent of his, or any person who is not a parent of his but who has parental responsibility for him, has been infrequent;

(ii) where any child whom they are looking after has not visited or been visited by (or lived with) a parent of his, or any person who is not a parent of his but who has parental responsibility for him, during the preceding twelve months (paragraph 17(1) of Schedule 2).

6.10. If either of these threshold criteria is satisfied, the authority has to assess whether it would be in the child's best interests for an independent visitor to be appointed (paragraph 17(1) of Schedule 2). In reaching their decision, the local authority has to have regard to the general duty in relation to children whom they are looking after (section 22(4)) to ascertain as far as is reasonably practicable the wishes and feelings of a range of persons, including the child. The wishes of the child are of particular importance. The authority must also take into consideration in reaching the decision not only the wishes and feelings of these persons but also the child's religious persuasion, racial origin and cultural and linguistic background (section 22(5)). The local authority may not appoint an independent visitor for a child if the child objects to it and the authority are satisfied he has sufficient understanding to make an informed decision.

6.11. It is possible that, in certain circumstances, although the threshold criteria for appointing an independent visitor set out above exist, the local authority may decide that such an appointment is unnecessary and therefore not in the child's best interests. For example, a child (at the time the Children Act came into force) may be well settled in a permanent placement with foster carers and already have sufficient contacts, friends and – if necessary – opportunities to seek advice. In some cases members of his family other than his parents may be in regular contact making the appointment of an independent visitor unnecessary.

SELECTION OF AN INDEPENDENT VISITOR FOR A PARTICULAR CHILD

6.12. In matching a particular visitor with a particular child the authority, as they did in the question of whether or not to appoint a visitor, will need to have regard to the wishes of the child, his parents or those with parental responsibility and any other persons whose wishes and feelings are relevant. If the child objects to the authority's choice they may not make the appointment.

6.13. The child's social worker will have been involved in the process whereby the authority decided that an independent visitor was necessary and his advice in the matching of a potential visitor to the child is crucial.

6.14. The personal qualities required of an independent visitor will include an ability to relate to children generally and more specifically in a manner appropriate to the age and circumstances of the child for whom he is to be appointed.

6.15. A child's views about whom he would like as an independent visitor and the reasons why will vary greatly. The child in his teens may prefer an independent visitor to be more like an elder sibling than a parent in age and role. Other children and circumstances may suggest that a much older person, perhaps resembling a grandparent, would be the preferred choice. Some children will appreciate having an independent visitor who has himself been in care. The local authority will need to take into account the child's wishes and feelings and these may also include whether the independent visitor should share his religion, culture, language and racial background. Where it has not proved possible to make a placement which entirely reflects the child's race and culture the independent visitor could be a link with the child's racial and cultural background.

6.16. There will be a need for introductory meetings to provide an opportunity for mutual assessment and to enable the child to decide whether he wishes the appointment to be made. If the child does not, the local authority should consider whether the appointment of another person might be possible and appropriate.

6.17. In a very limited number of cases there may be a relative who would be appropriate to fulfil the role of independent visitor and this arrangement might be the child's preferred option. Local authorities will need to distinguish between the small minority of cases where the designation of a relative or friend as the child's visitor is appropriate and the more common situation where the child properly has ongoing contact with relatives and friends. In the latter situation the local authority should encourage such contacts and may pay expenses without the necessity of changing the status to that of independent visitor (paragraphs 15(1) and 16(2) of Schedule 2).

RECRUITMENT

6.18. The local authority will need to devise a strategy for the recruitment of appropriate persons to act as independent visitors. It may be helpful to consult with community groups, voluntary bodies and other organisations with an interest in children. Imaginative and energetic recruiting measures may have to be devised to ensure that the needs of the child can be met in terms of his religious persuasion, racial origin, cultural and linguistic background. Particular requirements may also arise in the case of children with disabilities. It may be acceptable in some circumstances for an independent visitor to fulfil that role for more than one child.

6.19. For a child in his early teens and likely to remain in care, the relationship with the independent visitor might last four or five years. A variety of factors will determine the length of the relationship, but since it has the potential to be long-term, there are clearly strong arguments for recruiting as independent visitors people who are able to make a long-term commitment to the role. However, recruitment procedures should not preclude those potential independent visitors who, although able only to offer their services for shorter periods, may have valuable qualities and could well be needed and play a valuable role.

6.20. Local authorities may wish to consider recruiting a pool of persons to act as independent visitors. This should allow the selection of an individual visitor for a particular child to take place more quickly than would be possible if the complete recruitment and appointment process had to be undertaken from the beginning. However, even if there is a pool of visitors with a variety of backgrounds and ages, there may still be situations where the local authority and the child identify specific requirements which cannot be met by those visitors who have already been recruited. Moreover, there are disadvantages to the pool approach. Individual independent visitors may become frustrated and disillusioned by over-long waiting periods between appointment to the pool and introductions to a child.

6.21 The recruitment, assessment and support of independent visitors requires the deployment of administrative and professional skills which have similarities to those needed to assess foster and adoptive parents. For this reason authorities may wish to consider locating the responsibility for the independent visitor service with such a specialist team. There are alternative settings such as the local authority's volunteer sector or an independent inspection unit.

6.22. The effectiveness of the independent visitor will depend principally on her personal qualities, ability to communicate with children, commitment and interest in children's welfare. These are pre-requisites. However, such qualities will be enhanced by the provision of an induction programme which will need to cover not only the formal aspects of their role and functions but also the duties and procedures of the local authority and the relevant aspects of the legislation. Some familiarity with the principles and practice of inter-agency working in child abuse matters would be helpful. It is not intended that independent visitors should be required to undertake intensive training beyond the induction phase but there may be occasions when, because of the circumstances of an individual child, the independent visitor would benefit from some additional training.

6.23. Induction training will also allow the opportunity to set expectations in respect of access to file information concerning the child and the extent to which the independent visitor himself keeps any record, over and above that required to claim expenses. On appointment of the independent visitor, the local authority will have to decide the amount of information to be given to him in the circumstances of the child's current situation and history. The general approach is likely to be based on "the need to know" principle but there will always be some situations where it would be judged preferable to give the independent visitor the maximum information possible. The child himself should be involved in deciding what information is made available. It should be noted that the independent visitor, although appointed by the local authority, has no formal right to inspect the child's case files.

6.24. In most situations it will neither be necessary nor appropriate for the independent visitor to keep detailed records of his discussions with the child. However, he may well wish to keep a note as an *aide memoire;* for example, the names of relatives the child mentions or birthdays. The independent visitor may also feel it appropriate to note the decisions of meetings such as reviews he has attended with the local authority. Induction training should stress the importance of ensuring that such confidential information is safely stored, in the context of wider discussion about general confidentiality issues. Furthermore, there should be a clear understanding that such records would be destroyed on termination of his appointment.

6.25. Independent visitors and local authorities should discuss at an early stage how to deal with any anxieties which the child's carers might understandably feel about the appointment of an independent visitor. Local authorities should arrange for the preparation of carers and provide any support or explanations to them and the child about the independent visitor's functions. Explanation should not be left to the independent visitor. He will of course require to be sensitive in all his dealings with the child and his carers particularly where the child is in a family placement and the independent visitor is visiting the family's home.

6.26. Independent visitors do not require supervision or day to day management – indeed such an approach might seriously prejudice their independence. However, they will require support. Many of the children they seek to befriend will have had a history of breakdowns of relationships. In these cases the independent visitor may have to overcome a barrier of cynicism and distrust before they can forge and maintain a good relationship with the child. They may welcome opportunities to discuss in a confidential setting individual situations or wider dilemmas perhaps being faced by a number of independent visitors. The task of the independent visitor may at times be stressful. Local authorities should recognise this and, in considering the overall organisation of the independent visitor service, should consider how best to provide appropriate support for them.

Appointment

6.27. Local authorities will need to take steps to avoid the risk that unsuitable persons who pose a serious threat to children's safety are inadvertently recruited. Appointment procedures need to be rigorous and formal. Applicants will need to submit detailed background information and provide the names of two personal references. Police references should always be sought under the terms of Circular LAC(88)19 (WO Circular 45/88) and a check made of the Department of Health Consultancy Service. Attention should be drawn to the Rehabilitation of Offenders Act 1974 (Exceptions) Order 1975 as amended by the Rehabilitation of Offenders Act 1974 (Exceptions) (Amendment) Order 1986, which allows convictions which are spent under the terms of the 1974 Act to be disclosed by the police and to be taken into account in deciding whether to appoint the applicant. The applicant therefore may properly be requested to list all convictions and cautions. The applicant must give his permission in writing for a police check to be carried out. Where appointments are made the independent visitor should be provided with a letter of authority and arrangements should also be made for the provision of authenticated photographs for identification purposes. These will need to be withdrawn when the appointment is terminated.

REVIEW AND TERMINATION OF APPOINTMENT

6.28. Local authorities will need to consider at each review under the Review of Children's Cases Regulations 1991 the appropriateness of the continuing appointment of the particular independent visitor and indeed of any independent visitor. The child's views will be highly relevant. The local authority will need to consider the most appropriate way of ascertaining the child's wishes about the continuation of an appointment which has been made. The older child should be given the opportunity from time to time to express his views about the value of the appointment. If he objects to it continuing and the authority are satisfied that he has sufficient understanding to make an informed decision, the authority must terminate the independent visitor's appointment in respect of that particular child (paragraph 17(6) of Schedule 2). They should then consider whether it would be appropriate to appoint another independent visitor.

6.29. The independent visitor ceases to be appointed if he gives notice in writing to the authority who appointed him that he resigns the appointment or the authority give him notice in writing that they have terminated it (paragraph 17(3) of Schedule 2). Such a termination is in respect of a visitor's appointment to an individual child but may also signal that the local authority does not wish the independent visitor to be appointed again for any child. However, where an independent visitor is acting in respect of a number of children, termination of appointment in respect of one of them does not terminate appointment in respect of the others. Each case should be considered separately.

6.30. The local authority must act with the greatest care to avoid any suggestion that the termination of an independent visitor's appointment is a consequence of that visitor acting with appropriate independence and, for example, challenging the validity of the authority's care planning or standards of service in respect of a particular child.

6.31. Where the independent visitor disagrees with the local authority's action regarding termination he may wish to make a formal representation and complaint. The local authority has discretion to decide whether the independent visitor is a person with sufficient interest in the child's welfare to warrant his representations being considered under section 26(3)(e). The situation may also arise where, notwithstanding the local authority's wish to terminate the appointment, the child wishes it to continue on a friendship basis. The local authority in considering the child's wishes may conclude on balance that acceptance of such a position is preferable to official opposition provided the child's welfare is not endangered.

6.32. There may be exceptional circumstances where the behaviour of the independent visitor, whilst falling short of criminal activity, is nevertheless totally inappropriate and constitutes a serious risk to the child's welfare. Failure to terminate the independent visitor's appointment would amount to a breach of the local authority's duty to safeguard and promote the welfare of the child. In these circumstances the local authority should review any other current and all previous appointments of that person as an independent visitor and carry out such investigations as are necessary. Authorities should place that person's particulars on the Department of Health Consultancy Services Register (see paragraph 6.27 above). The child may well need particular help and support. Consideration will have to be given to implementing child protection procedures.

THE ROLE AND FUNCTION OF THE INDEPENDENT VISITOR

6.33. The functions of the independent visitor comprise visiting, advising and befriending the child. These are specific duties set out in paragraph 17(2) of Schedule 2. It is recognised, that in some instances, independent visitors may have qualities, skills, experience and qualifications which in other settings entitle them to undertake work in a professional capacity with children. In general, however, the role is envisaged as being undertaken by volunteers from a lay perspective. This section of the guidance discusses further the role of the independent visitor and also a range of specific functions which, depending on the individual child and his circumstances, may have greater or lesser prominence.

6.34. How the independent visitor pursues his role in terms of a plan and timetable of more specific activities will vary depending on the circumstances. He will need to form his own judgements about how best to proceed. Taking into account the local authority's view of the child's needs, the child's wishes and his developing relationship with the child, the independent visitor must reach his own conclusions as to how, in this particular situation, his activities might best be focused. Whatever he does should be directed at contributing to the welfare of the child, and this includes promoting the child's developmental, social, emotional, educational, religious and cultural needs. It may also require him to encourage the child to exercise his rights and to participate in decisions which will affect him. It will also include (unless he feels that there is clear evidence to act differently) supporting the care plan for the child and his carers, such as residential workers who have day to day care for the child.

6.35. The independent visitor's role and functions can also be described in terms of what he is not intended to do. He is not to be anything other than child-focused, however sympathetic he may be to other points of view. His functions are not that of a substitute parent or carer but he should aim, as far as possible, to complement their activities. In bringing the lay perspective, he must not allow his personal prejudices to determine his actions. He is not expected to accept unquestioningly what those responsible for the child tell him is in the child's interests, but should remain open-minded and even sceptical.

Visiting

6.36. Face to face contact with the child is an important aspect of the independent visitor's role. The frequency and length of such visits will depend on the circumstances of each situation and may change in the course of the relationship between the child and independent visitor. A child may have often experienced the disappointment of the cancellation of an arranged visit from a parent or relative and the independent visitor will need to be particularly sensitive and reliable in this regard. The independent visitor will need to make arrangements in advance about visiting with the child's carers as well as with the child himself.

6.37. As the relationship develops it may well be appropriate for the independent visitor and child to go out somewhere. The type of outing will depend on the child's interests and the range of facilities in the area. The independent visitor will need to be sensitive to avoid being regarded and treated as the person who simply provides 'treats'. It is not intended that the independent visitor should provide compensating leisure experiences which ought more appropriately be the responsibility of the child's carers. However, such outings can afford privacy, ease communication and develop the relationship between independent visitor and child through a shared activity. There may be activities which the carers cannot provide, perhaps for example connected to the cultural background or religion of the child. The fact of the child being of a different culture or religion from that of the residential carers or foster parents may not only influence the selection of an independent visitor but also his choice of the type of activity in which he involves the child. He may be able to promote contacts in the area relevant to the child's cultural development.

6.38. In exceptional circumstances it may be appropriate if the relationship with the child has developed, for the independent visitor to invite the child to his own home. Again, such a step must be seen within the overall care plans for the child and agreed with the authority and carers with due sensitivity. This is not an area suited to spontaneous gestures. There are obvious dangers that the child's hopes for the future may be unrealistically aroused and carefully laid plans distorted. However, there is also a general principle that children in care should experience normal activities and they will know that other children in their class at school, for example, will often visit friends at their homes.

6.39. Similar arguments will apply, again in exceptional circumstances, where the independent visitor, child and local authority agree that an overnight stay or short holiday (perhaps with the independent visitor's own family, if he has one) would be appropriate. Although the independent visitor has been the subject of formal checks on appointment (see paragraph 6.27), the local authority will have to make further checks before such an arrangement is agreed.

Advising

6.40. There will be a range of issues about which an independent visitor might offer the child advice. Some of these may be quite straightforward such as where to find, or who to ask for, particular information. The advising role becomes more complex where it overlaps with counselling and the responsibilities of other professionals involved with the child. It is not intended that the independent visitor should engage the child in intensive counselling. Independent visitors need to recognise that it is not their role to counsel or advise the child in complex situations. They should rather encourage and support the child to seek and accept help from his social worker in the first instance.

Befriending

6.41. Whoever is appointed will need to try to establish with the child a sense of trust in the relationship which must form one of the basic elements in the befriending role. The independent visitor must also be prepared for the process of establishing trust to be a slow one and for there to be setbacks. For some of these children earlier relationships with adults have ended in disappointment and disillusionment. They may be reluctant or find it very difficult to establish rapport with adults and to place any trust in them.

6.42. The possible involvement of the independent visitor in meetings or consultation processes arises in some circumstances as a legal requirement and in others is on a discretionary basis.

6.43. The mandatory involvement is in respect of a child who has an independent visitor and who is in secure accommodation. Where the local authority intends to make an application to court to keep the child in that accommodation, the authority has to inform a range of persons, including the child's independent visitor if one has been appointed, of the intention—see Regulation 15 of the Secure Accommodation Regulations 1991. If the placement of the child in secure accommodation continues, Regulations 16 and 17 require reviews to take place and, if practicable, the wishes and feelings of a range of persons to be taken into account. The independent visitor is included here and may be able to give his views in person, in writing or both. The independent visitor is also entitled to know the outcome of the review (Regulation 17(3)).

6.44. The independent visitor will have the opportunity to provide contributions to the review of a child's case either in writing or at meetings where the child's case is to be discussed and to which he has been invited because he has something relevant to contribute or because the child has requested that the visitor attend with him. The independent visitor may wish to put views to the meeting as a friend of the child. The independent visitor will have to take care to distinguish between repeating what the child has asked him to say on his behalf, interpreting such information and offering his own view as to what is best for the child.

6.45. The child may wish the independent visitor to speak as a friend on his behalf in order to help resolve a particular issue or difficulty. This may involve the independent visitor's attendance at a meeting; perhaps a review meeting, or an oral hearing of a complaint being made under the representations procedure. Independent visitors do not constitute the independent element of the representations procedure, but the child might wish the independent visitor to accompany him in the capacity of a friend to an oral hearing convened under the representations procedure (see Chapter 5).

6.46. The Children Act also offers the opportunity for an independent visitor to contribute views outside the formal review arrangements. The child may be involved in family proceedings where the court has requested a welfare report (section 7). Another possibility in relation to court proceedings is that a guardian ad litem has been appointed (section 41). The views of the independent visitor about the child may well be of relevance to such proceedings and the independent visitor may need to take the initiative in seeking out the relevant person in order to convey his views. He will wish to consult with the child before taking such action.

ADVOCACY

6.47. In some situations, the position of the child may be an unhappy one. The child may be dissatisfied with the current arrangements for his care or the absence of progress in achieving a plan for the future. He may dislike and distrust his carers and those in the authority who have responsibility for him. He may feel that his views are ignored or never sought and that he has no realistic opportunity to complain or challenge the validity of the legal processes which affect him. He may disclose that he is being abused by his carers. In such a bleak scenario the child has an urgent need for skilled advocacy. This is not a role the independent visitor is expected to play.

6.48. Instead, the independent visitor must be able to recognise the needs of the child in such serious situations and with the child's agreement draw their concerns to the attention of the child's social worker or, if necessary, a more senior officer in the social services department. In certain cases it may be appropriate to refer the matter to one of the voluntary organisations which specialises in advocacy.

Expenses

6.49. The independent visitor is entitled to recover from the authority who appointed him reasonable expenses incurred by him for the purpose of his functions in visiting, advising and befriending the child (paragraph 17(2)(b) of Schedule 2). The term 'expenses' is meant to cover travel and out of pocket payments but is not meant to equate to a regular payment or salary for undertaking the role of independent visitor. Whether anticipated expenditure may form a pattern or be a one-off amount, the local authority and independent visitor will need to reach some prior agreement about normal spending limits and authorisation for additional expenditure. The independent visitor will also need to keep records for the purpose of submitting expenses claims.

When a Child ceases to be looked after

6.50. The need for an independent visitor to continue his relationship with a young person once he ceases to be looked after by the local authority, where the young person seeks this, should not be overlooked. Such continuing arrangements would be on an informal basis but the local authority should consider whether it would be appropriate to continue to meet the cost of reasonable expenses associated with this continued role until such time as its own after-care responsibilities expire.

CHAPTER 7 · AFTER-CARE: ADVICE AND ASSISTANCE

SUMMARY

7.1. This guidance describes the statutory framework in section 24 of the Children Act 1989, dealing with the duty of local authorities to prepare young people they are looking after for the time when they cease to be so looked after and the powers and duties of local authorities to provide after-care advice and assistance to such young people and certain other defined young people who were accommodated by other bodies. The guidance also deals with the preparation of children accommodated by or on behalf of voluntary organisations (section 61(1)(c)) and those accommodated in registered children's homes (section 64(1)(c)).

7.2. For the purpose of simplicity the guidance describes young people as being 'cared for' or 'leaving care'. This is intended to refer to the concept of caring rather than the young person's legal status: it encompasses all the young people referred to in the previous paragraph and it does so whether they are being cared for under voluntary arrangements or on a compulsory basis. Young people who are privately fostered are covered by the arrangements.

INTRODUCTION

7.3. The successful re-integration of a young person with his family or other responsible person, or the establishment of the ability in the young person to become as self-supporting as possible, where this is necessary, is the culmination of a young person's experience in being cared for by a local authority, or a voluntary organisation or in a registered children's home.

7.4. It is of vital importance that young people are properly prepared for this step and are given access to support afterwards. Young people coming towards this stage will do so from a wide variety of backgrounds and in a wide variety of circumstances, at various ages and with various levels of support available to them from families and friends. All of this implies the need for a very flexible service to meet such a wide range of potentially differing experiences and needs. The quality of preparation for leaving care, and of the after care subsequently provided, may profoundly affect the rest of a young person's life.

7.5. Whether or not the local authority has parental responsibility (under a care order) it adopts, in effect, part of the role of the parent of a young person it is looking after and may provide subsequent advice and assistance. The Act lays powers and, in certain cases, duties, on each local authority to provide this help until a young person reaches the age of 21. (Note: in certain cases, help given to meet expenses concerned with education or training may continue beyond a young person's 21st birthday – see sections 24(8) and (9) of the Act).

7.6. In acting in this way, a local authority will wish to work in partnership with the young person's parents if possible. (It may not, of course, always be possible; for example, they may have died, or they may have rejected the young person or have been rejected by him).

7.7. In so far as these responsibilities are laid on local authorities they are laid on them as corporate bodies. The social services department (SSD) is likely to play a leading role in discharging them, but it will need to liaise with many other agencies, both internally and externally. For example, with housing and education departments, health authorities, careers advice and social security offices. This does not, of course, mean that the SSD should take on duties more properly performed by these other agencies.

7.8. The Act recognises the need for inter-agency liaison, and section 27 gives a local authority (in effect the SSD) the right to request help in its discharge of these functions from any other local authority, any local education authority, any local housing authority, any health authority and "any person authorised by the Secretary of State". Any such request is bound to be complied with "if it is compatible with (the other agency's) own statutory or other duties and obligations and does not unduly prejudice the discharge of any of their functions". With this reservation, therefore, any such request must be complied with as far as possible.

THE LEGAL FRAMEWORK

7.9. The powers and duties of local authorities to prepare young people they are looking after for the time when they cease to be so looked after, and the provision of after-care advice and assistance, are described in section 24 of the Act. These are more clearly defined and comprehensive than those in the former legislation (sections 27–29 of the Child Care Act 1980) and the *duty* to prepare young people for this change in their circumstances is new. A comparable new duty to prepare young people for the time when they are no longer cared for is also placed on voluntary organisations (section 61(1)(c)) and those carrying on registered children's homes (section 64(1)(c)). All of these powers and duties need to be carried out in the light of the general child care principles on which the Act is based.

SECTION 24: LOCAL AUTHORITY POWERS AND DUTIES

7.10. Broadly speaking, the powers and duties of local authorities in section 24 of the Act cover all young people leaving a variety of forms of care when aged 16 or over; and they continue until each young person reaches the age of 21.

Section 24(1): If a young person of any age is being looked after by a local authority, it is the duty of the authority to advise, assist and befriend him so as to promote his welfare when he ceases to be looked after by it. Although this has always been a matter of good practice, it is now a duty.

Section 24(2): In addition, a local authority has responsibilities to advise and befriend any young person who "qualifies for advice and assistance". This applies to any young person aged under 21 who ceases, after reaching the age of 16, to be:

(a) looked after by a local authority;

(b) accommodated by or on behalf of a voluntary organisation;

(c) accommodated in a registered children's home; or

(d) accommodated by any health authority, NHS trust or local education authority, or in any residential care home, nursing home or mental nursing home, (provided that he was accommodated for at least 3 months).

Section 24(3): section 24(2)(d) applies even if the 3 month period began before the young person reached the age of 16.

These responsibilities may be a duty or a power, according to the form of care that the young person has left (see sections 24(4) and (5) below).

Sections 24(4) and (5): Where a local authority knows that a person described in section 24(2) is in their area, they have:

(a) a duty to advise and befriend him if he was formerly looked after by a local authority or accommodated by or on behalf of a voluntary organisation; and

(b) a power to advise and befriend him in all other cases provided that:

- the young person has asked for such help; and
- the authority considers that he needs to be advised and befriended; and
- the person who formerly looked after him (if not the local authority) does not have the necessary facilities for advising and befriending him.

Sections 24(6) and (7): If a local authority has a duty or a power to advise and befriend someone, they may also give him assistance. This assistance may be in kind or, in exceptional circumstances, in cash.

Section 24(8): A local authority also has a power to give assistance to anyone who "qualifies for advice and assistance" and who was formerly looked after by the local authority (section 24(2)(a)) in the following ways:

- by contributing to expenses incurred by him in living near the place where he is, or will be, employed, or seeking employment, or in receipt of education or training;
- by making a grant to enable him to meet expenses connected with his education or training.

Section 24(9): If a local authority is making a contribution or grant under section 24(8) to meet expenses connected with education or training, it may continue to do so until the end of the course, even if the young person reaches the age of 21 before the end of the course. It may also disregard any interruption in his attendance on the course if he resumes it as soon as is reasonably practicable.

Section 24(10): Assistance given by a local authority under section 24 may be given unconditionally or may be repayable in part or in whole. However, no-one shall be liable to repay any assistance at any time when in receipt of income support or family credit. Before giving any assistance or imposing any conditions about repayment, the local authority shall take into account the means of the young person concerned and of each of his parents. (Note: these conditions do not apply to assistance given under section 24(8), which is always unconditional and not repayable).

Section 24(11): If a local authority has been advising and befriending a young person under section 24 and becomes aware that he proposes to live, or does live, in the area of another local authority, it must inform the other local authority.

Section 24(12): If a young person ceases, after reaching the age of 16, to be accommodated:

(a) by a voluntary organisation or in a registered children's home; or

(b) by any health authority, NHS trust or local education authority; or

(c) in any residential care home, nursing home or mental nursing home;

– then the organisation, authority or person carrying on the home (as appropriate) must inform the local authority in whose area the young person proposes to live.

Section 24(13): sections 24(12)(b) and (c) only apply if the accommodation has been provided for a consecutive period of at least 3 months.

The Courts and Legal Services Act 1990 inserts two more subsections into section 24 of the Children Act. These are as follows:

Section 24(14): "Every local authority shall establish a procedure for considering any representations (including any complaint) made to them by a person qualifying for advice and assistance about the discharge of their functions under this Part (of the Act) in relation to him". (See Chapter 5.)

This will (*inter alia*) allow young people to complain if they consider that the local authority has not given them adequate preparation for leaving care, or adequate aftercare. It will enable them to make a complaint even if they have left the care of the local authority or another agency. (The general complaints procedure specified at section 26(3) of the Act only applies to a young person who is a 'child', ie under 18 years of age).

7.11. Transitional Arrangements: These are set out in paragraph 22 of schedule 14 to the Act. Under these arrangements, a local authority's powers and duties under section 24 of the Act extend to any young person who:

(i)   left voluntary or compulsory care or ceased to be subject to a criminal care order before the Act came into force (see paragraphs 15(1)(a) to (g), 20(1) and 36 of Schedule 14 to the Act);

(ii) was at least 16 when he left care; and

(iii) is not yet 21.

These transitional arrangements will be in force for five years, ie until anyone qualifying for advice and assistance under these arrangements has reached his 21st birthday.

SECTION 61(1)(c): DUTIES OF VOLUNTARY ORGANISATIONS

7.12. Section 61(1)(c) of the Act stipulates that where a young person of any age is accommodated by or on behalf of a voluntary organisation, it is the duty of that organisation "to advise, assist and befriend him with a view to promoting his welfare when he ceases to be so accommodated". The voluntary organisation does not have a statutory duty to provide aftercare for the young person once he has ceased to be accommodated by the organisation or on its behalf. However, it is desirable to link the provision of care with that of aftercare. As a matter of good practice, the voluntary organisation should consider the provision of appropriate aftercare services for any young person ceasing to be accommodated by it, or on its behalf, after reaching the age of 16. Social services departments of local authorities should therefore encourage the provision of such services by all voluntary child care organisations within their local authority areas.

7.13. In addition, a voluntary organisation has a duty under section 24(12) of the Act (see paragraph 7.10) to inform the local authority if it is ceasing to accommodate a young person aged 16 or more. The local authority so informed will be the authority in whose area the young person proposes to live after ceasing to be accommodated by the voluntary organisation.

7.14. The voluntary organisation will need to inform the local authority as early as possible, ie as soon as it is known on what date the young person will cease to be accommodated by the organisation or on its behalf.

This will alert the local authority to the fact that it may have a responsibility to provide aftercare for the young person under section 24 of the Act (see section 24(5)(b)). The voluntary organisation should also keep the young person informed at all stages, by telling him as early as possible when he is likely to cease to be accommodated by the organisation and by letting him know what provision for aftercare will be made and by which agency.

SECTION 64(1)(c): DUTIES OF REGISTERED CHILDREN'S HOMES

7.15. Section 64(1)(c) of the Act stipulates that where a young person is accommodated in a registered children's home, it is the duty of the person carrying on the home to "advise, assist and befriend him with a view to promoting his welfare when he ceases to be so accommodated". The person carrying on the home does not have any duty to provide aftercare once the young person has ceased to be accommodated in the home. Again, however, it is desirable to link the provision of care with that of aftercare. As a matter of good practice, the person carrying on the home should consider the provision of appropriate aftercare services for any young person ceasing to be accommodated in the home after reaching the age of 16. Social services departments of local authorities should therefore encourage the provision of such services by all registered children's homes within their local authority areas.

7.16. In addition, the person carrying on the home has a duty under section 24(12) of the Act (see paragraph 7.10) to notify the local authority if the home is ceasing to accommodate a young person aged 16 or more. The local authority so informed will be the local authority in whose area the young person proposes to live after ceasing to be accommodated in the registered children's home.

7.17. The person carrying on the home will need to inform the local authority as early as possible, ie as soon as it is known on what date the young person will cease to be accommodated by the home. This will alert the local authority to the fact that it may have a responsibility to provide aftercare for the young person under section 24 of the Act (see section 24(5)(b)). The person carrying on the home should also keep the young person informed at all stages, by telling him as early as possible when he is likely to cease to be accommodated in the home, and by letting him know what provision for aftercare will be made and by which agency.

PRINCIPLES UNDERLYING PREPARATION FOR LEAVING CARE

7.18. The principles underlying preparation for leaving care should reflect good child care practice generally, following the principles of the 1989 Act:

● Services for young people must take account of the lengthy process of transition from childhood to adulthood, to reflect the gradual transition of a young person from dependence to independence. The support provided should be, broadly, the support that a good parent might be expected to give.

● Young people should be fully involved in discussions and plans for their future. Well before a young person leaves care, a continuing care plan should be formulated with him. This should specify the type of help the young person will be receiving and from whom. This plan should incorporate contingency arrangements in the event of a breakdown in the young person's living arrangements after he has left care since such breakdowns in arrangements are not uncommon. Such arrangements might include, for example, the possibility of a return to a community home.

● Parents should be invited to help formulate the plan (if they are not estranged from the young person).

● Preparation for leaving care should help develop a young person's capacity to make satisfactory relationships, develop his self-esteem and enable him to acquire the necessary practical skills for independent living.

● In helping young people to develop socially and culturally, carers must be prepared to take some risks and to take responsibility for doing so; to let young people take some risks, eg in attempting relationships that do not work; and to take responsibility for supporting young people through breakdowns in relationships.

● All preparation for leaving care and provision of aftercare must take account of the religious persuasion, racial origin, cultural and linguistic background and other needs of a young person (section 22(5)(c)).

● Preparation for leaving care and the provision of aftercare must be planned in conjunction with all other interested agencies, eg education and housing authorities, health authorities and, where appropriate, other local authorities. These agencies should be invited to contribute to a young person's continuing care plan.

7.19. Each local authority should take the above principles into account in developing leaving care and aftercare policies and in applying those policies to the needs of individual young people.

7.20. To help ensure this, each SSD should provide a written statement of its philosophy and practice on the preparation of young people for leaving care and the provision of aftercare support. It is a requirement of paragraph 1(2) of schedule 2 that each local authority must publish information about services provided by them under section 24 and take such steps as are reasonably practicable to ensure that those who might benefit from the services receive the relevant information. The statement should be comprehensive, acknowledging the different leaving care and aftercare needs of different young people, according to their age, sex and maturity. It should take into account the special needs of certain groups of young people, eg young people with disabilities and those with a statement of special educational needs (see paragraphs 7.28 to 7.42 below), pregnant girls and girls with young babies and young people from a range of cultural, racial and linguistic backgrounds. The statement should be revised periodically by the local authority to ensure that it remains up-to-date. It is suggested that 3-yearly revisions would be appropriate.

7.21. The statement should also cover the role of other agencies, who should be asked to provide contributions to the statement on the part they play in the preparation of young people leaving care and the provision of aftercare. They should be invited to revise their contributions to the statement when the statement itself is being revised by the local authority (see paragraph 7.20). The roles of other agencies are considered below, in more detail, at paragraphs 7.28 to 7.42 and 7.75 to 7.102.

7.22. The statement should be informed by the views of young people who are, or have been, cared for in those ways referred to in section 24(2) (paragraph 7.10). There should be a formal means of ensuring that the local authority continues to take their views into account, both when the statement of policy is being revised and at other times. One way of doing this might be to encourage young people who are being, or have been, cared for, to set up their own groups. Such groups would also enable these young people to meet each other and discuss matters of common interest; and they would help to overcome the common problem of loneliness felt by many young people who have left care. The local authority might also consider establishing a newsletter or other means of communication to inform young people who are being, or have been, cared for and to seek their views on matters such as these.

7.23. It would also be desirable for the statement to be informed by the views of the parents of these young people and by those of foster parents where a young person is fostered privately or by the local authority. There may be no formal mechanism for seeking these views, particularly since a local authority may have responsibility for providing aftercare for a young person whom they did not look after. However, a local authority may wish to consider obtaining a sample of views from parents and foster parents whenever a statement is prepared or revised. This might be done by sending copies of the statement to the parents and foster parents of at least some of the young people looked after by the local authority itself and seeking their comments on it.

7.24. The statement should be drafted so as to be easily comprehensible to young people and to their parents and foster parents. The local authority will need to provide translations of the policy statement in relevant ethnic minority languages. It will also need to consider how to provide the statement in versions that can be understood by young people with communication difficulties: for example a sign language video version might be particularly helpful for hearing-impaired young people whose preferred choice of communication is in sign language.

7.25. In addition, each SSD should provide an easy to read guide to its services for young people when they leave care. Like the policy statement, this should include a brief guide to services available from other agencies, based on information provided by those other agencies. The guide should be informed by the views of young people who are being, or have been, cared for, and their parents and foster parents. The local authority will need to provide translations of the guide in relevant ethnic minority languages. It will also need to consider how to provide the guide in a form that can be understood by young people with communication problems. For instance, a large print, braille or tape version may be helpful for blind or visually-impaired young people. A sign language video of the guide may be appropriate for hearing-impaired young people, or advice and information could be provided by workers trained in the needs of, and communication with, hearing-impaired young people.

7.26. The guide should include the following information:

● The advice and befriending services available to young people who have left care, under section 24(2) of the Act;

● The local authority's policy and practice on making payments in cash or in kind, under sections 24(6) and (8) of the Act, to young people who have left care;

● The nature of the help, including financial advice, that other agencies can give in preparing young people for leaving care and supporting them when they have left care; and the ways in which young people can obtain this help;

● Details of youth counselling services run by the local authority or the voluntary sector;

● The local authority's policy on giving young people access to their social services records;

● The local authority's complaints procedure, under sections 24(14) and 26(3) in case any young person considers that he is being denied appropriate advice and assistance (for further guidance see Chapter 5 of this volume);

● The name, address and telephone number of a contact point in each of the agencies mentioned in the guide.

7.27. Each local authority should nominate a designated officer in the social services department, of sufficiently senior rank, to ensure that the authority fulfils the responsibilities set out in paragraphs 7.19 to 7.26 above. In fulfilling his responsibilities, the designated officer may need to persuade the authority that it is legitimate to use staff time both to carry out aftercare work and to train staff to carry out this work properly. It may be useful if the designated officer is also the local authority's 'Appropriate Officer' for the purpose of the Disabled Persons (Services, Consultation and Representation) Act 1986.

YOUNG PEOPLE WITH DISABILITIES: PARTICULAR NEEDS

7.28. Young people with disabilities are, for the purpose of this guidance, young people who are "blind, deaf, or dumb, or (suffer) from mental disorder of any kind or (are) substantially and permanently handicapped by illness, injury or congenital deformity. . . ." (section 17(11) of the Children Act).

7.29. Young people with disabilities may well have particular needs over and above the needs of other young people who are being cared for. It is essential to ensure that these needs are met when preparing these young people for leaving care and subsequently, providing aftercare. At the same time, care must be taken to ensure that these young people do not fail to achieve their full potential as a result of under-expectation on the part of those caring for them.

7.30. The following paragraphs refer specifically to the responsibilities of local authorities (particularly SSDs). However, apart from paragraphs 7.34 to 7.39, they also apply to voluntary organisations and registered children's homes, who have a duty to prepare young people whom they are caring for, for the time when they leave care, and who may also provide aftercare for these young people.

7.31. SSDs should ensure that they have access to information on special resources and services necessary to meet the needs of young people with disabilities who are leaving care. They will also need to liaise closely with education departments and health authorities to ensure that the particular needs of these young people are met at all times. And they will need to take any steps necessary to ensure that the views of these young people about their needs, and the ways in which these can be met, are taken into account. This may necessitate the use of skilled appropriate communicators to enable better communication to take place between young people with disabilities and the various agencies.

7.32. SSDs will need to note, in addition, that they have a duty to assist local education authorities with the provision of services for any young person who is subject to a statement of special educational needs (section 27(4) of the Children Act).

7.33. SSDs will also need to liaise with housing authorities over the housing needs of young people with disabilities. They should ask the relevant housing authority to consider the particular needs of any young person with a disability who is leaving care.

7.34. In discharging these responsibilities, local authorities will need to take account of their powers and duties under other Acts of Parliament, as set out below. These powers and duties are not, of course, limited to young people who are being looked after by local authorities. Voluntary organisations and registered childrens homes may therefore consider what help the local authority can give, under these Acts, to young people whom they themselves are preparing for leaving care or providing with aftercare.

7.35. Section 2(1) of the Chronically Sick and Disabled Persons Act 1970 lays on each local authority a duty to provide various welfare services to any person living within its area if this is necessary in order to meet the needs of that person.

7.36. Sections 5 and 6 of the Disabled Persons (Services, Consultation and Representation) Act 1986 are also relevant since they are designed to ensure a smooth transition from full-time education to adult life for a young person who is subject to a "statement of special educational needs". Their effect is to require the relevant education department to obtain the view of the SSD as to whether such a young person is disabled. This is done at the first annual review of the statement of special educational needs, or the first reassessment of the young person's educational needs, following the young person's 14th birthday. If the SSD does consider that the young person is disabled, it must assess his needs, before he leaves full-time education, to decide what welfare services it has a duty to provide him with. (See the relevant sections of the 1986 Act for details).

7.37. Local authorities should, as a matter of good practice, also provide communication support for all young people who require it. This could take the form, for instance, of text telephones or interpreters.

7.38. When a child is being looked after by a local authority and placed in accommodation which provides education on the premises, the local authority is required to inform the appropriate education department when the child leaves that accommodation (section 28(3)).

7.39. In deciding the young person's future needs, the SSD should continue to liaise with the education department, which is responsible for providing "adequate facilities for further education" and which needs to "have regard to the requirements of persons over compulsory school age who have learning difficulties" (section 41 of the Education Act 1944 as substituted by section 120(2) of the Education Reform Act 1988).

7.40. More generally, local authorities will wish to note that some disabilities inhibit natural maturity and may delay learning processes and this must be taken account of in preparing a young person for leaving care and in providing aftercare.

7.41. Specific health requirements may also continue into adulthood. The transition from child to adult health services is not always easily made by a young person, who may well require help and support from the local authority, acting as a "good parent". In providing this help and support, local authorities should, of course, liaise closely with health authorities.

7.42. The particular needs of young people with disabilities will – as mentioned above – need to be taken into account in preparing them for leaving care and also in providing the necessary aftercare. It is important to note that the needs of young people with disabilities will not suddenly and fundamentally cease when they do leave care. Liaison between the various agencies concerned with a young person's welfare should continue after he has left care.

THE NATURE OF PREPARATION FOR LEAVING CARE

General

7.43. Sections 24(1), 61(1)(c) and 64(1)(c) make it clear that preparation for leaving care must start well before a young person ceases to be looked after or accommodated and is likely to continue until well after he has done so. Preparation for this process should be incorporated in the care plan for the young person as soon as he starts to be looked after or accommodated. The relevant SSD, voluntary organisation or registered children's home will play a leading role in preparing young people for the time when they leave care, but other agencies will need to be involved. Schools and the Careers Service, for instance, will need to be consulted about the long-term educational and training needs of a young person; and the relevant health authority may need to be involved if the young person is disabled.

7.44. Thus, preparation should be regarded as an integral part of the care process. A stable care relationship is, in its turn, an important basis on which to plan the preparation of a young person for leaving care.

7.45. There are three broad aspects to preparation for leaving care:
- enabling young people to build and maintain relationships with others, (both general and sexual relationships);
- enabling young people to develop their self-esteem;
- teaching practical and financial skills and knowledge.

Each of these is considered in more detail below. SSDs, voluntary organisations and registered children's homes should ensure that social workers and residential staff are trained so that they can help young people to be properly prepared for leaving care.

Enabling Young People to Build and Maintain Relationships With Others: General

7.46. The capacity to form satisfying relationships and achieve inter-dependence with others is crucial to the future well-being of the young person. With such a capacity, he is much more likely to cope with the transition to adulthood and the special difficulties associated with leaving care. It is crucial, therefore, that the experience of being cared for provides both the opportunity for such personal development and the attention that is required when special help is needed. This experience should be planned so as to cover the following points:

- Changes in care placements should be kept to the minimum consistent with the young person's welfare. This will provide continuity of care and of relationships, thereby showing young people how to relate to others.

- Social workers and residential staff, as well as other young people who are being cared for, will therefore be able to help a young person to relate to other people.

- However, a young person's friends should not all come from the care system since, if they do, he may be very lonely when he leaves care.

- It is therefore well worth encouraging young people who are being cared for to make friends with young people outside the care system, eg through school or local youth clubs.

- Young people who are being cared for should also be encouraged to develop friendships with suitable adults outside the care system who can provide role models. Volunteer adult befrienders who have been carefully vetted through a volunteer befriending scheme and who can stay in touch with a young person after he has left care can play a very important role here. The befriender will need to be 'matched' with the young person, eg he should preferably be from the same cultural, linguistic, racial and religious background. It is desirable for the young person to decide who is to act as his befriender. The befriender should be prepared to give time to his task; should be remunerated if appropriate; and should be allowed to make contributions to reviews and on other occasions, if the young person so wishes. (See also Chapter 6 – "Independent Visitors").

- The foster parents of a fostered young person can also be encouraged to continue to take an interest in him even when the fostering placement has ended.

- A young person's parents (and his relatives generally) should also be encouraged to stay in touch with him unless this would not be in his best interests.

- Young people from ethnic minorities will need to have contact with adults and young people from their own cultural background and may find it helpful to be put in touch with youth clubs or other voluntary organisations set up for people from their cultures.

- Young people with disabilities may have particular needs, and it may be useful to refer them to suitable materials, and to voluntary organisations of and for people with disabilities, to support them in finding friends and developing social skills.

The process of preparation should ensure that when a young person does leave care, he has a supportive network of friends, many of whom will be from outside the care system; and that he is well equipped to enter into relationships with others.

7.47. A local authority, in preparing a young person for leaving care, should also take account, where appropriate, of the need to enable the young person to relate better to his own family. Indeed, the local authority has a duty to make arrangements to enable a young person whom it is looking after to live with parents, relatives or friends "unless that would not be reasonably practicable or consistent with his welfare" (section 23(6)). Even if it is proved to be impracticable or undesirable to make such arrangements, any improvement in relationships between a young person and his family that can be achieved is usually to be welcomed and will contribute to the young person's capacity to cope in adult life. Similarly, general contact with family and friends should be promoted where consistent with a young person's welfare (paragraph 15 of schedule 2). Similar responsibilities are reflected in the duties of voluntary organisations and persons carrying on registered children's homes under Regulation 6 of the Arrangements for Placement of Children (General) Regulations 1991 (see Chapter 2).

Enabling Young People to Build and Maintain Relationships with Others: Sexual Relationships

7.48. The experience of being cared for should also include the sexual education of the young person. This may, of course, be provided by the young person's school, but if it is not, the SSD or other caring agency responsible for the young person should provide sexual education for him. This is absolutely vital since sexuality will be one of the most potent forces affecting any young person in the transition from childhood to adulthood.

7.49. Sexual education will need to cover practical issues such as contraception, particularly in view of the spread of AIDS. However, it must also cover the emotional aspects of sexuality, such as the part that sexuality plays in the young person's sense of identity; the emotional implications of entering into a sexual relationship with another person; and the need to treat sexual partners with consideration and not as objects to be used. The emotional and practical implications of becoming a parent also need to be explained in some detail.

7.50. Those responsible for the sexual education of young people will need to bear in mind the particular needs of different young people: the fact that young people with mental or physical disabilities have sexual needs should be acknowledged, for instance. And young people who have been abused, or have been in touch with abused young people, may need special counselling if they are not to regard sexual feelings as a matter for shame or to regard sexual relationships as impersonal and exploitive. The needs and concerns of gay young men and women must also be recognised and approached sympathetically.

Enabling Young People to Develop Their Self-esteem

7.51. Many young people who are being, or have been, cared for, have described feelings of shame about being cared for. These are frequently compounded by misunderstandings on the part of others, eg that most young people being cared for have committed criminal offences, or that there is something wrong with them, or that their parents are inadequate and unable to cope. It is therefore all the more necessary to encourage young people, from the day they begin to be cared for, to value themselves; to regard their experience of being cared for without embarrassment; and to be able to explain calmly to other people why they are being cared for and how they feel about it.

7.52. In doing this, it is particularly helpful if young people are told as much as possible about their family background and about all aspects of their cultural and individual identity, eg race, language, culture, sex, religion and any physical or mental disability. It is also helpful for young people to understand how they came to be cared for. A young person's individual identity and his cultural background should be presented to him in a positive light and not as something about which he should feel defensive. The use of life-story books may be helpful in achieving this end, but local authorities and other caring agencies will need to note that young people should be enabled to accept themselves emotionally and not simply intellectually.

7.53. Some young people may need considerable counselling before they do come to accept themselves. Young people who have been rejected by their parents may need a lot of help before they can accept, emotionally, that this is no reflection on their own worth. Young people with disabilities may also require a lot of counselling to enable them to accept themselves and to develop a sense of self-esteem. Gay young men and women may require very sympathetic carers to enable them to accept their sexuality and to develop their own self-esteem. And young people from ethnic minorities may need help – preferably from someone with the same background – to enable them to take a pride in their racial, cultural, linguistic and religious background.

7.54. If necessary the local authority or other caring agency may also act as an advocate for all young people leaving care in dealing with departments, organisations and people who may display prejudice.

Practical and Financial Skills and Knowledge

7.55. Many young people leave care without adequate preparation in practical and financial skills and knowledge. These include:

- How to shop for, prepare and cook food.
- Eating a balanced diet.
- Laundry, sewing and mending and other housekeeping skills.
- How to carry out basic household jobs such as mending fuses (which will involve basic electrical and other knowledge).
- Safety in the home and first aid.
- The cost of living.
- Household budgeting, including the matching of expenditure to income, the regular payment of bills and avoidance of the excessive use of credit.
- Health education, including personal hygiene.
- Sexual education, including contraception and preparation for parenthood. (This is particularly vital given the spread of AIDS).
- Applying for, and being interviewed for, a job.
- The rights and responsibilities of being an employee.
- Applying for a course of education or training.
- Applying for social security benefits.
- Applying for housing and locating and maintaining it.
- Registering with a doctor and dentist.
- Knowledge of emergency services (fire, police, ambulance).
- Finding and using community services and resources.
- Contacting the social services department and other caring agencies.
- Contacting organisations and groups set up to help young people who are, or have been, in care.
- The role of agencies such as the Citizens Advice Bureau, local councillors and MPs.
- How to write a letter (a) of complaint; (b) to obtain advice.

7.56. Some young people who are being cared for, particularly those in children's homes, do not have any opportunity of learning such skills. It may therefore be necessary to change the regime at the homes concerned to give them that opportunity. Young people who are being cared for should – like any other young people – start to learn these skills at a basic level when entering their teens and should be well advanced in them by the time they leave care. Young people with disabilities may need additional specific training and rehabilitation programmes to enable them to acquire these skills and to promote their independence. The nature of the programme will depend on the nature of the disability, eg sight replacement or sight enhancement techniques for visually-impaired young people. In addition, young people with communication difficulties, eg those who are hearing-impaired or speech-impaired, may need interpreters to facilitate their acquisition of these skills through sign language and also to improve their prospects at job interviews.

AFTER LEAVING CARE

7.57. Most young people will continue to need some help after they have left care. The continuing needs of young people may differ widely according to their individual circumstances and they may include any or all of the following examples:

- Advice and information.

- A continued interest in their welfare, possibly from a person specified to advise and befriend the young person.
- Assistance in cash or in kind.
- A return to care, if necessary.
- Education and training (education department).
- Accommodation (housing department: but social services departments have some responsibilities under section 20 of the Act – see paragraph 7.86 below).

The first four of these are social services responsibilities. It is impossible to specify precisely what services each local authority should offer within these broad headings. However, aftercare programmes of some kind should be available to all young people leaving care and should be organised so as to enable them to take control of their own lives. They should be flexible enough to meet the needs of all young people leaving care, including those with particular needs, eg disabled young people, those from religious, racial, cultural or linguistic minorities, young mothers and pregnant young women and gay young men and women. Each programme might be targeted at a particular group of clients, eg one might provide particularly extensive support for young people who are obliged to live independently after leaving care. The views of each young person should be sought on his needs, as he sees them, and the degree to which the local authority is meeting them. The senior officer responsible for ensuring that the local authority prepares young people properly for leaving care might usefully be responsible for ensuring that the local authority also provides a suitable range of aftercare services.

7.58. Aftercare programmes may also be offered by voluntary organisations and other caring agencies.

7.59. The possibility of encouraging young people to form their own groups has already been mentioned (paragraph 7.22). It may also be useful to set up "drop-in" bases where young people who have already left care can call for advice; to talk over any problems; or simply to keep in touch with their social workers and residential care workers. The Youth Service, both statutory and voluntary, may be able to help in developing such facilities. The role that the voluntary Youth Service can play is worth stressing. Many young people will prefer voluntary facilities to statutory ones since they will regard them as particularly able to help them escape from the stigma of being, or having been, cared for. Young people should, of course, also be encouraged to develop a social life outside care circles as well.

7.60. Some young people will also have had independent visitors appointed to visit them during their stay in care because they have infrequent or no contact with their families (paragraph 17 of schedule 2). Even when a young person has left care, he may wish to keep in touch with his independent visitor and the visitor may be a valuable source of advice, support and friendship. (See the detailed guidance on Independent Visitors in Chapter 6 of this Volume). If a young person has been fostered, his foster parents may continue to give him advice, support and friendship after the end of the foster placement.

7.61. It is desirable to monitor aftercare schemes and to evaluate them to establish how effective they are. This should be done at regular intervals. The local authority should include in these exercises representatives of the groups set up by young people who are being, or have been, cared for. This will ensure that the views of young people continue to be heard.

7.62. Young people may move to a different part of the country after leaving care and it is important to ensure that they do not fall through the net of local authority support if they require it. The local authority that has been helping them must inform the local authority into whose area they have moved, (section 24(11)) and in doing so should inform the second local authority of any particular needs of the young person. The second local authority will then assume the relevant powers and duties under section 24.

7.63. Furthermore, if a young person leaves certain forms of care other than local authority accommodation, after reaching the age of 16, the organisation or agency formerly accommodating him must inform the local authority in whose area he proposes to live (section 24(12)). The local authority should then consider what powers and duties to invoke in order to provide the young person with the appropriate aftercare.

THE DELIVERY OF SERVICES

7.64. Many local authorities are developing specialist services for young people leaving care. A number of models now exist, but it is probably too early to assess their respective merits. Where authorities have established separate aftercare teams, it is important that the person who has been most closely involved with the young person whilst in care maintains contact and provides continued support directly to him as well as contributing to the team's planned approach. This will necessitate close liaison between the aftercare team and the social services staff responsible for residential child care. The principle that preparation for leaving care is to be regarded as an integral part of any care placement from the outset should underpin the development of specialist services. (See principle 16 on page 9 of "The Care of Children: Principles and Practice in Regulations and Guidance" (HMSO, 1990)).

7.65. In discharging the responsibilities outlined above, the 'key' person working with a particular young person will need to liaise closely with any services provided by the local authority and the voluntary sector for young people with special needs, eg those who are disabled.

7.66. It is important that managers provide sufficient time and resources for staff, including staff of residential establishments, to undertake and develop the necessary skills associated with leaving care and continuing support. Local authorities should take account of the need to train staff to do this difficult job properly. The local authority's designated officer (paragraph 7.27) will need to assume responsibility for ensuring that all this is done.

7.67. The guidance given above relates to the local authority's own responsibilities. However, the authority's policy statement on leaving care and aftercare services, and its easy to read guide to those services, needs to refer to the role of other agencies in helping young people who are leaving care. In preparing both documents, and providing services accordingly, the local authority will wish to note the help that it can require from other agencies under section 27 of the Children Act (see paragraph 7.8).

7.68. These other agencies will include those who are caring for young people, who might be encouraged to assume responsibility for preparing the young people they are caring for, for the time when they leave care (voluntary organisations and registered children's homes do, of course, have a duty to do this). Local authorities will also wish to encourage them to provide aftercare for young people who have left their care. (See also paragraphs 7.12 to 7.17 and 7.76).

PROVISION OF FINANCIAL ASSISTANCE

7.69. The primary income-support role lies with the Department of Social Security. However, local authorities may also give financial assistance to young people leaving care on account of their particular needs over and above those of other young people.

7.70. Where a local authority has either a duty or a power to advise and befriend young people who have left care (section 24(4)) it may also give assistance which may be in kind or, in exceptional circumstances, in cash (sections 24(6) and (7)). Many young people leaving care, particularly those who are required to live independently because they have no family home to return to, can face very severe financial difficulties at this time – both immediately and during their transition to full independence. It is already the policy of many local authorities to provide all young people leaving care with a leaving care grant of sufficient amount to ease this transitional process, and this is to be encouraged. It should, however, be borne in mind that the local authority's power to provide assistance extends until every young person referred to in section 24(2) reaches the age of 21. Where a young person has no parent to turn to for help, or where a parent does not have the capacity to provide assistance, it is to be expected that they will turn to the local authority, which has in many cases been a major influence in their lives, for such help.

7.71. Local authorities are encouraged to be pro-active in advising young people of the circumstances in which assistance can be provided and to take into account the fact that the reference to the provision of financial assistance "in exceptional circumstances" in section 24(7) refers to the individual young person rather than the general policy of the authority. It will be for the authority to decide in each case whether the provision of financial assistance would be appropriate, but the presumption should be that such assistance should be provided where this is necessary to protect the young person's welfare and it cannot be made available by any other agency. Local authorities are encouraged to be flexible in deciding what leaving care grants can be given for; and to consider a young person's wishes about the way in which any grant given should be spent.

7.72. In addition to the general powers to provide assistance under section 24(6) of the Act, local authorities have a specific power to provide financial assistance to young people they formerly looked after where this is connected with the young person's further education, employment or training (section 24(8)). This provision enables an authority to contribute towards the costs of accommodation which enables the young person to live near the place where he is employed, seeking employment, or receiving education or training. It should be noted that the "exceptional circumstances" qualification to the provision of cash assistance in section 24(7) does not apply to assistance given under section 24(8) nor are the provisions of section 17(7)–(9) applied in such cases (section 24(10)). Bearing in mind the serious problems experienced by many young people in obtaining suitable and affordable accommodation, and the importance to be attached to the ability of young people to gain stable employment or further their education, local authorities are encouraged to exercise their powers under section 24(8) flexibly. Provision is also made for local authorities to make grants to young people to help them meet expenses connected with their further education or training (for example the purchase of books, tools or materials). It should be noted that any such financial assistance or grant provided under section 24(8) where this is connected to a course of education or training, may continue even though the young person reaches the age of 21 before completing the course (section 24(9)).

7.73. It is important that young people, residential social workers and parents should be aware of the assistance that the local authority can provide. This can be achieved through the provision of a clear statement of policy on financial assistance, which should be incorporated in the published statement of the authority's services under section 24 and in its easy to read guide to those services. Young people with disabilities may be particularly in need of financial assistance, especially if they have communication problems that make it difficult for them to apply to other agencies, such as voluntary organisations, for help.

7.74. It should be noted that financial assistance provided under section 24 is disregarded for the purposes of calculating entitlement to Income Support, Housing Benefit, Community Charge Benefit or Family Credit. It is also disregarded in assessing the maintenance grant of a student on a designated course. It is important to note that a young person does not have to qualify for Income Support before being given financial assistance under section 24.

THE ROLE OF THE VOLUNTARY SECTOR

7.75. There are two separate, but related, aspects to the work of the voluntary sector in preparing young people for leaving their care. Voluntary organisations may accommodate young people in one of their homes. In such a case, the voluntary organisation must assume the responsibility for preparing the young person concerned for leaving its care (section 61(1)(c) – see paragraphs 7.12 to 7.14). The duty of ensuring that this is done should fall to a designated senior member of staff within the voluntary organisation. When a young person ceases to be accommodated by the voluntary organisation and is aged 16 or over, the voluntary organisation must inform the local authority in whose area the young person proposes to live. The notification should be made by the designated member of staff referred to above. The notification is necessary because the local authority will have certain powers and duties to provide aftercare; therefore the voluntary organisation and the local authority must liaise closely in preparing these young people to leave the voluntary organisation's care and in providing aftercare for them. The care and aftercare services should be closely linked to each other (see also paragraph 7.43). Young people aged 16–20 who are being, or have been, cared for by a voluntary organisation, should be made aware by that organisation of the statutory amenities open to them.

7.76. The other aspect of the voluntary sector's role lies in the aftercare services provided by it. Voluntary organisations are not under a duty to provide these services, but local authorities will wish to encourage them to provide them for young people whom the organisations concerned formerly cared for. In some cases, local authorities will also be able to "purchase" aftercare services from voluntary organisations to help young people whose care was not provided by those organisations. Local authorities are therefore encouraged to liaise with voluntary organisations in their areas to make use, where appropriate, of any aftercare services they may offer (see in particular section 17(5)).

7.77. These aftercare services may include: drop-in centres; counselling; advocacy for young care-leavers – both individually and as a group; and various forms of accommodation, eg sheltered and half-way housing, refuges for young people at risk, and supported lodgings. The role of housing associations in providing suitable accommodation is particularly important. So, too, is the specialised information and advice that voluntary organisations can give to young people with a wide range of disabilities. It is important for local authorities and other caring agencies to put young people with disabilities in touch with the appropriate voluntary organisations in order to provide them with additional opportunities for involvement with particular self-help or interest groups.

7.78. Local authorities will also wish to bear in mind the help that young people leaving care can obtain from the Homelessness Advice Service. The Service operates through the national network of Citizens' Advice Bureaux. It is particularly concerned with the prevention of homelessness, the provision of advice on the dangers of leaving home without access to accommodation, the provision of access to suitable accommodation and financial counselling. Specialist and detailed advice is provided by Shelter and SHAC organisations if necessary.

THE ROLE OF THE PROBATION SERVICE

7.79. A minority of young people who are being or have been cared for will have committed criminal offences. Some of these young people will be subject to a probation order or to a supervision order designating the probation service as the supervisor. The probation service are naturally concerned to ensure, as far as possible, that these young people do not re-offend. In trying to achieve their aim, they will concern themselves not only with a young person's offending and its consequences but with his development into a self-reliant adult who has "grown out" of offending. It is therefore important for each local authority to consult the probation service when drawing up its written statement of policies on leaving care and aftercare services and its easy to read guide to those services; and to cover the role of the probation service in both documents. It is also necessary for the SSD or other caring agency to involve the probation service closely when preparing one of these young people for leaving care or providing him with aftercare.

THE ROLE OF THE HOUSING DEPARTMENT

7.80. When a young person leaves care, it may not be possible for him to return to his family: he may have none, or he may be estranged from them. Young people who have left care are over-represented among the single homeless and this emphasises the need to consider the housing needs of young people who are about to leave care. This is particularly necessary if they have disabilities (see paragraph 7.33).

7.81. The primary responsibility for housing lies with the housing department of a local authority. Close liaison between SSDs and housing departments ("housing authorities") is therefore necessary. This may best be achieved through the establishment of formal arrangements, particularly as social services and housing may be provided by different tiers of government; the SSD in a shire county, for instance, will have to deal with several district council housing departments. It is suggested that liaison should take place between the designated senior officer in the SSD and designated colleagues in the housing department(s), whether or not housing and social services are provided by the same tier of government. They should, between them, agree the arrangements for referring young people to the housing departments. At the same time, housing departments can make clear what priority they can give to young people leaving care in general and to those who have disabilities or who are otherwise vulnerable in particular. The housing departments' policies on these issues will, of course, need to be spelt out in their contribution to the local authority's written statement of leaving care and aftercare services and in its easy-to-read guide to those services – see paragraphs 7.20 and 7.25.

7.82. The priority afforded to providing housing for young people leaving care is a matter for consideration locally. However, local authorities do have a statutory duty (exercised primarily by housing departments) to ensure that accommodation is provided for single homeless people whom they assess as vulnerable. In fulfilling their duties, local authorities must bear in mind the advice contained in the Code of Guidance on homelessness accompanying the Housing Act 1985. Careful consideration should be given to the vulnerability of homeless young people who have left care and in particular those who are disabled or are at risk of sexual or financial exploitation. Many housing associations provide accommodation specifically for young people. Authorities are strongly encouraged to liaise with housing associations, who may prove receptive to the needs of those young people leaving care who are not judged to be a priority for council housing. (Note: Whether housing is provided by a local authority or another organisation, it should be adapted as soon as possible to the needs of any disabled young people living there).

7.83. The local authority's housing department may provide sheltered or halfway accommodation for young people leaving care and it may also wish to consider reserving some of its stock of conventional accommodation to meet the needs of young people leaving care who are capable of living independently. It may also wish to liaise with the voluntary sector, which may well provide accommodation and advice itself. In all cases (including those in which the local authority is not the caring agency) the SSD should consider well in advance whether a young person is likely to need help with housing when he leaves care. If he is, the SSD will need to discuss his housing needs with the housing department in time to make the necessary arrangements before he leaves care. The housing department may be able to offer accommodation. However, even if they cannot help a particular young person in this way, the SSD will know this in good time and will be able to approach other agencies offering housing, such as housing associations.

7.84. Young people who have left care are over-represented amongst young homeless people, including those who are sleeping rough. Studies suggest that as many as a third or more of young rough sleepers have been in local authority care at some point in their lives. In formulating a policy to meet the housing needs of young people leaving care, the housing and social services departments should consider:

- the ability of the young people to live independently;
- the extent to which some supervision may still be necessary;
- the personal preferences of young people leaving care;
- the possibility of arranging a private interview with a Housing Officer for any young person applying for assistance with accommodation;
- the need to clearly inform any such young person of the decision and advice of the housing department as soon as possible;
- how best to provide advice and assistance on housing;
- the contribution that the voluntary sector can make towards the provision of accommodation;
- how far landlords and landladies can contribute towards getting young people into independent living.

7.85. Housing and social services departments will also wish to consider how best to meet the following needs in providing local authority housing:

- The provision of some sheltered or halfway housing, with appropriate support services;
- The provision of a reasonable quality and range of accommodation (Note: Young people leaving care may move from sheltered accommodation to increasingly independent forms of accommodation);
- The provision, where necessary, of housing adapted to meet the needs of disabled young people;
- Good housing management and maintenance and upkeep of properties;
- A regular and simple system of rent collection;
- A system to select and match the tenants of shared properties;
- Clear tenancy agreements;
- Training for housing personnel in the special needs of young people who have left care, who may well be younger than most local authority tenants and less used to looking after themselves. Training for the staff of sheltered or halfway housing is particularly necessary.

7.86. Local authorities should also note that they have powers under section 20(5) to provide accommodation for young people aged 16–20 in their area if this is necessary to safeguard or promote their welfare. The provision of accommodation under section 20 of the Act may be a desirable course of action if it is not possible to provide suitable accommodation in any other way for a young person who has left care. There is, of course, a duty to provide accommodation if a child is in need and section 20(3) applies.

THE ROLE OF THE YOUTH SERVICE

7.87. Local authorities will wish to note the help that the youth service – both statutory and voluntary – can give to young people who are being, or who used to be, cared for. This help may include advocacy of the interests of individual young people. More particularly, the youth service can offer support to vulnerable young people and give them the opportunity of extending their social network outside the care system. Disabled young people may need advice and help to enable them to integrate into local youth services and they may need to be enabled to choose to use special youth services (eg deaf clubs) if they think these are right for them.

7.88. Young people from ethnic and cultural minorities may also find the youth service particularly helpful in enabling them to meet other young people, and adult youth leaders, from their own ethnic and cultural background. This, in turn, should help them to develop a sense of pride in their cultural identity.

THE ROLE OF THE SCHOOL

7.89. For a variety of reasons, many young people leaving care have few, if any, academic qualifications. It is essential that every effort be made to enable a young person to fulfil his potential and to reduce the degree of disadvantage experienced by many of those leaving care. To this end, SSDs and other caring agencies will need to liaise closely with schools and to support them in promoting the welfare of these young people.

7.90. It is important for schools to be aware of the dangers of under-expectation regarding the academic potential of young people who are being cared for and to ensure that such young people are given every encouragement to obtain academic qualifications and to develop their emotional, social and intellectual potential generally. Young people who are under-achieving at school will need attention to remedy this well before they leave care. The role of the SSD or other caring agency in this is that of a good parent. In exercising parental responsibility the young person's carer should ensure that the school is made fully aware of all relevant information regarding the young person's abilities and interests and that the school receives the support and reinforcement that would be expected from a concerned parent. Such support should include supervising homework and attending meetings at school with teachers, headteachers and careers staff. (Note: under education legislation, 'parent' is defined to include the carer).

7.91. The SSD or other caring agency should also encourage the young person to continue his education beyond the minimum school-leaving age unless he will quite clearly not benefit from this. It is important to note that a lot of disabled people, including many with impaired sight, hearing or speech, are quite capable of benefiting from further education and should be encouraged to undertake it. They may, of course, need special facilities such as interpreters, note takers and readers.

7.92. Where the young person concerned has a statement of special educational needs, the SSD, voluntary organisation or person carrying on a registered children's home will often, in effect, be exercising the responsibilities normally exercised by parents in ensuring that the young person's special educational needs are appropriately identified and met. This will entail close liaison with the education department, including attendance at assessment meetings and at annual reviews and ensuring that the SSD liaises closely with the education department in order to discharge its duties under sections 5 and 6 of the Disabled Persons (Services, Consultation and Representation) Act 1986. (See paragraphs 7.36 and 7.39).

7.93. Like any other young person, a young person who is being cared for will receive careers education and guidance at school. The SSD or other caring agency should ensure that this is received in good time, is appropriate and includes advice on the possibilities of undertaking a course of further education. The young person's carer should be involved in considering such advice and should discuss the available options with the young person, assisting him or her to reach a considered decision in full knowledge of the short and long term advantages and disadvantages of any choice.

TRAINING

7.94. Training is covered separately from education in this guidance in order to explain the role of the different agencies concerned.

7.95. The SSD or other caring agency involved should be ready to inform the young person of the existence of training, eg Youth Training and training schemes geared to a particular occupation. Although it will not be able to advise in detail on such training schemes, it should be able to refer the young person to those best able to advise him. This referral may be to the school careers advisory service, the local Careers Officer (for Youth Training) and the relevant occupational body for schemes geared to a particular occupation. If the young person has a disability, it may be useful to refer him to a Disablement Resettlement Officer at a Job Centre.

THE ROLE OF THE CAREERS SERVICE

7.96. The Careers Service provides the link between the worlds of work and further education. The Service is a prime source of contact for employers, training providers, teachers, those involved in higher and further education and others responsible for helping young people. The Careers Service aims to ensure that young people understand all the options open to them, including both the short-term and the long-term prospects in any particular career, so that they can make informed choices. The Careers Service gives information to young people on employment and training opportunities; it is the main placing agent with Youth Training (YT); and it gives young people information on what YT programmes are available. Careers Officers work closely with careers teachers in schools and generally contact pupils in their 3rd year at school. SSDs and other caring agencies will, as good parents, need to ensure that all young people whom they are caring for do receive this advice from the Careers Service. Young people with disabilities should receive careers advice like other young people in care. It is important to ensure that they are not advised to take up an undemanding job unless their disability really does prevent them from embarking on a challenging career.

RETURNING TO TAKE UP COURSES OF EDUCATION OR TRAINING

7.97. Many young people have left care without qualifications but have effectively returned to school in order to obtain qualifications or training. SSDs may wish to consider advising those who have left school without qualifications that it is not too late for them to remedy this situation and they may wish to provide advice on finance for educational and training courses. If the SSD is still exercising parental responsibility, the carer might support the young person by attending meetings at the school to discuss an appropriate programme of study. The SSD may also need to liaise with the education department, which has responsibility for further education.

LOCAL AUTHORITY ASSISTANCE TO YOUNG PEOPLE RECEIVING EDUCATION OR TRAINING; OR EMPLOYED; OR SEEKING EMPLOYMENT

7.98. SSDs should bear in mind the powers they have to assist young people who left local authority care when aged 16 or over and who are employed, or seeking employment, or in receipt of education or training (section 24(8)). These powers last until a young person reaches the age of 21 and they can therefore be invoked well after the young person has left the local authority's care. (See paragraph 7.72).

SOCIAL SECURITY

7.99. Local authority powers to give assistance in cash or in kind are designed to meet the special needs of young people leaving care over and above the needs of other young people. They are not designed simply to duplicate the social security system, which is why the making of these payments is at the discretion of the local authority.

7.100. However, local authorities should advise young people who are in, or have left, care on the social security benefits they may be entitled to and the way in which they can claim them. This can most easily be done by obtaining the relevant social security leaflets from the local social security office, or material specially prepared for young people by youth organisations, and making them available to the young people concerned as a first step. This material should be made available in ethnic minority languages where appropriate. Regulations for awarding income support to 16 and 17 year olds are linked to the provision of Youth Training (YT) placements. Specialist advice is sometimes required to ensure that young people receive their full entitlement and where advice is not readily available within an SSD, reference to an agency such as the Citizens' Advice Bureau may be considered.

7.101. If a young person has a disability, advice on benefits for disability should be available as a priority. If the local authority has a welfare rights officer, he should be able to give this advice. The services of an interpreter may be necessary if the young person's disability involves problems in communicating.

7.102. Local authorities will wish to note that any payments made to a young person under section 24 are not regarded as a part of his income or capital when his entitlement to Income Support, Housing Benefit, Community Charge Benefit or Family Credit is being calculated.

CHAPTER 8 <u>SECURE ACCOMMODATION</u>

8.1. This guidance describes the statutory framework in section 25 of the Act governing the restriction of liberty of children being looked after by local authorities; how this statutory protection has been extended to children in other types of accommodation, and the further provisions which have been included in the Children (Secure Accommodation) Regulations 1991 (Annex G).

8.2. Since 1983 local authorities have been precluded from placing children in their care in secure accommodation unless statutory criteria have applied, and moreover have been required to seek the authority of the court to continue such placements beyond a period of 72 hours. Children in a variety of other settings, however, have had no such statutory protection. For this reason the opportunity has been taken to extend the same statutory controls, which currently apply to local authority placements, to children accommodated by health and local education authorities, or accommodated in residential care, nursing or mental nursing homes. A subsequent set of Regulations will, it is intended, provide that applications to court in these cases should be made by health and education authorities or those carrying on residential care, nursing or mental nursing homes rather than local authorities.

8.3. The Act also gives the Secretary of State specific power to prohibit the restriction of liberty of children accommodated in voluntary and registered children's homes, and Regulations have been made to this effect.

8.4. Where reference is made to applications being made to the 'court' for authority to keep a child in secure accommodation, this means a juvenile or magistrates' court, as appropriate, where the child is the subject of criminal proceedings (ie remand to local authority accommodation). In all other cases applications are to be made to the family proceedings court unless the matter arises in the context of a case already before a County or High Court, in which case applications should be made to that court. In addition to a child's entitlement to be legally represented when applications to restrict liberty are being considered by *any* court, children appearing before a civil or magistrates' court for such purposes will be entitled to have a guardian ad litem appointed to safeguard their interests.

Placements in secure accommodation

8.5. Secure accommodation has an important role to play amongst the range of residential services and facilities provided by local authorities. Both in terms of the safety and security of the premises, the skills and enhanced levels of staff available, and the specialist programmes which can be provided, a secure placement may be the most appropriate, and only, way of responding to the likelihood of a child suffering significant harm or injuring himself or others. However, restricting the liberty of children is a serious step which must be taken only when there is no appropriate alternative. It must be a 'last resort' in the sense that all else must first have been comprehensively considered and rejected — never because no other placement was available at the relevant time, because of inadequacies in staffing, because the child is simply being a nuisance or runs away from his accommodation and is not likely to suffer significant harm in doing so, and never as a form of punishment. It is important, in considering the possibility of a secure placement, that there is a clear view of the aims and objectives of such a placement and that those providing the accommodation can fully meet those aims and objectives. Secure placements, once made, should be only for so long as is necessary and unavoidable. Care should be taken to ensure that children are not retained in security simply to complete a pre-determined assessment of 'treatment' programme. It is important that plans are made for continuity of care, education and, where appropriate, access to professional (eg psychiatric) support when the child leaves secure accommodation.

8.6. Local authorities have a new duty under the Act to take reasonable steps designed to avoid the need for children within their area to be placed in secure accommodation (Schedule 2, paragraph 7(c)). Careful consideration should be given to the existing range of alternative facilities and services available locally, identifying any gaps or inadequacies in such provision, and how these might best be met either by the authority itself or in co-operation with other agencies. In addition, steps should be taken to ensure that all decisions to seek a placement for a child in secure accommodation are taken at a senior level within the authority. This should be not less than at Assistant Director level and such a person should be accountable to the Director of Social Services for that decision. Local authorities managing secure units have a particular responsibility to ensure that children accommodated in the non-secure part of the home are not unnecessarily placed in the associated secure facility, and that the criteria for restricting liberty are applied equally rigorously to such children as to those being considered for admission from outside the home.

General Principles

8.7. The placement of a child it is looking after in secure accommodation should, wherever practicable, arise as part of the local authority's overall plan for the child's welfare. In planning such a placement, and in considering any decision with respect to a child looked after in such accommodation, a local authority must have regard to its general duties under section 22 of the Act, including the duty to safeguard and promote the child's welfare (section 22(3)(a)) and, so far as is reasonably practicable, ascertain the wishes and feelings regarding the matter of the child, his parents, any other person who has parental responsibility for him and any other person whose wishes and feelings they consider relevant (section 22(4)). For children who are provided with accommodation on a voluntary basis under section 20(1) of the Act, a person with parental responsibility for a child may, at any time, remove him from accommodation which has been provided (section 20(8)), unless the exceptions in section 20(9) apply. This includes removal from placements in secure accommodation, whether or not the authority of the court to restrict the liberty of the child has been obtained. However, in line with the requirements of the regulations and guidance covering voluntary arrangements, a written agreement about the placement made between the local authority and the parents should include the expected duration of the placement and the arrangements for bringing the placement to an end.

Statutory Framework for Restriction of Liberty

8.8. Section 25 of the Act sets out the statutory criteria which must be met before a child being looked after by a local authority can be placed and if placed, kept in secure accommodation. It also enables the Secretary of State to make regulations governing the associated court process, and makes further provision about applications, authorisations, appeals and legal representation. The associated regulations are the Children (Secure Accommodation) Regulations 1991, which replace the Secure Accommodation (No. 2) Regulations 1983 and the Secure Accommodation (No. 2) (Amendment) Regulations 1986. Section 1(5) of the Act requires that the court should not make an order unless this would be better for the child than making no order. Section 1(1) requires that the child's welfare must be the court's paramount consideration. Careful scrutiny by the court is therefore required before a secure order is made. Because restricting a child's liberty is such a serious matter proceedings under section 25 have been specified under the Rules of Court as requiring the appointment of a guardian ad litem except where the court does not consider this is necessary to protect the welfare of the child.

8.9. The purpose of the statutory framework governing the restriction of liberty of children being looked after by local authorities or accommodated by other agencies, is to protect them from unnecessary and inappropriate placement in secure accommodation; to ensure that administrative decisions taken by the local authority or others within that framework are scrutinised and endorsed by the court, and to ensure that any such placements are only for so long as is necessary and appropriate. When an application is made to the court to keep a child in secure accommodation, it is the responsibility of that court to safeguard the rights of the child by satisfying itself that adequate evidence has been produced by the applicant to demonstrate that the statutory criteria are met in the particular case. When it is so satisfied and, having had regard to the provisions of section 1 of the Act is also satisfied that giving paramount consideration to the child's welfare requires the making of a secure order (S. 1(1)) and that it will be better for the child to make an order rather than not (S. 1(5)), the court is required to make an order for such maximum duration (within the terms of the regulations) as it considers appropriate having had regard to the evidence provided. If at any stage the criteria for keeping the child in secure accommodation do not apply he should be released and put in alternative accommodation, as the court's authorisation is merely that — an authorisation.

Definition of "restriction of liberty"

8.10. The interpretation of the term "accommodation provided for the purpose of restricting liberty ("secure accommodation") in section 25(1) of the Act is ultimately a matter to be determined by the court. However, it is important to recognise that any practice or measure which prevents a child from leaving a room or building of his own free will may be deemed by the court to constitute "restriction of liberty". For example, while it is clear that the locking of a child in a room, or part of a building, to prevent him leaving voluntarily is caught by the statutory definition, other practices which place restrictions on freedom of mobility (for example, creating a human barrier) are not so clear cut. In the latter case, the views of the authority's legal department should be sought in the first instance as to the legality of the practice or measure. The views of the Social Services Inspectorate might also be sought.

Restriction of liberty of children looked after by local authorities

8.11. Within the community homes system the liberty of children may be restricted only in secure accommodation approved by the Secretary of State for such use under Regulation 3. In granting his approval the Secretary of State may impose such terms and conditions (eg a maximum length of stay) as he considers appropriate. Any such accommodation approved under Regulation 3 of the (No. 2) Regulations 1983 on the date the 1991 Regulations come into force, will be considered by the Secretary of State as having been approved under the 1991 Regulations.

8.12. Children being looked after by a local authority may also find themselves placed in secure accommodation provided outside the community homes system. This would include the Youth Treatment Centres provided in accordance with arrangements made by the Secretary of State under section 82(5) of the Act. As regards other such placements, as mentioned in paragraph 8.10 the interpretation of the term "accommodation provided for the purpose of restricting liberty ("secure accommodation")" in section 25(1) of the Act is a matter for the court, but it is likely that the placement of a child being looked after by a local authority in any accommodation outside the community homes system in which his liberty is restricted will be covered by the provisions of that section. The exceptions to this general principle are where an order exists under other legislation (eg the Mental Health Act 1983) to detain such a child. In any cases of doubt, local authorities are advised to apply to a court (which would determine whether an application under section 25 is necessary in any particular case).

Restriction of liberty of children provided with accommodation by Health and Education Authorities

8.13. The statutory safeguards governing restriction of liberty in section 25 of the Act have been extended to children accommodated by health (including National Health Service Trusts) and local education authorities (Regulation 7(1)(a)). Such an authority is 'accommodating a child' for the purpose of this section if it is either accommodating him in a directly provided establishment, or has responsibility for placing the child in accommodation provided by some other body or organisation under a contractual arrangement (eg through the payment of fees). The exclusions from this provision are described in regulation 5, namely those detained under any provision of the Mental Health Act 1983 or subject to any of the other legal provisions described in that regulation.

8.14. The practical effect of Regulation 7(1) is that, subject to the exclusions mentioned in paragraph 8.13, no child, other than one looked after by a local authority who is accommodated in the circumstances defined may have his liberty restricted unless the statutory criteria for the use of secure accommodation in section 25(1) of the Act applies. This applies equally to any proposed short-term placement of a child in a locked room for 'time-out' or seclusion purposes. The maximum period such a child may be kept in secure accommodation without the authority of a court is 72 hours, whether consecutively or in aggregate in any period of 28 consecutive days (Regulation 10(1)). The arrangements for the seeking and granting of such authority, the duration of any such court authorisation, adjournments, appeals and legal aid are as described elsewhere in the following sections of this guidance, modified as described in paragraph 8.15 below.

8.15. Regulation 7(2)(a) modifies the effect of section 25(1) of the Act by replacing the reference to a child "who is being looked after by a local authority", with one referring to a child "who is being provided with accommodation by a health authority or, as the case may be, a local education authority". Regulation 7(2)(b) amends section 25(2)(c) of the Act to enable regulations to provide that health authorities, or as the case may be, local education authorities shall make application to the court to place, or keep, a child in secure accommodation. Such regulations will be made in due course.

8.16. It is recommended that applications to the court (ie the family proceedings court) to keep a child in secure accommodation should be authorised at a senior level within the authority. Within the health authority establishment this might be the Consultant or other person with line management responsibility for the ward or establishment in which the child is accommodated. For children accommodated by local education authorities authority might be given at Assistant Director level (in line with recommendations for social services departments). In all cases it is also important that the authority's legal department be consulted at an early stage.

8.17. Under section 85 of the Act, where a child is provided with accommodation by any health or local education authority for at least three months there is a requirement to notify the responsible (local) authority of the case. It is recommended that the local authority should be notified about the restriction of liberty of a child in such accommodation, irrespective of whether or not the child has been accommodated for three months or more.

Restriction of liberty of children accommodated in residential care homes, nursing homes or mental nursing homes

8.18. The section 25 safeguards have also been extended to children, other than those looked after by local authorities, who are accommodated in residential care homes, nursing homes and mental nursing homes (Regulation

7(1)(b)). The practical effect of this provision is as described in paragraph 8.14 above.

8.19. Regulation 7(3)(a) modifies the effect of section 25(1) of the Act by replacing the reference to a child "who is being looked after by a local authority" with one referring to a child "who is being provided with accommodation in a residential care home or, as the case may be, a nursing home or mental nursing home". Regulation 7(3)(b) amends section 25(2)(c) of the Act to enable regulations to provide that persons carrying on the residential care homes or, as the case may be, nursing homes or mental nursing homes shall make applications to the court to place, or keep, a child in secure accommodation. Such regulations will be made in due course.

8.20. It is important to recognise that the purpose of extending the provisions of section 25 to such homes is not to authorise the restriction of liberty of children in them. As described in paragraph 8.9, it is to prevent children being locked-up except in the wholly exceptional circumstances described in section 25(1) and to ensure that, if they are, they have access to legal advice and judicial oversight if the placement is to continue for more than a short period.

8.21. It is recommended that the manager of the home should prepare a written statement of policy regarding the restriction of liberty of children in the home. Where, exceptionally, this is deemed to be appropriate, the statement should specify who is responsible for authorising such action (normally the person responsible for the day to day running of the home), maximum periods to be authorised, arrangements for observation and supervision and the steps which need to be taken to notify those placing the child in the home.

Restriction of liberty of children in voluntary homes and registered childrens homes.

8.22. Regulation 18 prohibits voluntary homes and registered children's homes from providing accommodation for the purpose of restricting the liberty of children. This regulation is made under powers in Schedule 5 (paragraph 7(2)(f) (voluntary homes) and Schedule 6 (paragraph 10(2)(j) (registered children's homes) of the Act. Contravention of, or failure to comply with, this provision without reasonable excuse is an offence. Any person guilty of such an offence is liable on conviction to a fine not exceeding level 4 on the standard scale (Schedule 5 (paragraph 7(3) and (4)); Schedule 6 (paragraph 10(3) and (4)).

Application of Secure Accommodation Regulations 1991

8.23. The various provisions of the Children (Secure Accommodation) Regulations 1991 refer to either "secure accommodation in community homes" or "secure accommodation". The regulations as a whole apply to the placement of children in secure accommodation in community homes; placements in secure accommodation outside the community homes system are subject only to those regulations which refer to "secure accommodation" (ie regulations 5, 6, 7, 8, 10, 11, 12 and 13). Agencies restricting the liberty of children, other than local authorities in community homes (ie those described in paragraphs 8.13–8.21), are recommended to apply administratively the principles set out in regulations 4, 9, and 14–17 which the Secretary of State has thought it appropriate to apply to the use of secure accommodation in community homes.

Minimum Age

8.24. Regulation 4 states that no child under the age of 13 years may be placed in secure accommodation in a community home without the prior approval of the Secretary of State to the placement (this replaces the previous minimum age of 10 years). A local authority wishing to restrict the liberty of a child under the age of 13 should first discuss the case with the Social Services Inspectorate. Subject to their advice a formal written submission should then be submitted to the Secretary of State for his consideration, providing details of why restriction of liberty is considered the only appropriate way of dealing with the child.

Children to whom Section 25 does not apply

8.25. Regulation 5 describes various groups of children to whom section 25 of the Act does not apply. Two broad categories of children are excluded from these provisions:

Regulation 5(1) describes children who may have their liberty restricted without section 25 applying — these are children detained under any provision of the Mental Health Act 1983 and those sentenced under section 53 of the Children and Young Persons Act 1933. In both these cases lawful authority already exists, by virtue of these statutory provisions, to restrict the child's liberty, if considered appropriate in exceptional circumstances;

Regulation 5(2) describes children who may not have their liberty restricted in any circumstances — these are (a) people aged 16 or over but under 21 provided with accommodation in a community home under section 20(5) of the Act, and (b) children subject to a child assessment order under section 43 of the Act.

Criteria for restriction of liberty

8.26. Section 25 of the Act specifies the criteria which must apply before a child may have his liberty restricted. They are that:

"(a) i. he has history of absconding and is likely to abscond from any other description of accommodation; *and*

ii. if he absconds, he is likely to suffer significant harm;

or

(b) that if he is kept in any other description of accommodation he is likely to injure himself or other persons."

It should be noted in this context that by virtue of section 105 of the Act (Interpretation), "harm" has the same meaning as in section 31(9) and the question of whether harm is significant shall be determined in accordance with section 31(10).

8.27. Subject to what is said in paragraphs 8.28 and 8.29 below, it is unlawful for the liberty of a child to be restricted unless one of these criteria is met, no matter how short the period in security. Similarly, a child must not continue to have his liberty restricted once the criteria cease to apply, even if there is a court order authorising restriction of liberty when currently in existence.

Remanded and detained Children

8.28. Regulation 6 exempts two groups of children from the application of the criteria in section 25(1)(a) and (b), and provides different criteria. These are defined in Regulation 6(1) as being:

(a) children detained under section 38(6) of the Police and Criminal Evidence Act 1984 (detained children), and

(b) certain children remanded to local authority accommodation under section 23 of the Children and Young Persons Act 1969, who are:

(i) charged with or convicted of an offence imprisonable, in the case of a person aged 21 or over, for 14 years or more, or

(ii) charged with or convicted of an offence of violence, or has been previously convicted of an offence of violence.

8.29. For both groups of children described in paragraph 8.28 above, Regulation 6(2) modifies the criteria in section 25(1) to be applied in such cases. Such children may not be placed, and, if placed, may not be kept in accommodation provided for the purpose of restricting liberty ("secure accommodation"):

"unless it appears that any accommodation other than that provided for the purpose of restricting liberty is inappropriate because:—

(a) the child is likely to abscond from such other accommodation, or

(b) the child is likely to injure himself or other people if he is kept in any such other accommodation."

It should be noted that children detained under section 38(6) of the Police and Criminal Evidence Act 1984 are brought within the scope of these arrangements for the first time.

8.30. Children remanded to local authority accommodation under section 23 of the 1969 Act who do not meet the definition set out in Regulation 6(1)(b) (see paragraph 8.28 above) may be placed in secure accommodation only if the general criteria specified in section 25(1) of the Act apply.

8.31. Under section 130 of the Criminal Justice Act 1988 all children remanded to local authority accommodation and placed in secure accommodation will have time so spent deducted from an eventual custodial sentence. The arrangements were described in local authority circular LAC(88)23. Local authorities are reminded of the need to maintain accurate records of the duration of such placements and to ensure that the information is available at the court on the day the case is finally dealt with.

Notifications

8.32. Regulation 9 requires that when a child is placed in secure accommodation in a community home which is not managed by the authority which is looking after him, the managing authority must notify the other authority within 12 hours of the placement (this replaces the previous requirement to provide such notification within 24 hours). The purpose of the notification is to enable the managing authority to obtain the agreement of the local authority looking after the child to continue the placement and, if necessary, to initiate the process of seeking the authority of the court. Notifications should preferably be done by telephone, as soon as possible after the placement, and it is essential that managing authorities are informed of officers who may be contacted for this purpose out of normal office hours (eg at night, weekends and public holidays).

8.33. Where a child is kept in secure accommodation in a community home and it is intended to seek the authority of the court to continue the placement, Regulation 14 places a duty on the local authority looking after the child, wherever practicable and as soon as possible, to notify the child's parent; any person not a parent but who has parental responsibility for him; the child's independent visitor, if one has been appointed, and any other person who the local authority consider should be informed, of this intention. This could include, for example, any 'Independent Representative' attached to the secure unit. This regulation applies both to court applications after the first 72 hour period (Regulation 10) and to applications to keep a child in secure accommodation beyond a period authorised by a court. The requirements of Regulation 14 should be considered in conjunction with the Magistrates' Court (Children Act 1989) Rules 1991 (which in effect require the local authority to notify a child's parent or guardian of the date, place and time of a court hearing). Local authorities will, where appropriate, no doubt wish to combine their duty under the Rules with the notification requirements of Regulation 14.

Maximum period of restriction of liberty without court authority

8.34. Regulation 10(1) places a limit on the maximum period a child, to whom section 25 of the Act applies, may have his liberty restricted without the authority of the court. The maximum period is one of 72 hours, either consecutively or in aggregate in any period of 28 consecutive days.

8.35. Some easement of this provision is provided by Regulation 10(3) to meet difficulties which may be faced by local authorities and other agencies in arranging applications to be heard at short notice where the 72 hours period expires late on a Saturday, a Sunday or public holiday. The regulation provides that where a child is placed in secure accommodation at any time between 12 midday on the day before and 12 midday on the day after a public holiday or a Sunday, and:

(a) during that period the maximum period of 72 hours expires, and

(b) in the 27 days before the day on which he was placed in secure accommodation been placed and kept in secure accommodation for an aggregate of more than 48 hours,

the maximum period (of 72 hours) shall be treated as if it did not expire until 12 midday on the first working day after the public holiday or Sunday.

8.36. This limited extension of the 72 hours rule is intended to cater for the emergency placement of a child in secure accommodation at a time when both the major proportion of that 72 hours has already been used up and it is unlikely to be possible to arrange for an application to be heard by a court before the 72 hour limit expires. In any other type of placement an application must be brought before the court within the 72 hour period if it is intended the placement should continue beyond that period, especially in those cases where the period would expire on a day when courts do not normally sit.

8.37. Regulation 10(2) provides that where a court has authorised a child to be kept in secure accommodation, any time which a child had been kept in such accommodation before that authority was given shall be disregarded for the purposes of calculating the maximum period in relation to any subsequent occasion on which the child is placed in such accommodation after the period authorised by the court has expired. The practical effect of this regulation is that the 28 day period mentioned in Regulation 10(1) will restart on the expiry of any authority which the court has given. This is intended to meet the case of a child who may need to be readmitted to security as an emergency, and where –

(a) during the previous 28 days the child has had his liberty restricted for up to 72 hours, and

(b) a court has authorised such a placement for a period of less than 28 days.

Applications to court

8.38. Regulation 8 requires that applications to the court under section 25 of the Act to keep a child in secure accommodation shall be made only by the local authority looking after the child or when further Regulations are made dealing with court applications by other authorities and persons, in cases where Regulation 7(1)(a) or (b) applies, the health authority, local education authority, or person carrying on the residential care home, nursing home or mental nursing home (see paragraphs 8.13–8.21 above). The regulation does not prevent an application being made on behalf of the local authority looking after the child, or (when the further Regulations are made) other authority or person referred to in the Regulation. For example, an application could be made on behalf of the local authority looking after a child by the local authority managing the secure accommodation in which he is accommodated, where different. Similarly, in the case of a Youth Treatment Centre, applications may be made by the Director of the Centre on behalf of the local authority looking after the child. In all cases, however, the application must only be made with the agreement of, and in the name of, the authority or person, as appropriate, specified by the Regulation.

8.39. Staff working in accommodation which restricts liberty and, for example, field social workers will be aware of the need to prepare children adequately for the court hearing and, in this respect, particular regard should be paid to the age and understanding of the child. The child's entitlement to legal aid (see paragraph 8.40 below) should be carefully explained. Staff themselves may require some guidance on the preparation of reports and on the need to ensure that the court is provided with precise evidence of the way in which it is considered that the child meets the statutory criteria for placing or keeping him in secure accommodation.

Legal representation

8.40. A court is unable to exercise its powers to authorise a period of restriction of liberty under section 25 of the Act if the child is not legally represented in court. The only exception is where the child, having been informed of his right to apply for legal aid and having had an opportunity to do so, has refused or failed to apply (section 25(6)). Children should be encouraged to appoint a legal representative in such proceedings and given every assistance to make such arrangements. The provision of legal aid in such proceedings is described in section 99 of the Act. This adds a new subsection (3B) to section 15 of the Legal Aid Act 1988 which says that "representation . . . must be granted where a child who is brought before a court under section 25 of the 1989 Act (use of accommodation for restricting liberty) is not, but wishes to be, legally represented before the court". The child in such circumstances should have details of local solicitors on the Law Society's Child Care Panel made available to him and should be assisted in making contact with the solicitor of his choice.

Appointment of Guardians Ad Litem

8.41. Applications to the court for authority to restrict the liberty of children are 'specified proceedings' within the meaning of section 41 of the Act. As such, the court is required to appoint a guardian ad litem unless it is of the opinion that it is unnecessary to do so in order to safeguard the child's interests. This is an important new provision designed to ensure that the welfare of children in such circumstances, and particularly those provided with accommodation under section 20(1), is adequately safeguarded.

Court's powers in considering secure accommodation applications

8.42. In applying to a court the local authority looking after the child, or other authority or person as appropriate, will be seeking to satisfy the court that the appropriate criteria are met in respect of the child. Where the court is satisfied, and having regard to the provisions of section 1 of the Act (see paragraph 8.47 below), it must, where appropriate, make an order. The order is permissive; it enables but does not oblige the authority or person making the application to continue the placement for the duration of the order. Neither does it empower the authority or person to continue the placement once the criteria under which the order was made cease to apply.

8.43. Regulation 11 provides that, subject to Regulations 12 and 13 (the latter making special provision for remanded children – see paragraph 8.46 below), the maximum period a court may authorise a child to be kept in secure accommodation is three months. This regulation refers to orders made on a first application (ie within the 72 hour period referred to in Regulation 10(1), or the extended period referred to in Regulation 10(3)).

8.44. Where the local authority looking after the child, or other authority of person as appropriate, believes his placement in secure accommodation should continue beyond the period specified in the initial order, a further application must be made to the court following the procedures outlined in paragraphs 8.32, 8.33, and 8.38–8.40 above.

8.45. Regulation 12 enables a court to authorise a child (other than a remanded child as specified in Regulation 13) to be kept in secure accommodation for further periods of up to six months beyond that authorised under Regulation 11, on each application to the court.

8.46. The maximum periods a court may authorise restriction of liberty for children remanded to local authority accommodation under section 23 of the Children and Young Persons Act 1969 are described in Regulation 13. Other than when a child is committed to a Crown Court for trial, the maximum period will be the period of remand. Where such a child needs to have his liberty restricted, authority for the placement to continue must be sought on each occasion the child returns to the court for his remand case to be reviewed. In the case of a child committed for trial in the Crown Court, different remand arrangements apply. In this case a 28 day limitation on the duration of secure accommodation authorisations will apply. This is a change from the previous arrangements.

8.47. When the court is considering whether to authorise any of the orders described in paragraphs 8.42 to 8.46 above, it must also have regard to the provisions of section 1 of the Act. The child's welfare is the paramount consideration. In broad terms this means that the court must be satisfied that the order will positively contribute to the child's welfare and it must have regard to the fact that any delay in determining questions relating to the upbringing of the child is likely to prejudice his welfare. It must not make the order unless it considers that doing so would be better for the child than making no order at all (section 1(5)).

8.48. Where the court adjourns consideration of an application, it may make an interim order authorising the child to be kept in secure accommodation during the period of the adjournment (section 25(5)). An interim order will be made only where the court is not in a position to decide whether the criteria in section 25(1), or the provisions of Regulation 6 in respect of certain remanded children, have been met. If the court adjourns consideration of an application and does not make an interim order, the child may not be placed in secure accommodation during the period of the adjournment unless his circumstances subsequently change, when the normal procedures will apply (see paragraphs 8.34 to 8.37 above).

Appeals

8.49. Section 94 of the Act makes provisions for appeals to the High Court against decisions to authorise, or refusal to authorise, applications for restriction of liberty. Where such an appeal is against an authorisation, a child's placement in secure accommodation may continue during consideration of the appeal. Where a court has refused to authorise restriction of liberty, and the local authority looking after the child, or other authority or person as appropriate, is appealing against that decision, the child must not be retained or placed in secure accommodation during consideration of the appeal.

Wardship and Inherent Jurisdiction of High Court

8.50. The impact of the Children Act on the inherent jurisdiction of the High Court, which will be considerable, is described in detail in paragraphs 3.98–3.103 of Volume 1 (Court Orders) in the Children Act Guidance and Regulations series. The important point to note, as far as restriction of liberty is concerned, is that wardship will no longer be available as a route into secure accommodation for a child looked after by a local authority. There are also important additions and modifications to Schedule 14 of the Act, relating to wardship and placement in secure accommodation, in the Schedule to The Children Act 1989 (Commencement and Transitional Provisions) Order 1991 (SI 1991 No 828 (C 19)). Paragraphs 2 and 3 of that Schedule make court directions relating to secure accommodation subject to:

(a) the provisions of section 25 of the Act and any regulations made under that section; and

(b) a new sub-paragraph 16(6) to Schedule 14 of the Act (which provides that any such directions shall cease to have effect after the maximum period specified by regulations made under section 25(2)) (the effect of this is to qualify court directions which would otherwise be preserved by virtue of paragraph 16(5) of Schedule 14 to the 1989 Act).

8.51. For children who, on commencement, are wards of court and have their liberty restricted as a result of directions given under the High Court's inherent jurisdiction, the directions will cease to have effect upon expiry of the maximum period specified in Regulation 11 or 12, calculated from 14th October 1991. In practice, this means a maximum period of three months from that date if directions had been sought and granted on a single occasion in relation to that secure placement, and a maximum of six months from that date in all other cases. Local authorities should consider whether it would be appropriate to seek a discharge or variation of any such direction.

8.52. The Children (Secure Accommodation) Regulations 1991, unlike their predecessors, make no special provision for children who are subject to the inherent jurisdiction of the High Court. This, coupled with the modifications to paragraph 16 of Schedule 14 to the Act referred to in paragraph 8.50 above, means that in the exceptional circumstances of an application being made to the High Court to exercise its inherent jurisdiction to give directions as to the placement of a child in secure accommodation, such applications will be subject to the full provisions of section 25 of the Act and the associated Secure Accommodation Regulations from 14 October 1991. In practice, this means that under the new arrangements, the court will be unable to give directions to place a child under the age of 13 in secure accommodation in a community home without the local authority having obtained the prior approval of the Secretary of State (Regulation 4); the child will be entitled to be legally represented at the hearing of the application (section 25(6) of the Act), and the maximum duration of any direction to restrict the child's liberty will be three or six months, as appropriate (Regulations 11 and 12). The provisions of section 25(8) of the Act will not prejudice the position described above in relation to directions concerning other aspects of the child's upbringing.

Reviews

8.53. Regulations 15 and 16 deal with the review by local authorities looking after children of the placements of such children in secure accommodation in community homes. This review is additional to the review required by section 26 of the Act. Regulation 15 requires each local authority looking after a child in secure accommodation to ensure that his case is reviewed within one month of the start of the placement and thereafter at intervals not exceeding three months. The first review within one month is a new provision. Each local authority is required to appoint at least three persons to undertake such reviews, one of whom must not be employed by the local authority looking after the child or by the local authority managing the secure accommodation in which he is accommodated. This 'independent' element in the review process is a new provision. The voluntary organisation 'Voice for the Child in Care', may be able to assist in providing such an independent person from their panel of Independent Representatives for children in secure accommodation. It should be noted that responsibility for undertaking such reviews rests solely on the local authority looking after the child, and not with the local authority managing the secure unit in which he is accommodated, where different.

8.54. Regulation 16(1) requires the persons appointed under Regulation 15 to satisfy themselves, in respect of each case they review, that:

(a) the criteria for keeping the child in secure accommodation in a community home continue to apply, and

(b) such a placement continues to be necessary and whether or not any other description of accommodation would be appropriate for him;

and in doing so they must have regard to the welfare of the child.

8.55. Regulations 16(2) and (3) require the persons appointed to undertake the review to ascertain and take into account, as far as is practicable, the wishes and feelings of:

(a) the child,

(b) any parent of his,

(c) any person not being a parent of his but who has parental responsibility for him,

(d) any other person who has had the care of the child, whose views the persons appointed consider should be taken into account,

(e) the child's independent visitor if one has been appointed, and

(f) the local authority managing the secure accommodation in which the child is placed if that authority is not the authority looking after the child.

These parties must, if practicable, all be informed of the outcome of the review, and the reasons for such outcome.

8.56. If a conclusion of the reviewing panel is that the criteria for restricting liberty no longer apply, the placement is no longer necessary or other accommodation is appropriate, the authority looking after the child must immediately review the child's placement.

Records

8.57. Regulation 17 requires each local authority responsible for the management of secure accommodation to keep records giving:

(a) the name, date of birth and sex of the child,

(b) details of the care order or other statutory provision under which the child is in the community home and particulars of any other local authority involved with the placement of the child in that home,

(c) the date, time and reason for the placement, the name of the officer authorising the placement and where the child was living before placement,

(d) persons informed under the provisions of regulations 9, 14 and 16,

(e) court orders made under section 25 of the Act,

(f) reviews undertaken under regulation 15,

(g) the date and time of any occasion when the child is locked on his own in any room (including his bedroom) in the secure unit, other than his bedroom during usual bedtime hours; the name of the person authorising this action; the reason for it, and the date on which and time at which the child ceases to be locked in the room,

(h) the date and time of his discharge from secure accommodation and the address of his subsequent placement.

These records must be made available for inspection by the Secretary of State, who may require copies to be sent to him at any time.

Children sentenced to detention

8.58. Where a child is sentenced to detention under Section 53 of the Children and Young Persons Act 1933, and a local authority agrees to detain him in secure accommodation in a community home, the local authority will receive detailed instructions and guidance from the Department of Health in respect of a child normally resident in England and from the Welsh Office in respect of a child normally resident in Wales. The only requirements in the Regulations that apply are those relating to the keeping of records (described in paragraph 8.57 above). As mentioned in paragraph 25 above, any child sentenced under Section 53 of the 1933 Act who is also being looked after by a local authority is specifically excluded from the provisions of section 25 of the Act.

CHAPTER 9 REFUGES FOR CHILDREN AT RISK

9.1. Section 51 of the Children Act 1989 provides a scheme under which bona fide organisations, which provide refuges for runaway youngsters, can be exempted from prosecution for assisting or inducing youngsters to run away or stay away or for harbouring them or for child abduction.

9.2. Refuges can provide a breathing space for runaway youngsters. Refuge workers can work with the youngsters to help them to return to parents or local authority care, or to sort out some other solution if a return home is not appropriate (eg where a child has been, or may have been, sexually or physically or emotionally abused at home.) The Department believes there is a legitimate and valuable role for such provision operated in a well-structured and responsible way, as evidenced in a study produced by the Children's Society on a project for runaway youngsters in London (Young Runaways: findings from Britain's first safe house, C Newman, ISBN 0 907324 51 7). It is important that those running such facilities have a clear legal framework within which to work.

PROVISIONS OF SECTION 51(1)

9.3. The Secretary of State is given power under section 51(1) to issue certificates with respect to voluntary or registered homes or foster parents approved by local authorities or voluntary organisations. The issue of such certificates has the effect that the following provisions do not apply to that home or foster parent:

(a) Section 49 of the Children Act 1989 (abduction of children in care etc),

(b) Section 2 of the Child Abduction Act 1984 (offence of abduction of child by persons [other than parent], etc),

(c) Section 32(3) of the Children and Young Persons Act 1969 (compelling, persuading, inciting or assisting any person to be absent from detention etc),

(d) Section 71 of the Social Work (Scotland) Act 1968 (harbouring children who have absconded from residential establishments etc).

REGULATIONS

9.4. Provisions as to the issue and withdrawal of certificates and requirements while a certificate is in force are contained in the Refuges for Children at Risk (Children's Homes and Foster Placements) Regulations 1991 and in this guidance.

APPLICATIONS

9.5. Applications should be made on an application form obtainable from the Department of Health, Community Services Division (CS2C). A copy of the application form is annexed to this circular. Any applicant will normally be expected first to have registered the home as a voluntary or private children's home or have made an application in respect of a foster parent approved by the voluntary organisation (under the Children (Foster Placement) Regulations 1991).

9.6. It is believed unlikely that any local authority, or local authority foster parent, should be, or potentially be, at risk of being prosecuted under any of the provisions listed at paragraph 9.3 above. It would have to be proved that the authority were acting with intent and without lawful authority or reasonable excuse.

9.7. The objectives of the project will be expected to include the rehabilitation of the young person with his or her parent(s) or whoever else is responsible for the young person, provided this is consistent with the welfare of the child.

ADDITIONAL GUIDANCE

9.8. While a certificate is in force the provisions of Regulation 3 will apply, eg the child must appear to be at risk of harm before he is accepted into the refuge and when he is in the refuge he must be at risk of harm if he were not staying at the refuge; moreover the police have to be notified of every admission within 24 hours with a view to the parent or other specified person being notified that the child is in a refuge and provided with a telephone contact number, but not the address, of the project. The police should also be notified by the refuge when the child leaves.

9.9. Where a child remains in the refuge for more than 14 consecutive days, or more than 21 days in any period of three months, the protection from prosecution which a certificate provides will apply but the certificate can be withdrawn altogether from the refuge as it will not be being used in accordance with the basis upon which the certificate was granted.

9.10. It should be noted that the protection from prosecution given by such certificates extends to the organisation itself and to those persons providing the home in which the refuge is situated, or the foster parent providing the refuge as the case may be. However, it would appear that those involved in outreach work, whether or not they are employed by the refuge, would not be protected from prosecution by the certificate.

9.11. Under Regulation 4 a certificate may be withdrawn at any time, where Regulation 3 of the Refuges Regulations or of Part II of the Children's Homes Regulations 1991, or Schedule 2 Part II or Schedule 3 Part II of the Children (Foster Placement) Regulations 1991 are not complied with.

9.12. The Rules of Court will require notice to be given in any proceedings brought under the Act where it is alleged that the child is in a refuge. The person providing the refuge can then seek leave to be joined as a party should he wish to challenge the application to make the order. It is expected that similar arrangements will exist in relation to wardship proceedings. Additionally such person(s) or organisations may apply for an emergency protection order (section 44(1)) or ask the police to take the child into police protection (section 46) if they believe the child would suffer significant harm by being removed from the refuge. An emergency protection order or police protection in the last resort takes precedence over a care order. The police can arrange for a child who is in police protection to be placed in a refuge (section 46(3)(f)(ii)). The Emergency Protection Order (Transfer of Responsibilities) Regulations (section 52(3) and (4)) will not require a child to be removed from a refuge when an emergency protection order is in force.

9.13. Certificates will not be issued lightly. The local authority social services department and the police will have had the opportunity to express a view on whether a certificate should be issued. The Department of Health will give very careful consideration to such views and will require a report from the Social Services Inspectorate before issue of a certificate will be considered. Contravention of the provisions of Part II of the Children's Homes Regulations or paragraphs 4 to 9 of Schedule 2 and paragraphs 4 to 8 of Schedule 3 or of Regulation 3 of the Refuges for Children at Risk (Children's Homes and Foster Placements) Regulations 1991 would be grounds for refusal or withdrawal of a certificate. If any person providing a refuge or any person assisting him has had proceedings instituted against him in relation to or has been convicted of any criminal offence this could also be grounds for refusal or withdrawal of a certificate. Homes will of course first have had to be registered by the local authority or the Secretary of State and foster parent arrangements will have had to be checked for compliance with the Foster Placement Regulations. Police checks will have been undertaken as will checks as to whether people are on the list maintained by the Department of Health of people considered unsuitable for work with children. The Social Services Inspectorate will also inspect, and report to the Department on homes and foster parent arrangements before issue of section 51 certificates is considered and at regular intervals thereafter.

9.14. There is no formal right of appeal against refusal or withdrawal of a certificate though any representations about such steps would of course be properly and thoroughly considered. The Secretary of State will operate the procedure in relation to certificates in a reasonable way having regard to the rules of natural justice as to the process which is adopted for consideration of applications, their refusal, and withdrawal of certificates.

9.15. SSDs should aim to work together with refuges in their area to establish a satisfactory basis for operation.

9.16. Guidance is expected to be issued to the police on the legal framework within which refuges will have to operate and on the need to work in co-operation with SSDs. The importance of maintaining the confidentiality of the address of a refuge will also be emphasised.

**ANNEX TO
CHAPTER 9**

CONFIDENTIAL

CHILDREN ACT 1989

SECTION 51 (REFUGES FOR CHILDREN AT RISK)

APPLICATION FOR CERTIFICATE

1. Full name(s) of applicant person(s) or organisation.

2. Address of proposed refuge.

3. Numbers/sex/age range of persons for whom this service is proposed to be provided.

4. Objectives of proposed service.

5. Proposed contact address and telephone number.

6. Signature of applicant (with designation in the case of an organisation).

A SEPARATE COPY OF THE APPLICATION SHOULD NOW BE PASSED UNDER CONFIDENTIAL COVER—WITH DOCUMENTARY EVIDENCE OF REGISTRATION OR FOSTER PARENT STATUS — TO:

1. The local Director of Social Services, who should be requested to provide his comments if any to the application and then send it and any comments to the Department at the address given in this circular.*

2. The Chief Officer for the police area within which the proposed refuge is situated, who should be requested to provide his comments if any to the application and then send it and any comments to the Department at the address given in this circular.*

– FOR COMMENT AND ONWARD TRANSMISSION TO THE DEPARTMENT OF HEALTH, (CS2C), ROOM 216, WELLINGTON HOUSE, 133–155 WATERLOO ROAD, LONDON SE1 8UG.

DH
CS2(C)

February 1991

  *Comments should include whether there is a need for the refuge, whether the organisation or person or persons proposing to provide the refuge are suitable to run such a service, whether there is any impediment to such persons providing such a service.

STATUTORY INSTRUMENTS

1991 No. 1506

CHILDREN AND YOUNG PERSONS

Children's Homes Regulations 1991

Made -   -   -   -   *30th June 1991*

Laid before Parliament   *8th July 1991*

Coming into force   *14th October 1991*

ARRANGEMENT OF REGULATIONS

The Secretary of State for Health, in exercise of the powers conferred by sections 62(3), 63(3)(b), 64(4), and 104(4) of, and paragraph 4 of Schedule 4, paragraphs 1, 6 and 7 of Schedule 5, paragraphs 1(2), (4), (5) and (6) and 10 of Schedule 6 to the Children Act 1989(**a**) and of all other powers enabling him in that behalf hereby makes the following Regulations:

PART I — Introductory

Citation and commencement

1. These Regulations may be cited as the Children's Homes Regulations 1991 and shall come into force on 14th October 1991.

Interpretation

2.—(1) In these Regulations unless the context otherwise requires–

"the Act" means the Children Act 1989;

"children's home" means a registered children's home, a community home or a voluntary home;

"maintained community home" means a community home proivded, managed, equipped and maintained by a local pursuant to section 53(3)(a) of the Act (Provision of community homes by local authorities);

"medicinal product" means anything in respect of which a product licence under the Medicines Act 1968(**b**) is required;

"person in charge" means in relation to a home the person appointed as the person in charge of it by the responsible authority;

"registered dental practitioner" means a person registered in the dentists register under the Dentists Act 1984(**c**);

"registration authority" means–

   (a) in the case of a voluntary home, the Secretary of State; and

   (b) in the case of a registered children's home, the local authority in whose area the home is situated;

"responsible authority" means–

   (a) in the case of a maintained community home, the local authority(**d**) by whom it is maintained;

   (b) in the case of a controlled or assisted community home, the body of managers, except in respect of a matter which is reserved, by the Act or the instrument of management, to the local authority or the voluntary

---

(**a**) 1989 c.41, (for the definition of "prescribed" *see* section 105(1) and, in relation to Schedule 6, paragraph 1(3) of that Schedule).
(**b**) 1968 c.67.
(**c**) 1984 c.24.
(**d**) "Local authority" is defined in section 105(1) of the Act as the council of a county, a metropolitan district, a London Borough of the Common Council of the City of London. Pursuant to section 2 of the Local Authority Social Services Act 1970 (c.42) local authority functions under the Children Act 1989 stand referred to the social services committee of a local authority.

organisation providing the home, and in that case means the local authority or the voluntary organisation providing the home;

(c) in the case of a voluntary home, the voluntary organisation by whom it is provided; and

(d) in the case of a registered children's home, the person carrying it on.

(2) In the Regulations unless the context otherwise requires–

(a) any reference to a numbered section is to the section of the Act bearing that number;

(b) any reference to a numbered regulation is to the regulation in these Regulations bearing that number, and any reference in a regulation to a numbered paragraph is to the paragraph of that regulation bearing that number; and

(c) any reference to a numbered schedule is to that numbered Schedule to these Regulations.

Application of Regulations

3.—(1) Subject to paragraph (2)–

(a) This Part, Part II and Part III of these Regulations apply to all children's homes.

(b) Part IV of these Regulations applies only to community homes.

(c) Part VI of these Regulations applies only to registered children's homes.

(d) Parts V and VII of these Regulations apply only to voluntary homes.

(e) Part VIII of these Regulations applies only to registered children's homes and to voluntary homes.

(2) These Regulations shall not apply to premises used only to accommodate children for the purpose of a holiday for periods of less than 28 days at a time in the case of any one child.

PART II — Conduct of Children's Homes

Statement of purpose and function of children's homes

4.—(1) The responsible authority shall within three months of the coming into force of these Regulations compile, and thereafter maintain, and keep up to date, a written statement of the particulars mentioned in Part I of Schedule 1 relating to each children's home for which it is the responsible authority.

(2) The statement referred to in paragraph (1) shall be made available for inspection by the persons referred to in Part II of Schedule 1 (in addition to those who have a right under the Act to inspect this statement).

Staffing of children's homes

5.—(1) The responsible authority shall ensure that the number of staff of each children's home and their experience and qualifications are adequate to ensure that the welfare of the children accommodated there is safeguarded and promoted at all times.

(2) The responsible authority shall ensure that the particulars specified in Part I of Schedule 1 are brought to the notice of all staff in each children's home.

Accommodation for individual children

6.—(1) The responsible authority shall ensure that, so far as is reasonably practicable, each child in a children's home shall be provided with an area within the home which is suitable for his needs, and is equipped in accordance with the following paragraphs of this regulation.

(2) The area referred to in paragraph (1) shall be equipped with furniture, bedding and furnishings appropriate to the needs of the child.

(3) Where the child concerned is disabled the area referred to in paragraph (1) shall be

equipped with what is reasonably necessary in order to meet the child's needs arising from his disability so as to enable him to live as normal a life as possible.

Accommodation—general provisions

7.—(1) The responsible authority shall ensure that there is provided within the home for the use of children accommodated there–
- (a) a sufficient number of wash basins, baths and showers supplied with hot and cold running water; and
- (b) a sufficient number of lavatories,

for the number of children accommodated.

(2) The responsible authority shall ensure that all parts of the home used by children accommodated are–
- (a) adequately lit, heated and ventilated;
- (b) kept in good structural repair, clean and reasonably decorated and maintained for the purpose of accommodating children.

(3) The responsible authority shall ensure that there are provided within the children's home suitable facilities for any child accommodated there to meet privately–
- (a) his parent;
- (b) any person who is not a parent but who has parental responsibility for him;
- (c) his relatives or friends;
- (d) his solicitor;
- (e) his guardian ad litem;
- (f) any independent person appointed in respect of any requirement of the procedure specified in the Representations Procedure (Children) Regulations 1991(**a**);
- (g) any visitor appointed for the child in accordance with paragraph 17 of Schedule 2 to the Act;
- (h) any person authorised in accordance with section 80(2) by the Secretary of State to conduct an inspection of the children's home and the children there;
- (i) in the case of a registered children's home any person authorised by the registration authority;
- (j) in the case of an assisted community home, any person authorised by the local authority named in the instrument of management.

(4) The responsible authority shall ensure that there are provided in the children's home adequate facilities for laundering linen and clothing used by children accommodated there, and, for children wishing to do so, to wash, dry and iron their own clothes.

(5) The responsible authority shall ensure that a pay telephone is available for children accommodated in the home in a setting where it is possible to make and receive telephone calls in private.

Control and discipline

8.—(1) Except as otherwise directed by the Secretary of State in accordance with section 53(2) of the Children and Young Persons Act 1933(**b**) or section 22(7) of the Act, only such disciplinary measures as are for the time being approved by the responsible authority shall be used in a children's home.

(2) Subject to paragraph (3), the following measures shall not be used in a children's home–
- (a) any form of corporal punishment;
- (b) any deprivation of food or drink;
- (c) any restriction on visits to or by any child or any restriction on or delay in communications by telephone or post with–
    - (i) his parent,

(**a**) S.I. 1991/894.
(**b**) 1933 c.12. Section 53(2) was amended by Schedule 10, Part I of the Criminal Justice Act 1948 (c.58), and by section 2(1) of the Criminal Justice Act 1961 (c.39).

5

(ii) any person who is not a parent of his but who has parental responsibility for him,

(iii) his relatives or friends,

(iv) any visitor appointed for the child in accordance with paragraph 17 of Schedule 2 to the Act,

(v) any social worker for the time being assigned to the child by the local authority who are looking after him or voluntary organisation who are caring for him,

(vi) any guardian ad litem of the child,

(vii) any solicitor for the time being acting for the child or whom the child wishes to instruct;

(d) any requirement that a child wear distinctive or inappropriate clothes;

(e) the use or withholding of medication or medical or dental treatment;

(f) the intentional deprivation of sleep;

(g) the imposition of fines (except by way of reparation);

(h) any intimate physical examination of the child.

(3) Nothing in this regulation shall prohibit–

(a) the taking of any action by, or in accordance with the instructions of, a registered medical or dental practitioner which is necessary to protect the health of a child;

(b) the taking of any action immediately necessary to prevent injury to any person or serious damage to property;

(c) the imposition of a requirement that a child wear distinctive clothing, for purposes connected with his education or with any organisation whose members customarily wear uniform in connection with its activities;

(d) the imposition by the responsible authority or the person in charge of the home having obtained a court order where necessary of any prohibition, restriction or condition upon contact between the child and any person if they or the person in charge of the home are satisfied that the prohibition, restriction or condition is necessary in order to protect or promote the welfare of the child.

(4) Full particulars of the use made of any disciplinary measures including–

(a) the date on which they were used;

(b) the reason why they were used; and

(c) the person by whom they were used;

shall be recorded by a duly authorised person on behalf of the responsible authority in permanent form in the home within 24 hours of their use and shall be signed by him.

Storage of medicinal products

9.—(1) Subject to paragraph (3), the responsible authority shall ensure that any medicinal product which is kept in a children's home shall be stored in a secure place so as to prevent any child accommodated there having access to it otherwise than under the supervision of a member of the staff of the home.

(2) Subject to paragraph (3), the person in charge of a children's home shall ensure that no medicinal product shall be administered to a child otherwise than by a member of the staff of the children's home, a registered nurse or registered medical practitioner.

(3) Paragraphs (1) and (2) do not apply to a medicinal product which–

(a) is stored by the child for whom it is provided in such a way that others are prevented from using it; and

(b) may safely be self-administered by that child.

Employment and education of older children

10. Where any child in a children's home has attained the age where he is no longer required to receive compulsory full-time education, the responsible authority shall assist with the making of, and give effect to, the arrangements made for him in respect of his education, training and employment.

Religious observance

11. The responsible authority shall ensure that each child accommodated in each children's home is enabled, so far as practicable, to attend the services of, to receive instruction in, and to observe any requirement (whether as to dress, diet or otherwise) of, the religious persuasion to which he belongs.

Food provided for children and cooking facilities

12.—(1) The responsible authority shall ensure that children accommodated in each children's home are provided with food, in adequate quantities for their needs, which is properly prepared, wholesome and nutritious.

(2) So far as is practicable the responsible authority shall ensure that at each main meal there is a choice for each course.

(3) The responsible authority shall ensure that any special dietary need of a child accommodated in the home, which is due to his health, religious persuasion, racial origin or cultural background, is met.

(4) The responsible authority shall provide within a home–
  (a) suitable and sufficient catering equipment, crockery and cutlery to provide for the needs of children accommodated in the home;
  (b) proper facilities for the refrigeration and storage of food; and
  (c) so far as is practicable, adequate facilities for children to prepare their own food if they so wish.

Purchase of clothes

13.—(1) So far as is practicable the responsible authority shall enable each child accommodated in the home to purchase clothes according to his needs.

(2) Where a child accommodated in the home does not wish to, or is not able to, purchase his own clothes, the responsible authority shall purchase clothes for him to meet his needs.

Fire precautions

14.—(1) The responsible authority shall ensure, before any child is accommodated in a children's home and at all times when children are accommodated, that the fire authority within whose area the home is or will be situated are notified in writing of the following particulars–
  (a) the location of the home;
  (b) the number of children accommodated or to be accommodated there;
  (c) the minimum and maximum age of children accommodated or to be accommodated there;
  (d) whether children suffering from any impairment of movement or intellect are accommodated or are to be accommodated there, and if so the nature of the impairment.

(2) The responsible authority shall ensure that in respect of the home–
  (a) adequate precautions are taken against the risk of fire,
  (b) adequate means of escape in the event of fire are provided,
  (c) adequate arrangements are made for detecting, containing and extinguishing fire,
  (d) adequate arrangements are made for warning of an outbreak of fire and for evacuation in the event of fire, and
  (e) adequate fire fighting equipment is provided.

(3) The responsible authority shall ensure that arrangements are made so that–
  (a) the staff, and
  (b) so far as is practicable, the children accommodated in the home,
are aware of the procedure to be followed in the event of fire at the home.

(4) The arrangements referred to in paragraph (3) shall include practices of the

evacuation procedure for the home and the techniques of resuscitation and the saving of life.

(5) The responsible authority shall make arrangements to ensure that any outbreak of fire requiring an evacuation of children accommodated in the home from it or any part of it is notified to them immediately.

PART III — Administration of Children's Homes

Confidential records with respect to children in children's homes

15.—(1) The responsible authority shall arrange that there shall be kept in each children's home a record in permanent form with respect to each child who is accommodated there, which shall so far as practicable include the information specified in Schedule 2.

(2) The record mentioned in paragraph (1) shall be kept securely and treated as confidential subject only to–

(a) any provision under or by virtue of a statute under which access may be obtained or given to records and information concerning a child;

(b) any court order, in respect of access to records and information concerning a child.

(3) The records mentioned in paragraph (1) shall be retained for at least seventy-five years from the date of birth of the child to whom they relate or, if the child dies before attaining the age of 18, for a period of 15 years from the date of his death.

Access by guardians ad litem to records and register

16.—(1) Each voluntary organisation, where they are not acting as an authorised person(a), and every person carrying on a registered children's home shall provide a guardian ad litem of a child–

(a) such access as may be required to–

(i) records in so far as they relate to the child maintained in accordance with these Regulations; and

(ii) the information from such records held in whatever form (such as by means of computer).

(b) such copies of the records as he may require.

Other records with respect to children in children's homes

17.—(1) The responsible authority shall keep in each children's home the records specified in Schedule 3 and shall ensure that the details are kept up to date.

(2) The records referred to in paragraph (1) shall be retained for at least fifteen years, except for records of menus which need be kept only for one year.

Regulations and guidance

18. A copy of these Regulations and of any relevant guidance issued by the Secretary of State under Section 7 of the Local Authority Social Services Act 1970(b) shall be kept in the home and made available when required to–

(a) all staff;

(b) every child accommodated in the home;

(c) the parents or guardians of any child accommodated in the home;

(a) Section 42 of the Act as amended by paragraph 18 of Schedule 16 to the Court and Legal Services Act 1990 (c.41) provides for guardians ad litem to have right of access to local authority and authorised persons' records. "Authorised person" is defined in section 31 of the Children Act 1989.
(b) 1970 c.42. The guidance referred to in regulation 18 is published by Her Majesty's Stationery Office and is available from any of their sale outlets, or direct from them by post from HMSO Publications Centre, PO Box 276, London SW8 5DT.

(d) any person who is not a parent of a child accommodated in the home but has parental responsibility for him.

Notification of significant events

19.—(1) In respect of the events at any children's home mentioned in paragraph (2), the responsible authority shall forthwith notify–

    (a) insofar as it is reasonably practicable–

        (i) the parents of any child concerned,

        (ii) any person who is not a parent of any child concerned but who has parental responsibility for such a child, and

        (iii) any other person who has undertaken to meet any fees or expenses incurred in accommodating any child concerned at the home;

    (b) except in the case of the event mentioned in paragraph (2)(b), the District Health Authority within whose district the children's home is situated;

    (c) where the responsible authority is not a local authority–

        (i) the local authority within whose area the home is situated, and

        (ii) the registration authority;

    (d) in respect of the events mentioned in paragraph (2)(a), (b) and (c), the Secretary of State, except, in relation to paragraph (2)(a) where the child is being looked after by a local authority(**a**);

    (e) in respect of the event mentioned in paragraph (2)(c), a constable.

(2) The events referred to in paragraph (1) are–

    (a) the death of a child accommodated at the home;

    (b) any conduct on the part of a member of staff of the home which is or may be such, in the opinion of the responsible authority, that he is not, or as the case may be would not be, a suitable person to be employed in work involving children;

    (c) the suffering of serious harm by a child accommodated at the home;

    (d) any serious accident involving a child accommodated at the home;

    (e) any serious illness of a child accommodated at the home; and

    (f) the outbreak in the home of any notifiable infectious disease to which the Public Health (Control of Disease) Act 1984(**b**) applies or disease to which provisions of that Act are applied by Regulation made under that Act(**c**).

(3) Any notification given with respect to the death of a child shall give such detail as to the circumstances as is known to the responsible authority.

Absence of a child without authority

20.—(1) The responsible authority shall draw up and cause to be recorded in writing the procedure to be followed when any child accommodated in a children's home is absent without permission.

(2) The responsible authority shall ensure that the procedure mentioned in paragraph (1) is drawn to the attention of the children accommodated in the home and the staff of, and others working in, the home.

Absence of person in charge of voluntary or registered children's home

21.—(1) Subject to paragraphs (2) and (4), where the person in charge of a voluntary home or registered children's home proposes to be absent from the home for a continuous period of four weeks or more, he shall give written notice to that effect to the registration authority at least four weeks before the absence is due to begin.

(2) Subject to paragraph (4), where it is necessary for the person in charge to be absent from the home for a continuous period of four weeks or more in circumstances where it would be impracticable to give the period of notice mentioned in paragraph (1) the registration authority may accept such shorter notice as appears reasonable.

(**a**) Equivalent provision is made in these circumstances by paragraph 20(1) of Schedule 2 to the Act.
(**b**) 1984 c.22.
(**c**) The relevant regulations are the Public Health (Infectious Disease) Regulations 1988 (S.I. 1988/1546).

(3) Subject to paragraph (4), where paragraph (1) applies, the person for the time being in charge of a voluntary or registered children's home shall inform the registration authority at least seven days before the beginning of the absence of–

(a) its occurrence and anticipated duration;

(b) the reason for it;

(c) the number of children accommodated when the information is given;

(d) the arrangements which have been made for the running of the home;

(e) the name, address and qualifications of the person who will for the time being be in charge.

(4) Nothing in this regulation shall require notification to be given to the registration authority if in a case falling within paragraph (1) or (2) no child is to be accommodated during the period of the absence.

(5) If, in any case referred to in paragraph (4) of this regulation, a child is provided with accommodation in the home during the period of absence, the person for the time being in charge shall, within seven days of the child first being provided with accommodation, inform the registration authority of the matters mentioned in paragraph (3).

(6) Within seven days of the return of the person in charge, or the appointment of some other person in his place, the responsible authority shall notify the registration authority of that fact.

(7) If, in the case of a registered children's home the person in charge is also the responsible authority, anything required to be done by or to the responsible authority shall be done by or to (as the case may require) the person for the time being in charge of the home.

Accountability and visiting on behalf of responsible authority

22.—(1) If the person carrying on a voluntary home or registered children's home, is an individual but is not also the person in charge of the home, he shall visit the home once a month, or cause some other person to do so on his behalf and to report to him in writing on the conduct of the home.

(2) Where the person carrying on a voluntary home or registered children's home is a body of persons (whether incorporated or not), the directors, or other persons responsible for the conduct of the body, shall cause one of their number to visit the home once a month and to report to them in writing on the conduct of the home.

(3) The managers of a controlled or assisted community home shall cause one of their number to visit the home once a month and to report to them in writing on the conduct of the home.

(4) The local authority who maintain a maintained community home shall cause the home to be visited once a month and to report to them in writing upon the conduct of the home.

PART IV — Community Homes

Secretary of State's directions

23. The Secretary of State may give and revoke directions requiring–

(a) the local authority by whom a community home is provided or who are specified in the instrument of management for a controlled community home, or

(b) the voluntary organisation by which an assisted community home is provided

to accommodate in the home a child looked after by a local authority for whom no places are made available in that home or to take such action in relation to a child accommodated in the home as may be specified in the directions.

PART V — Registration of Voluntary Homes

Application for registration of voluntary home

24. An application for registration under paragraph 1 of Schedule 5 to the Act (registration of voluntary homes) shall be–

    (a) made in writing to the Secretary of State; and

    (b) accompanied by the particulars specified in, or referred to in, Schedule 4.

PART VI — Registered Children's Homes

Application for registration of children's home

25.—(1) An application under paragraph 1 of Schedule 6 to the Act (registration of a children's home) shall be made in writing.

(2) Where the applicant is a natural person his application shall be accompanied by the particulars specified in Part I of Schedule 5.

(3) Where the applicant is a body corporate or unincorporate the application shall be accompanied by the particulars specified in Part II of Schedule 5.

(4) Whether the applicant is a natural person or a body corporate or unincorporate his application shall also be accompanied by the particulars specified in, or referred to in, Part III of Schedule 5.

Limits on number of children accommodated

26. The registration authority may limit the number of children to be accommodated in a registered children's home to such number as it may specify by means of a condition imposed under paragraph 2 of Schedule 6 to the Act.

Annual review of registration

27. In connection with an annual review of registration under paragraph 3 of Schedule 6 to the Act, the person carrying on the registered children's home shall notify the registration authority of any changes which there may have been since the previous review, or the original application where there has been no review, in any of the particulars furnished under regulation 25(2), (3) or (4).

Inspection of registered children's homes

28.—(1) Where an application has been made for the registration of a children's home, the registration authority shall cause it to be inspected before deciding whether or not to grant the application.

(2) Within the period of one month ending upon the anniversary of the registration of a registered children's home, the registration authority shall cause the home to be inspected.

(3) On at least one other occasion in any year the registration authority shall cause the home to be inspected.

(4) The registration authority may notify the person in charge of the home of its intention to conduct the inspection required by paragraph (2), but shall not do so with regard to any inspection pursuant to paragraph (3).

(5) The registration authority shall consider the report of any inspection of the home conducted in accordance with this regulation when determining whether or not the registration of the home shall be reviewed or cancelled.

Cancellation of registration

29. An application under paragraph 4(1) of Schedule 6 to the Act (cancellation of registration) shall be made in writing and shall include–

    (a) particulars of the date on which the person carrying on the home wishes the cancellation of the registration of the home to take effect, being a date no earlier than one month after the date on which the application is made;

    (b) particulars of the action which he intends should be taken with regard to alternative accommodation for any child then accommodated in the home.

Change of person in charge

30. The responsible authority shall give at least one month's prior notice in writing to the registration authority of any proposal to change the person in charge of a registered children's home, giving the particulars mentioned in Schedule 6.

PART VII — Notification of Particulars with respect to Voluntary Homes

Particulars on establishment of a voluntary home

31.—(1) The particulars set out in Schedule 7 are hereby prescribed as the particulars with respect to a voluntary home for the purpose of–

    (a) paragraph 6(1) of Schedule 5 to the Act (particulars to be sent to the Secretary of State within 3 months from the establishment after the commencement of the Act of a home); and

    (b) paragraph 6(2) of Schedule 5 to the Act (particulars to be sent to the Secretary of State annually).

(2) The date prescribed for the purposes of paragraph 6(3) of Schedule 5 to the Act (by which particulars must be sent annually) is 3rd April.

PART VIII — Local Authority Visits

Circumstances necessitating visits by Local Authorities

32. Every local authority shall arrange for one of their officers to visit every child who is accommodated within their area in a registered children's home or in a voluntary home in any of the following circumstances and within the periods specified–

    (a) where they are informed that a child not in the care of, nor looked after by, any local authority has been placed in such accommodation, within 28 days of being so informed;

    (b) where the voluntary organisation or the person carrying on a registered children's home providing such accommodation makes representations to the local authority that there are circumstances relating to the child which require a visit, within 14 days of receipt of those representations;

    (c) when they are informed that the welfare of a child may not be being safeguarded or promoted, within 7 days of being so informed.

Further visits

33.—(1) After a visit ("the first visit") has been made under regulation 32, the local authority shall arrange for such further visits to the child by one of their officers as appear to them to be necessary, (whether in the light of a change of circumstances or not), and shall in any event arrange for the further visits provided for by paragraphs (2) to (3).

(2) Where the local authority are satisfied following the first visit that the child's welfare is being safeguarded and promoted they shall arrange for a further visit by one of their officers where the first visit was made in the circumstances specified in regulation 32(a), within 6 months of the first visit.

(3) Where the local authority are not satisfied following the first visit that the child's welfare is being safeguarded and promoted but have decided that the child should continue to reside in the same accommodation, they shall arrange for a further visit by one of their officers within 28 days of the first visit.

Requirements for visits

34.—(1) Every local authority shall ensure that in the course of visits to which regulations 32 and 33 refer an officer of the authority–

(a) sees the child alone (unless exceptionally he considers it unnecessary);

(b) reads all relevant case papers and records concerning the child kept by the voluntary organisation or the person carrying on the registered children's home, and signs and dates them to indicate that he has seen them;

(c) makes a written report of his visit which shall be copied to the voluntary organisation or person carrying on the registered children's home.

(2) The voluntary organisation or the person carrying on the home shall provide suitable accommodation for a visit made under regulation 32 or regulation 33.

PART IX — Revocations

Revocation of Regulations

35. The following Regulations are revoked–

(a) the Administration of Children's Homes Regulations 1951(**a**);

(b) the Community Homes Regulations 1972(**b**);

(c) the Children's Homes (Control and Discipline) Regulations 1990(**c**).

Signed by authority of the Secretary of State for Health.

Virginia Bottomley
Minister of State,
30th June 1991   Department of Health

SCHEDULE 1   Regulation 4

STATEMENT TO BE KEPT RELATING TO CHILDREN'S HOMES

PART I
PARTICULARS TO BE INCLUDED IN STATEMENT

1. The purpose for which the children's home is established, and the objectives to be attained with regard to children accommodated in the home.

2. The name and address of the responsible body, and of the person in charge of the children's home if different.

3. The following details about the children for whom it is intended that accommodation should be provided–

(a) their age-range;

(b) their sex;

(**a**) S.I. 1951/1217.
(**b**) S.I. 1972/319.
(**c**) S.I. 1990/87.

(c) the number of children;

(d) whether children are selected by reference to other criteria than age or sex, and if so those criteria.

4.   The organisational structure of the children's home.

5.   The experience of the person in charge of the children's home, the staff and others working there, and details of qualifications held by any of those persons relevant to their work in the home, or to the care of children.

6.   The facilities and services to be provided within the children's home for the children accommodated there.

7.   The arrangements made to protect and promote the health of the children accommodated there.

8.   The fire precautions and associated emergency procedures.

9.   The arrangements made for religious observance by any child accommodated there.

10.   The arrangements made for contact between a child accommodated there and his parents, any person who is not a parent of his but who has parental responsibility for him, relatives and friends.

11.   The methods of control and discipline and the disciplinary measures used there, the circumstances in which any such measures will be used and who will be permitted to authorise them.

12.   The procedure for dealing with any unauthorised absence of a child from the home.

13.   The arrangements for dealing with any representation (including any complaint).

14.   The arrangements for the education of any child accommodated there.

15.   The arrangements for dealing with reviews under section 26 of the cases of every child accommodated there.

PART II
PERSONS TO WHOM STATEMENT IS TO BE MADE AVAILABLE FOR INSPECTION

1.   The person in charge of the children's home.

2.   The staff of the children's home and any other person working there.

3.   The children accommodated in the children's home.

4.   The parent of any child accommodated in the children's home.

5.   Any person who is not a parent of a child accommodated in the children's home, but who has parental responsibility for such a child.

6.   Any local authority looking after or having the care of a child accommodated in the children's home where they are not responsible for the management of the home.

7.   Any voluntary organisation providing accommodation for a child accommodated in the children's home where they are not responsible for the management of the home.

8.   Any local education authority which has placed a child in the children's home or is considering doing so.

SCHEDULE 2 Regulation 15(1)

INFORMATION TO BE INCLUDED IN CONFIDENTIAL RECORDS CONCERNING CHILDREN IN CHILDREN'S HOMES

1. The child's name and any name by which the child has previously been known other than a name used by the child prior to adoption.

2. The child's sex and date of birth.

3. The child's religious persuasion, if any.

4. A description of the child's racial origin, cultural and linguistic background.

5. Where the child came from before he was accommodated in the home.

6. The person by whose authority the child is provided with care and accommodation in the home, and the statutory provision under which he is so provided.

7. The name, address and telephone number and the religious persuasion, if any, of–
(a) the child's parents;
(b) any person who is not a parent of the child but who has parental responsibility for him.

8. The name, address and telephone number of any social worker for the time being assigned to the child by the local authority looking after him, or by the voluntary organisation or the person carrying on the registered children's home who are providing him with accommodation.

9. The date and circumstances of any absence of the child from the home including whether the absence was authorised and where the child went during the period of absence.

10. The date and circumstances of any visit to the child whilst in the home by any of the persons referred to in regulation 8(2)(c).

11. A copy of any statement of special educational needs under section 7 of the Education Act 1981 **(a)** maintained in relation to the child, with details of any such needs.

12. The name and address of any school or college attended by the child, and of any employer of the child.

13. Every school report received by the child while accommodated in the home.

14. The date and circumstances of any disciplinary measures imposed on the child.

15. Any special dietary or health needs of the child.

16. Arrangements for, including any restrictions on, contact between the child and–
(a) his parents;
(b) any person who is not a parent of his but who has parental responsibility for him;
(c) any other person.

17. The date and result of any review of the child's case.

18. The name and address of the medical practitioner with whom the child is registered.

19. Details of any accident involving the child.

20. Details of any immunisation, illness, allergy, or medical examination of the child and of any medical or dental need of the child.

21. Details of any health examination or developmental test conducted with respect to the child at or in connection with his school.

(a) 1981 c.60, as amended by Schedule 12 of the Education Reform Act 1988 (c.40).

22. Details of all medicinal products taken by the child while in the home and by whom they were administered, including those which the child was permitted to administer to himself.

23. The date on which any money or valuables are deposited by or on behalf of a child for safe-keeping, and the date on which such money is withdrawn, and the date on which any valuables are returned.

24. Where the child goes to when he ceases to be accommodated in the home.

SCHEDULE 3   Regulation 17

OTHER RECORDS WITH RESPECT TO CHILDREN IN CHILDREN'S HOMES

1. A record showing–
   (a) a date on which each child was first accommodated in the children's home;
   (b) the date on which any child ceased to be accommodated in the children's home;
   (c) where each child came from before he was accommodated in the children's home;
   (d) where each child who had ceased to be accommodated went when he left the children's home;
   (e) the identity of the person, authority or organisation responsible for the child being placed in the children's home;
   (f) which, if any, child accommodated in the children's home was being looked after, or in the care of, any authority or organisation and under what legal authority.

2. A record showing–
   (a) the full names;
   (b) the sex;
   (c) the date of birth;
   (d) the qualifications relevant to, and experience of work involving children,
of every person who–
         (i) is employed at the children's home,
         (ii) works at the home, or
         (iii) is intended by the responsible authority to work at the home,
showing whether they work at the home full-time or part-time, (whether paid or not) and if part-time the average number of hours worked per week, and whether or not they reside at the home or are intended to do so.

3. A record of all those persons resident at the children's home, other than the persons mentioned in paragraph 2 of this Schedule and children accommodated in the home.

4. A record of accidents occuring in the home.

5. A record of any medicinal product administered to any child in the home, including the date and circumstances of its administration and by whom it was administered, including medicinal products which the child is permitted to administer to himself.

6. A record of every fire drill or fire alarm test conducted, with details of any deficiency in either the procedure or the equipment concerned, together with details of the steps taken to remedy that deficiency.

7. A record of all money deposited by a child for safekeeping, together with the date on which that money was withdrawn, or the date of its return.

8. A record of all valuables deposited by a child and the date of their return.

9. Records of all accounts kept in the children's home.

10. A record of menus.

11. A record of every disciplinary measure imposed, giving the information required by regulation 8.

12. Records of duty rosters.

13. A daily log of events occurring in the home, including the names of visitors to any child accommodated in the home.

SCHEDULE 4 Regulation 24

PARTICULARS TO ACCOMPANY APPLICATION FOR REGISTRATION OF VOLUNTARY HOMES

1. The name of the voluntary organisation making the application.

2. The address and telephone number of the registered office or principal office of the voluntary organisation.

3. The names and addresses of the chairman and secretary of, or any other person responsible for the management of, the organisation, their dates of birth and, if the Secretary of State has requested, their qualifications and experience (if any) of running a home.

4. The name, address and telephone number of premises in respect of which registration is sought.

5. The name and address of any other home within the scope of Parts VI, VII or VIII of the Act, or Parts I or II of the Registered Homes Act 1984 (**a**) in respect of which the voluntary organisation has or at any time had a financial interest, and details of that interest.

6. A description of the premises and the area in which the premises are situated and details of any comments made by the health officer or environmental health officer for the area.

7. Particulars of the accommodation provided for residents in the home and for the employees and volunteers at the home.

8. The date on which the home was established or is to be established.

9. Particulars of any other business which is or will be carried on in or from the same premises as the home.

10. The name, sex, date of birth of the person in charge or intended to be in charge of the home and whether or not he resides or is to reside in the home, together with–
    (a) the name and address of each person by whom he is or has been employed in the past ten years;
    (b) the names and addresses of two persons, in addition to those referred to in sub paragraph (a) who are willing and able to give a reference as to his suitability to be in charge of a home;
    (c) particulars of his health and an undertaking to provide a report by a registered medical practitioner where the Secretary of State considers it necessary.

11. The number and sex of every person working or whom it is proposed should work in the home (as an employee or otherwise) with particulars of–
    (a) whether they are or will be resident;
    (b) whether they are full-time or part-time, and, if part-time the number of hours for which they are or will be employed;
    (c) the positions they hold or will hold;
    (d) any relevant qualifications.

12. Particulars of the equipment, facilities and services provided or to be provided in the home, and any special arrangements or services for any particular category of children.

(**a**) 1984 c.23.

13. The arrangements for the storage and administration of medicinal products.

14. The arrangements for medical and dental examinations and treatment.

15. The scale of charges payable in respect of residents.

16. The arrangements for the education of the children and what contact there is with the local education authority.

17. Particulars of any children in residence, including their name, sex, date of birth, and details of who was responsible for their placement in the home.

18. Particulars of any prospectus or advertisement relating to the home.

19. The particulars set out in Part I of Schedule 1.

SCHEDULE 5 — Regulation 25(2), (3) and (4)

PARTICULARS TO ACCOMPANY APPLICATIONS FOR REGISTRATION AS REGISTERED CHILDREN'S HOME

PART I
PARTICULARS WHERE APPLICANT IS A NATURAL PERSON

1. The name, date of birth, address and telephone number of the applicant.

2. The qualifications and experience (if any) held by the applicant which are relevant to his suitability to carry on the home.

3. The names and addresses of any person by whom the applicant is, or has at any time in the preceding ten years been, employed.

4. The names and addresses of two persons, in addition to those referred to in paragraph 3, who are willing and able to give a reference as to the suitability of the applicant to carry on a children's home.

5. A report (where the registration authority consider it necessary) by a registered medical practitioner as to the physical and mental health of the applicant.

PART II
PARTICULARS WHERE APPLICANT IS A CORPORATE OR UNINCORPORATE BODY

6. The address of the registered office or principal place of business of the applicant.

7. The names, dates of birth and addresses of the chairman and secretary of the applicant.

8. The qualifications and experience (if any) held by the person whom the applicant intends to be in charge of the home which are relevant to his suitability to be in charge of the home.

9. The names and addresses of two persons who are willing and able to give a reference as to the suitability of the person mentioned in paragraph 8.

PART III
PARTICULARS REQUIRED IN ALL CASES

10. The name, address and telephone number of the premises in respect of which registration is sought.

11. A description of the premises and the area in which they are situated, and particulars of any comments made by the local fire or environmental health authorities.

12. The name and address of any other home within the scope of Parts VI, VII or VIII of the Act, or Parts I or II of the Registered Homes Act 1984(a) in respect of which the applicant has or at any time had a financial interest, or in the case of a natural person at which he was employed, and details of the interest or employment.

13. The date on which the home was established or is to be established.

14. Particulars of any children in residence, including their name, sex, date of birth, and the local authority in whose care they are.

15. The name, sex, date of birth and other particulars, including date of employment or proposed employment, of any person employed or proposed to be employed in the children's home as a manager, together with details of–
(a) his qualifications, insofar as they are relevant to his employment;
(b) his previous experience in work involving or related to the care of children; and
(c) whether he is intended to live on the premises;
and in this paragraph "manager" means any person to whom the day to day responsibility for the business of the home or any part of it is or is to be entrusted.

16. The name, sex, date of birth, and the responsibilities of every person working in the home (whether as an employee or otherwise) or whom it is proposed should work in the home, other than a person to whom paragraph 15 applies or a person working at the home only as a teacher.

17. The hours for which it is proposed any person mentioned in paragraphs 15 or 16 should work.

18. Details of which of the persons mentioned in paragraph 15 or 16 will be resident in the home.

19. The scale of charges payable for residents in the home.

20. Particulars of the equipment, facilities and services to be provided in the home, if any, and particular needs of children which are intended to be met by means of the equipment, facilities or services.

21. Particulars of the arrangements made or proposed for the education of resident children, and, if education is to be provided on the premises, information on the home's status as a school under the Education Act 1944(b).

22. Particulars of the accommodation provided for resident children and for others resident at the home.

23. The arrangements for medical and dental examinations and treatment.

24. The particulars set out in Part I of Schedule 1.

25. Particulars of any prospectus or advertisements relating to the home.

26. Particulars of any other business which is, or is proposed to be, carried on on or from the premises of the home.

27. Where the person carrying on, or intending to carry on, the home is not also the person in charge the particulars required by paragraphs 1 to 5 of Part I of this Schedule for the person in charge.

(a) 1984 c.23.
(b) 1944 c.31.

PARTICULARS OF CHANGE OF IDENTITY OF PROPOSED PERSON IN CHARGE OF REGISTERED CHILDREN'S HOME

1.   The name, date of birth, address and telephone number of the proposed person in charge.

2.   The qualifications and experience (if any) held by the proposed person which are relevant to his suitability to carry on the registered children's home.

3.   The names and addresses of any person by whom the proposed person in charge is, or has at any time in the preceding ten years been, employed.

4.   The names and addresses of two persons, in addition to those referred to in paragraph 3, who are willing and able to give a reference as to the suitability of the proposed person in charge to be in charge of a children's home.

5.   A report (where the registration authority considers it necessary) by a registered medical practitioner as to the physical and mental health of the proposed person in charge.

PARTICULARS RELATING TO VOLUNTARY HOMES

1.   The name, address and telephone number of the home.

2.   The name and date of birth of the person in charge of the home.

3.   The name, address and telephone number of the organisation or person carrying on the home.

4.   The name and address of the chairman and secretary.

5.   The maximum number of children who can be accommodated at one time in the home.

6.   The criteria if any for admission to the home.

7.   The religious persuasion or persuasions, if any, in which the home undertakes to bring up the children.

8.   The weekly charge made in respect of each child accommodated in the home.

9.   The name of any Government Department, other than the Department of Health, inspecting the home, and the date of the last inspection by each such Government Department.

10.   The details and number of staff employed by the voluntary organisation by reference to care staff, ancillary staff, full-time and part-time, and including volunteers who work in the home.

11.   The number of children accommodated in the home at the time the particulars were sent, giving–
      (a) the total number;
      (b) the number in the care of a local authority;
      (c) the number receiving full-time education or vocational training at the home;
      (d) the number receiving full-time education or vocational training outside the home;
      (e) the number who are in full-time employment within the home;
      (f) the number who are in full-time employment outside the home;
and giving the number by reference to sex and age bands of one to four, five to nine, ten to fifteen, and 16 years of age and over.

These Regulations supersede with modifications the existing regulations relating to children's homes, whether community homes, registered children's homes or voluntary homes.

The main changes effected by these Regulations are as follows–

    (a) Private children's homes are required to be registered with and regularly inspected by the local authority for the area in which they are situated. There was no previous such requirement as the Children's Homes Act 1982 (c.20) which dealt with this was never brought into force;

    (b) All types of children's home are subject to the same or similar provisions. Previously, quite different rules applied to voluntary homes and community homes, and none at all to private homes;

    (c) All homes will now have to provide a statement setting out their objectives;

    (d) Requirements about control and discipline have been strengthened. Corporal punishment is prohibited.

The Regulations provide for the conduct of children's homes.

They provide for each children's home to keep a statement of the particulars specified in Schedule 1, which shall be made available for inspection by those specified in Part II of that Schedule (regulation 4); in detail how children's homes should be conducted (regulations 5 to 14); provide for records to be kept about each child and about the running of the children's home and for guardians ad litem to have access to the records (regulations 15, 16 and 17 and Schedules 2 and 3).

They provide for regulations and guidance on them to be available in the home (regulation 18); certain events to be notified to specified persons (regulation 19); a procedure to be established when a child is absent from the home without authority (regulation 20); the procedure to be followed if the person in charge of a voluntary home or registered children's home proposes to be absent (regulation 21); and visits to homes on behalf of the repsonsible authority (regulation 22).

They provide for the Secretary of State to give and revoke directions in relation to a particular child accommodated or to be accommodated in a community home (regulation 23); particulars to be supplied with applications for registration of voluntary homes (regulation 24 and Schedule 4); the particulars to be supplied with applications for registration of registered children's homes and the number of children limited by the registration authority (regulations 25 and 26 and Schedule 5); the annual review of such registration and the inspection of registered children's homes before granting registration, and twice yearly thereafter (regulations 27 and 28); cancellation of registration of registered children's homes (regulation 29); the details to be supplied and notice to be given by the responsible authority to the registration authority if it is proposed to change the person in charge (regulation 30 and Schedule 6).

They provide for the particulars to be supplied on the establishment of a voluntary home (regulation 31 and Schedule 7); and for visits to be made by the local authority to all children's homes at prescribed intervals (regulations 32 to 34).

Regulation 35 revokes three sets of regulations which are superseded by these Regulations.

STATUTORY INSTRUMENTS

1991 No. 890

CHILDREN AND YOUNG PERSONS

Arrangements for Placement of Children (General) Regulations 1991

Made - - - -	*2nd April 1991*
Laid before Parliament	*10th April 1991*
Coming into force	*14th October 1991*

ARRANGEMENT OF REGULATIONS

SCHEDULES

The Secretary of State for Health, in exercise of the powers conferred by sections 23(2)(a) and (f)(ii) and (5), 59(2) and (3) and 104(4) of, and paragraphs 12, 13 and 14 of Schedule 2, 4(1) and (2)(d) of Schedule 4, 7(1) and (2)(g) of Schedule 5 and paragraph 10(1) and (2)(f) of Schedule 6 to the Children Act 1989(**a**) and of all other powers enabling him in that behalf hereby makes the following Regulations:–

Citation, commencement and interpretation

1.—(1) These Regulations may be cited as the Arrangements for Placement of Children (General) Regulations 1991 and shall come into force on 14th October 1991.

(2) In these Regulations, unless the context otherwise requires–

"the Act" means the Children Act 1989;

"area authority" means, in relation to a child who is or is to be placed, the local authority(**b**) in whose area the child is or is to be placed, where the child is looked after by a different authority;

"care case" means a case in which the child is in the care of a local authority(**c**) ;

"placement" subject to regulation 13 means–

    (a) the provision of accommodation and maintenance by a local authority for any child whom they are looking after by any of the means specified in section 23(2)(a), (b), (c), (d) or (f) of the Act (accommodation and maintenance of child looked after by a local authority);

    (b) the provision of accommodation for a child by a voluntary organisation by any of the means specified in section 59(1)(a), (b), (c), (d) or (f) of the Act (provision of accommodation by voluntary organisations), and

    (c) the provision of accommodation for a child in a registered children's home,

and the expressions "place" and "placed" shall be construed accordingly;

"responsible authority" means–

    (a) in relation to a placement by a local authority (including one in which the child is accommodated and maintained in a voluntary home or a registered children's home), the local authority which place the child,

    (b) in relation to a placement by a voluntary organisation of a child who is not looked after by a local authority, the voluntary organisation which place the child, and

    (c) in relation to a placement in a registered children's home of a child who is neither looked after by a local authority nor accommodated in such a home by a voluntary organisation, the person carrying on the home.

(3) Any notice required under these Regulations is to be given in writing and may be sent by post.

(4) In these Regulations, unless the context otherwise requires–

    (a) any reference to a numbered regulation is to the regulation in these Regulations bearing that number and any reference in a regulation to a numbered paragraph is to the paragraph of that regulation bearing that number;

    (b) any reference to a numbered Schedule is to the Schedule to these Regulations bearing that number.

Application of Regulations

2. These Regulations apply to placements–

    (a) by a local authority of any child;

    (b) by a voluntary organisation of a child who is not looked after by a local authority;

(**a**) 1989 c.41. Paragraph 14 of Schedule 2 was amended by paragraph 26 of Schedule 16 to the Courts and Legal Services Act 1990 (c.41).

(**b**) "local authority" is defined in section 105(1) of the Act as the council of a county, a metropolitan district, a London Borough or the Common Council of the City of London. Pursuant to section 2 of the Local Authority Social Services Act 1970 (c.42), local authority functions under the Children Act 1989 stand referred to the social services committee of a local authority.

(**c**) *See* the definition of "care order" in section 105(1) of the Children Act 1989 and paragraphs 15 and 16 of Schedule 14 to that Act.

(c) in a registered children's home of a child who is neither looked after by a local authority nor accommodated in such a home by a voluntary organisation, by a person carrying on the home.

Making of arrangements

3.—(1) Before they place a child the responsible authority shall, so far as is reasonably practicable, make immediate and long-term arrangements for that placement, and for promoting the welfare of the child who is to be placed.

(2) Where it is not practicable to make those arrangements before the placement, the responsible authority shall make them as soon as reasonably practicable thereafter.

(3) In the case of a child to whom section 20(11) of the Act applies (child aged 16 or over agreeing to be provided with accommodation) the arrangements shall so far as reasonably practicable be agreed by the responsible authority with the child before a placement is made and if that is not practicable as soon as reasonably practicable thereafter.

(4) In any other case in which a child is looked after or accommodated but is not in care the arrangements shall so far as reasonably practicable be agreed by the responsible authority with–

(a) a person with parental responsibility for the child, or

(b) if there is no such person the person who is caring for the child

before a placement is made and if that is not practicable as soon as reasonably practicable thereafter.

(5) Any arrangements made by the responsible authority under this regulation shall be recorded in writing.

Considerations on making and contents of arrangements

4.—(1) The considerations to which the responsible authority are to have regard so far as reasonably practicable in making the arrangements referred to in regulation 3 in each case are the general considerations specified in Schedule 1, the considerations concerning the health of a child specified in Schedule 2 and the considerations concerning the education of a child specified in Schedule 3.

(2) Except in a care case, the arrangements referred to in regulation 3 shall include, where practicable, arrangements concerning the matters specified in Schedule 4.

Notification of arrangements

5.—(1) The responsible authority shall, so far as is reasonably practicable, notify the following persons in writing of the arrangements to place a child, before the placement is made–

(a) any person an indication of whose wishes and feelings have been sought under section 22(4), section 61(2) or section 64(2) of the Act (consultation prior to decision making in respect of children looked after by a local authority, provided with accommodation by a voluntary organisation or in a registered children's home);

(b) the district health authority for the district in which the child is living;

(c) the local education authority for the area in which the child is living;

(d) the child's registered medical practitioner;

(e) the local authority for the area in which the child is living where the child is not placed by such an authority;

(f) the area authority;

(g) any person, not being an officer of a local authority, who is caring for the child immediately before the arrangements are made;

(h) except in a care case, any person in whose favour a contact order is in force with respect to the child, and

(i) in a care case, any person who has contact with the child pursuant to section 34 of the Act (contact with a child in care by parents etc) or to an order under that section.

(2) Where it is not practicable to give the notification before the placement, it shall be given as soon as reasonably practicable thereafter.

(3) The responsible authority shall send a copy of the arrangements referred to in regulation 3 or such part of the arrangements as they consider will not prejudice the welfare of the child with the notification referred to in paragraph (1) but in the case of notification to those specified in paragraph (1)(b) to (i) they shall send details of only such part of the arrangements as they consider those persons need to know.

Arrangements for contact

6. In operating the arrangements referred to in paragraph 6 of Schedule 4, a voluntary organisation or a person carrying on a registered children's home shall, unless it is not reasonably practicable or consistent with the child's welfare, endeavour to promote contact between the child and the persons mentioned in that paragraph.

Health requirements

7.—(1) A responsible authority shall, so far as reasonably practicable before a placement is made and if that is not reasonably practicable as soon as practicable after the placement is made–

(a) ensure that arrangements are made for the child to be examined by a registered medical practitioner and

(b) require the practitioner who has carried out the examination to make a written assessment of the state of health of the child and his need for health care

unless the child has been so examined and such assessment has been made within a period of three months immediately preceding the placement or the child is of sufficient understanding and he refuses to submit to the examination.

(2) During the placement of the child the responsible authority shall ensure that arrangements are made for a child to be provided with health care services, including medical and dental care and treatment.

Establishment of records

8.—(1) A responsible authority shall establish, if one is not already in existence, a written case record in respect of each child whom it places.

(2) The record shall include–

(a) a copy of the arrangements referred to in regulation 3;

(b) a copy of any written report in its possession concerning the welfare of the child;

(c) a copy of any document considered or record established in the course of or as a result of a review of the child's case;

(d) details of arrangements for contact, of contact orders and of other court orders relating to the child; and

(e) details of any arrangements whereby another person acts on behalf of the local authority or organisation which placed the child.

Retention and confidentiality of records

9.—(1) A case record relating to a child who is placed shall be retained by the responsible authority until the seventy-fifth anniversary of the date of birth of the child to whom it relates or, if the child dies before attaining the age of 18, for a period of 15 years beginning with the date of his death.

(2) The requirements of paragraph (1) may be complied with either by retaining the original written record, or a copy of it, or by keeping all of the information from such record in some other accessible form (such as by means of a computer).

(3) A responsible authority shall secure the safe keeping of case records and shall take all necessary steps to ensure that information contained in them is treated as confidential, subject only to–

(a) any provision of or made under or by virtue of, a statute under which access to such records or information may be obtained or given;

(b) any court order under which access to such records or information may be obtained or given.

Register

10.—(1) A local authority, shall, in respect of every child placed in their area (by them and any other responsible authority) and every child placed by them outside their area enter into a register to be kept for the purpose–

    (a) the particulars specified in paragraph (3), and

    (b) such of the particulars specified in paragraph (4) as may be appropriate.

(2) A voluntary organisation and a person carrying on a registered children's home shall, in respect of every child placed by them, enter into a register to be kept for the purpose–

    (a) the particulars specified in paragraph (3), and

    (b) such of the particulars specified in paragraph (4) as may be appropriate.

(3) The particulars to be entered into the register in accordance with paragraphs (1) or (2) are–

    (a) the name, sex and date of birth of the child;

    (b) the name and address of the person with whom the child is placed and, if different, of those of the child's parent or other person not being a parent of his who has parental responsibility for him;

    (c) in the case of a child placed on behalf of a local authority by a voluntary organisation or in a registered children's home, the name of the authority;

    (d) whether the child's name is entered on any local authority register indicating that the child is at risk of being abused;

    (e) whether the child's name is entered on the register maintained under paragraph 2 of Schedule 2 to the Act (register of disabled children);

    (f) the date on which each placement of the child began and terminated and the reason for each termination;

    (g) in a care case the name of the local authority in whose care the child is;

    (h) the legal provisions under which the child is being looked after or cared for.

(4) The additional particulars to be entered in the register, where appropriate in accordance with paragraphs (1) or (2) are–

    (a) in the case of a child placed by a local authority in respect of whom arrangements have been made for the area authority to carry out functions pursuant to regulation 12 a note that the arrangements were made and the name of the other local authority with whom they were made; and

    (b) in the case of a child who has been placed, in respect of whom arrangements have been made for supervision of the placement to be carried out on behalf of a responsible authority (otherwise than pursuant to Regulation 12), a note that the arrangements were made and the name of person with whom the arrangements were made.

(5) Entries in registers kept in accordance with this regulation shall be retained until the child to whom the entry relates attains the age of 23 or, if the child has died before attaining 23, the period of 5 years beginning with the date of his death.

(6) The requirements of paragraph (1) may be complied with either by retaining the original register, or a copy of it, or by keeping all of the information from such a register in some other accessible form (such as by means of a computer).

(7) A responsible authority shall secure the safe keeping of registers kept in accordance with this regulation and shall take all necessary steps to ensure that information contained in them is treated as confidential, subject only to–

    (a) any provision of or made under or by virtue of a statute under which access to such registers or information may be obtained or given;

    (b) any court order under which access to such registers or information may be obtained or given.

Access by guardians ad litem to records and register

11. Each voluntary organisation, where they are not acting as an authorised person(**a**), and every person carrying on a registered children's home shall provide a guardian ad litem of a child–

(a) such access as may be required to–

(i) case records and registers maintained in accordance with these Regulations; and

(ii) the information from such records or registers held in whatever form (such as by means of computer);

(b) such copies of the records or entries in the registers as he may require.

Arrangements between local authorities and area authorities

12. Where arrangements are made by a local authority which is looking after a child with an area authority for the area authority to carry out functions in relation to a placement on behalf of the local authority–

(a) the local authority shall supply the area authority with all such information as is necessary to enable the area authority to carry out those functions on behalf of the local authority;

(b) the area authority shall keep the local authority informed of the progress of the child and, in particular, shall furnish reports to the local authority following each visit to the home in which the child is placed and following each review of the case of the child carried out by the area authority on behalf of the local authority;

(c) the local authority and the area authority shall consult each other from time to time as necessary, and as soon as reasonably practicable after each such review of the case of the child, with regard to what action is required in relation to him.

Application of Regulations to short-term placements

13.—(1) This regulation applies to a series of short-term placements at the same place where the following conditions are satisfied–

(a) all the placements occur within a period which does not exceed one year;

(b) no single placement is for a duration of more than four weeks; and

(c) the total duration of the placements does not exceed 90 days.

(2) Any series of short-term placements to which this regulation applies may be treated as a single placement for the purposes of these Regulations.

Signed by authority of the Secretary of State for Health.

Virginia Bottomley
Minister of State,
Department of Health

2nd April 1991

SCHEDULE 1   Regulation 4(1)

CONSIDERATIONS TO WHICH RESPONSIBLE AUTHORITIES ARE TO HAVE REGARD

1. In the case of a child who is in care, whether an application should be made to discharge the care order.

(**a**) For access by guardians ad litem to local authority and authorised person's records *see* section 42 of the 1989 Act as amended by paragraph 18 of Schedule 16 to the Courts and Legal Services Act 1990 (c.41). "Authorised person" is defined in section 31, of the 1989 Act.

2. Where the responsible authority is a local authority whether the authority should seek a change in the child's legal status.

3. Arrangements for contact, and whether there is any need for changes in the arrangements in order to promote contact with the child's family and others so far as is consistent with his welfare.

4. The responsible authority's immediate and long term arrangements for the child, previous arrangements in respect of the child, and whether a change in those arrangements is needed and consideration of alternative courses of action.

5. Where the responsible authority is a local authority, whether an independent visitor should be appointed if one has not already been appointed.

6. Whether arrangements need to be made for the time when the child will no longer be looked after by the responsible authority.

7. Whether plans need to be made to find a permanent substitute family for the child.

SCHEDULE 2   Regulation 4(1)

HEALTH CONSIDERATIONS TO WHICH RESPONSIBLE AUTHORITIES ARE TO HAVE REGARD

1. The child's state of health.

2. The child's health history.

3. The effect of the child's health and health history on his development.

4. Existing arrangements for the child's medical and dental care and treatment and health and dental surveillance.

5. The possible need for an appropriate course of action which should be identified to assist necessary change of such care, treatment or surveillance.

6. The possible need for preventive measures, such as vaccination and immunisation, and screening for vision and hearing.

SCHEDULE 3   Regulation 4(1)

EDUCATIONAL CONSIDERATIONS TO WHICH RESPONSIBLE AUTHORITIES ARE TO HAVE REGARD

1. the child's educational history.

2. The need to achieve continuity in the child's education.

3. The need to identify any educational need which the child may have and to take action to meet that need.

4. The need to carry out any assessment in respect of any special educational need under the Education Act 1981(**a**) and meet any such needs identified in a statement of special educational needs made under section 7 of that Act.

(**a**) 1981 c.60.

MATTERS TO BE INCLUDED IN ARRANGEMENTS TO ACCOMMODATE CHILDREN WHO ARE NOT IN CARE

1. The type of accommodation to be provided and its address together with the name of any person who will be responsible for the child at that accommodation on behalf of the responsible authority.

2. The details of any services to be provided for the child.

3. The respective responsibilities of the responsible authority and–
   (a) the child;
   (b) any parent of his; and
   (c) any person who is not a parent of his but who has parental responsibility for him.

4. What delegation there has been by the persons referred to in paragraph 3(b) and (c) of this Schedule to the responsible authority of parental responsibility for the child's day to day care.

5. The arrangements for involving those persons and the child in decision making with respect to the child having regard–
   (a) to the local authority's duty under sections 20(6) (involvement of children before provision of accommodation) and 22(3) to (5) of the Act (general duties of the local authority in relation to children looked after by them);
   (b) the duty of the voluntary organisation under section 61(1) and (2) of the Act (duties of voluntary organisations); and
   (c) the duty of the person carrying on a registered children's home under section 64(1) and (2) of the Act (welfare of children in registered children's homes).

6. The arrangements for contact between the child and–
   (a) his parents;
   (b) any person who is not a parent of his but who has parental responsibility for him; and
   (c) any relative, friend or other person connected with him,
and if appropriate, the reasons why contact with any such person would not be reasonably practicable or would be inconsistent with the child's welfare.

7. The arrangements for notifying changes in arrangements for contact to any of the persons referred to in paragraph 6.

8. In the case of a child aged 16 or over whether section 20(11) (accommodation of a child of 16 or over despite parental opposition) applies.

9. The expected duration of arrangements and the steps which should apply to bring the arrangements to an end, including arrangements for rehabilitation of the child with the person with whom he was living before the voluntary arrangements were made or some other suitable person, having regard in particular, in the case of a local authority looking after a child, to section 23(6) of the Act (duty to place children where practicable with parents etc.) and paragraph 15 of Schedule 2 to the Act (maintenance of contact between child and family).

EXPLANATORY NOTE

(This note does not form part of the Regulations)

These Regulations make provision for the arrangements for placement of children by local authorities, voluntary organisations and persons carrying on registered children's homes. These placements are with foster parents, in community homes, voluntary children's homes or registered children's homes and under other arrangements (but not in a home provided in accordance with arrangements made by the Secretary of State under section 82(5) of the Children Act 1989).

The Regulations make provision for the application of the regulations (regulation 2); the making of arrangements for accommodation and maintenance of and promotion of the welfare of children (regulation 3); the considerations to be given on making the arrangements and except in a care case the contents of those arrangements (regulation 4); notification of the arrangements (regulation 5); the arrangements for contact in respect of children placed by voluntary organisations or in a registered children's home (regulation 6); the health requirements (regulation 7); establishment of records (regulation 8); the retention and confidentiality of records (regulation 9); registers of relevant information (regulation 10); the access by guardians ad litem to records and registers (regulation 11); arrangements made between local authorities and other authorities for carrying out responsibilities in respect of those arrangements on their behalf (regulation 12) and short-term placements (regulation 13).

STATUTORY INSTRUMENTS

1991 No. 895

CHILDREN AND YOUNG PERSONS

Review of Children's Cases Regulations 1991

Made - - - -	*2nd April 1991*
Laid before Parliament	*10th April 1991*
Coming into force -	*14th October 1991*

ARRANGEMENT OF REGULATIONS

SCHEDULES

The Secretary of State for Health, in exercise of the powers conferred by sections 26(1) and (2), 59(4)(a) and (5) and 104(4) of and paragraph 10(1) and (2)(l) of Schedule 6 to the Children Act 1989**(a)** and of all other powers enabling him in that behalf hereby makes the following Regulations:–

(a) 1989 c.41.

Citation, commencement and interpretation

1.—(1) These Regulations may be cited as the Review of Children's Cases Regulations 1991 and shall come into force on 14th October 1991.

(2) In these Regulations, unless the context otherwise requires–

"the Act" means the Children Act 1989;

"guardian ad litem" means a guardian ad litem appointed pursuant to section 41 of the Act or rules made under section 65 of the Adoption Act 1976**(a)**;

"independent visitor" means an independent visitor appointed under paragraph 17 of Schedule 2 to the Act;

"responsible authority" means in relation to–

(a) a child who is being looked after by a local authority**(b)**, that authority,

(b) a child who is being provided with accommodation by a voluntary organisation otherwise than on behalf of a local authority, that voluntary organisation,

(c) a child who is being provided with accommodation in a registered children's home otherwise than on behalf of a local authority or voluntary organisation, the person carrying on that home;

(3) Any notice required under these Regulations is to be given in writing and may be sent by post.

(4) In these Regulations, unless the context otherwise requires–

(a) any reference to a numbered regulation is to the regulation in these Regulations bearing that number and any reference in any regulation to a numbered paragraph is to the paragraph of that regulation bearing that number;

(b) any reference to a numbered Schedule is to the Schedule to these Regulations bearing that number.

Review of children's cases

2. Each responsible authority shall review in accordance with these Regulations the case of each child while he is being looked after or provided with accommodation by them.

Time when case is to be reviewed

3.—(1) Each case is first to be reviewed within four weeks of the date upon which the child begins to be looked after or provided with accommodaton by a responsible authority.

(2) The second review shall be carried out not more than three months after the first and thereafter subsequent reviews shall be carried out not more than six months after the date of the previous review.

Manner in which cases are to be reviewed

4.—(1) Each responsible authority shall set out in writing their arrangements governing the manner in which the case of each child shall be reviewed and shall draw the written arrangements to the attention of those specified in regulation 7(1).

(2) The responsible authority which are looking after or providing accommodaton for a child shall make arrangements to coordinate the carrying out of all aspects of the review of that child's case.

(3) The responsible authority shall appoint one of their officers to assist the authority in the coordination of all the aspects of the review.

(4) The manner in which each case is reviewed shall, so far as practicable, include the elements specified in Schedule 1.

(a) 1976 c.36.
(b) "local authority" is defined in section 105(1) of the Act as the council of a county, a metropolitan district, a London Borough or Common Council of the City of London. Pursuant to section 2 of the Local Authority Social Services Act 1970 (c.42), local authority functions under the Children Act 1989 stand referred to the social services committee of a local authority.

(5) Nothing in these Regulations shall prevent the carrying out of any review under these Regulations and any other review, assessment or consideration under any other provision at the same time.

Considerations to which responsible authorities are to have regard

5. The considerations to which the responsible authority are to have regard so far as is reasonably practicable in reviewing each case are the general considerations specified in Schedule 2 and the considerations concerning the health of the child specified in Schedule 3.

Health reviews

6. The responsible authority shall make arrangements for a child who continues to be looked after or provided with accommodation by them to be examined by a registered medical practitioner and for a written assessment on the state of health of the child and his need for health care to be made–

    (a) at least once in every period of six months before the child's second birthday, and

    (b) at least once in every period of twelve months after the child's second birthday,

unless the child is of sufficient understanding and he refuses to submit to the examination.

Consultation, participation and notification

7.—(1) Before conducting any review the responsible authority shall, unless it is not reasonably practicable to do so, seek and take into account the views of–

    (a) the child;

    (b) his parents;

    (c) any person who is not a parent of his but who has parental responsibility for him; and

    (d) any other person whose views the authority consider to be relevant;

including, in particular, the views of those persons in relation to any particular matter which is to be considered in the course of the review.

(2) The responsible authority shall so far as is reasonably practicable involve the persons whose views are sought under paragraph (1) in the review including, where the authority consider appropriate, the attendance of those persons at part or all of any meeting which is to consider the child's case in connection with any aspect of the review of that case.

(3) The responsible authority shall, so far as is reasonably practicable, notify details of the result of the review and of any decision taken by them in consequence of the review to–

    (a) the child;

    (b) his parents;

    (c) any person who is not a parent of his but who has parental responsibility for him; and

    (d) any other person whom they consider ought to be notified.

Arrangements for implementation of decisions arising out of reviews

8. The responsible authority shall make arrangements themselves or with other persons to implement any decision which the authority propose to make in the course, or as a result, of the review of a child's case.

Monitoring arrangements for reviews

9. Each responsible authority shall monitor the arrangements which they have made with a view to ensuring that they comply with these Regulations.

Recording review information

10. Each responsible authority shall ensure that–
    (a) information obtained in respect of the review of a child's case,
    (b) details of the proceedings at any meeting arranged by the authority at which the child's case is considered in connection with any aspect of the review of that case, and
    (c) details of any decisions made in the course of or as a result of the review
are recorded in writing.

Application of Regulations to short periods

11.—(1) This regulation applies to cases in which a child is looked after or provided with accommodation by a responsible authority for a series of short periods at the same place where the following conditions are satisfied–
    (a) all the periods are included within a period which does not exceed one year;
    (b) no single period is for a duration of more than four weeks; and
    (c) the total duration of the periods does not exceed 90 days.

(2) Cases to which this regulation applies may be treated as a single case of a child being looked after or provided with accommodation by a responsible authority for the purpose of these Regulations.

Signed by authority of the Secretary of State for Health.

Virginia Bottomley
Minister of State,
Department of Health

2nd April 1991

SCHEDULE 1
Regulation 4(4)

ELEMENTS TO BE INCLUDED IN REVIEW

1. Keeping informed of the arrangements for looking after the child and of any relevant change in the child's circumstances.

2. Keeping informed of the name and address of any person whose views should be taken into account in the course of the review.

3. Making necessary preparations and providing any relevant information to the participants in any meeting of the responsible authority which considers the child's case in connection with any aspect of the review.

4. Initiating meetings of relevant personnel of the responsible authority and other relevant persons to consider the review of the child's case.

5. Explaining to the child any steps which he may take under the Act including, where appropriate–
    (a) his right to apply, with leave, for a section 8 order (residence, contact and other orders with respect to children),
    (b) where he is in care, his right to apply for the discharge of the care order, and
    (c) the availability of the procedure established under the Act for considering representations.

6. Making decisions or taking steps following review decisions arising out of or resulting from the review.

SCHEDULE 2

CONSIDERATIONS TO WHICH RESPONSIBLE AUTHORITIES ARE TO HAVE REGARD

1. In the case of a child who is in care, whether an application should be made to discharge the care order.

2. Where the responsible authority are a local authority whether they should seek a change in the child's legal status.

3. Arrangements for contact, and whether there is any need for changes in the arrangements in order to promote contact with the child's family and others so far as is consistent with his welfare.

4. Any special arrangements that have been made or need to be made for the child, including the carrying out of assessments either by a local authority or other persons, such as those in respect of special educational need under the Education Act 1981(a).

5. The responsible authority's immediate and long term arrangements for looking after the child or providing the child with accommodation (made pursuant to the provisions of the Arrangements for Placement of Children (General) Regulations 1991(b)), whether a change in those arrangements is needed and consideration of alternative courses of action.

6. Where the responsible authority are a local authority, whether an independent visitor should be appointed if one has not already been appointed.

7. The child's educational needs, progress and development.

8. Whether arrangements need to be made for the time when the child will no longer be looked after or provided with accommodation by the responsible authority.

9. Whether plans need to be made to find a permanent substitute family for the child.

SCHEDULE 3

HEALTH CONSIDERATIONS TO WHICH RESPONSIBLE AUTHORITIES ARE TO HAVE REGARD

1. The child's state of health.

2. The child's health history.

3. The effect of the child's health and health history on his development.

4. Existing arrangements for the child's medical and dental care and treatment and health and dental surveillance.

5. The possible need for an appropriate course of action which should be identified to assist necessary change of such care, treatment or surveillance.

6. The possible need for preventive measures, such as vaccination and immunisation, and screening for vision and hearing.

(a) 1981 c.60.
(b) S.I. 1991/890.

EXPLANATORY NOTE

(This note is not part of the Regulations)

These Regulations provide for the review of the cases of children who are looked after by a local authority or provided with accommodation by a voluntary organisation or in a registered children's home.

They make provision for the review of such cases (regulation 2); the time when cases are to be reviewed (regulation 3); the manner in which cases are to be reviewed (regulation 4); the considerations to which there should be regard (regulation 5); health reviews (regulation 6); consultation, participation and notification (regulation 7); the arrangements for implementation of decisions arising out of reviews (regulation 8); monitoring the arrangements for reviews (regulation 9); recording review information (regulation 10); and application of the Regulations to short periods (regulation 11).

STATUTORY INSTRUMENTS

1991 No. 891

CHILDREN AND YOUNG PERSONS

Contact with Children Regulations 1991

Made - - - -	*2nd April 1991*
Laid before Parliament	*10th April 1991*
Coming into force	*14th October 1991*

The Secretary of State for Health, in exercise of the powers conferred by section 34(8) of the Children Act 1989(**a**), and all other powers enabling him in that behalf, hereby makes the following Regulations:

Citation, commencement and interpretation

1.—(1) These Regulations may be cited as the Contact with Children Regulations 1991, and shall come into force on 14th October 1991.

(2) Any notice required under these Regulations is to be given in writing and may be sent by post.

(3) In these Regulations unless the context requires otherwise–
  (a) any reference to a numbered section is to the section in the Children Act 1989 bearing that number;
  (b) any reference to a numbered regulation is to the regulation in these Regulations bearing that number; and
  (c) any reference to a Schedule is to the Schedule to these Regulations.

Local authority refusal of contact with child

2. Where a local authority has decided under section 34(6) to refuse contact with a child that would otherwise be required by virtue of section 34(1) or a court order, the authority shall, as soon as the decision has been made, notify the following persons in writing of those parts of the information specified in the Schedule as the authority considers those persons need to know–
  (a) the child, if he is of sufficient understanding;
  (b) the child's parents;
  (c) any guardian of his;
  (d) where there was a residence order in force with respect to the child immediately before the care order was made, the person in whose favour the order was made;
  (e) where immediately before the care order was made, a person had care of the child by virtue of an order made in the exercise of the High Court's inherent jurisdiction with respect to children, that person; and
  (f) any other person whose wishes and feelings the authority consider to be relevant.

Departure from terms of court order on contact under section 34

3. The local authority may depart from the terms of any order under section 34 (parental contact etc with children in care) by agreement between the local authority and

---

(**a**) 1989 c.41.

the person in relation to whom the order is made and in the following circumstance and subject to the following condition–
  (a) where the child is of sufficient understanding, subject to agreement also with him; and
  (b) a written notification shall be sent to the persons specified in regulation 2 containing those parts of the information specified in the Schedule as the authority considers those persons need to know, within seven days of the agreement to depart from the terms of the order.

Notification of variation or suspension of contact arrangements

4. Where a local authority varies or suspends any arrangements made (otherwise than under an order made under section 34) with a view to affording any person contact with a child in the care of that local authority, written notification shall be sent to those persons specified in regulation 2 containing those parts of the information specified in the Schedule as the authority considers those persons need to know, as soon as the decision is made to vary or suspend the arrangements.

Signed by authority of the Secretary of State for Health.

Virginia Bottomley
Minister of State,
Department of Health

2nd April 1991

SCHEDULE   Regulations 2, 3, and 4
Information to be contained in written notification

1. Local authority's decision.
2. Date of the decision.
3. Reasons for the decision.
4. Duration (if applicable).
5. Remedies available in case of dissatisfaction.

EXPLANATORY NOTE

(This note is not part of the Regulations)

These Regulations provide for the steps to be taken by a local authority who have refused to allow contact between a child in care and parents and others specified in section 34(1), which include notifying those persons and anyone else whose wishes and feelings they consider to be relevant (regulation 2).

They provide for the authority to depart from the terms of any order as to contact, by agreement between the authority and the person about whom the order was made, where the child agrees, if he is of sufficient understanding, and where a written notification of details of the decision is sent to the person specified in regulation 2 (regulation 3). They provide for the authority to notify those persons of details of any decision to vary or suspend any arrangements made, other than under an order under section 34, so as to allow any person contact with a child in care (regulation 4).

The Schedule provides for the details of the information which may be given in each case.

STATUTORY INSTRUMENTS

1991 No. 894

CHILDREN AND YOUNG PERSONS

Representations Procedure (Children) Regulations 1991

Made - - - -	*2nd April 1991*
Laid before Parliament	*10th April 1991*
Coming into force	*14th October 1991*

ARRANGEMENT OF REGULATIONS

PART I

Introductory

PART II

Representations and their consideration

PART III

Review of procedure

PART IV

Application of the Regulations to voluntary organisations and registered children's homes

The Secretary of State for Health, in exercise of the powers conferred by sections 24(15) and 26(5) and (6), 59(4) and (5) and 104(4) of, and paragraph 10(2)(l) of Schedule 6 and paragraph 6 of Schedule 7 to, the Children Act 1989**(a)**, and all other powers enabling him in that behalf, hereby makes the following Regulations:—

PART I

INTRODUCTORY

Citation and commencement

1. These Regulations may be cited as the Representations Procedure (Children) Regulations 1991, and shall come into force on 14th October 1991.

Interpretation

2.—(1) In these Regulations, unless the context otherwise requires—

" the Act " means the Children Act 1989;

"complainant" means a person qualifying for advice and assistance about the discharge of their functions by a local authority under Part III of the Act in relation to him, or a person specified in section 26(3)(a) to (e) of the Act making any representations;

"independent person" means in relation to representations made to, or treated as being made to, a local authority, a person who is neither a member nor an officer of that authority;

" panel " means a panel of 3 persons;

" representations " means representations referred to in sections 24(14) or 26(3) of the Act.

(2) Any notice required under these Regulations is to be given in writing and may be sent by post.

(3) In these Regulations unless the context requires otherwise—

(a) any reference to a numbered section is to the section in the Act bearing that number;

(b) any reference to a numbered regulation is to the regulation in these Regulations bearing that number, and any reference in a regulation to a numbered paragraph is to the paragraph of that regulation bearing that number.

PART II

REPRESENTATIONS AND THEIR CONSIDERATION

Local authority action

3.—(1) The local authority shall appoint one of their officers to assist the authority in the co-ordination of all aspects of their consideration of the representations.

(2) The local authority shall take all reasonable steps to ensure that everyone involved in the handling of the representations, including independent persons, is familiar with the procedure set out in these Regulations.

(a) 1989 c.41. Section 24(14) and (15) were inserted by paragraph 9 of Schedule 16 to the Courts and Legal Services Act 1991 (c.41).

Preliminaries

4.—(1) Where a local authority receive representations from any complainant, except from a person to whom section 26(3)(e) may apply, they shall send to the complainant an explanation of the procedure set out in these Regulations, and offer assistance and guidance on the use of the procedure, or give advice on where he may obtain it.

(2) Where oral representations are made, the authority shall forthwith cause them to be recorded in writing, and sent to the complainant, who shall be given the opportunity to agree that they are accurately recorded in writing.

(3) For all other purposes of these Regulations the written record to which paragraph (2) refers shall be deemed to be the representations.

(4) Where a local authority receive representations from a person to whom they consider section 26(3)(e) may apply they shall—

    (a) forthwith consider whether the person has a sufficient interest in the child's welfare to warrant his representations being considered by them;

    (b) if they consider that he has a sufficient interest, cause the representations to be dealt with in accordance with the provisions of these Regulations, and send to the complainant an explanation of the procedure set out in the Regulations, and offer assistance and guidance on the use of the procedure, or give advice on where he may obtain it;

    (c) if they consider that he has not got a sufficient interest they shall notify him accordingly in writing, and inform him that no further action will be taken;

    (d) if they consider it appropriate to do so having regard to his understanding, they shall notify the child of the result of their consideration.

(5) Where paragraph (4)(b) applies, the date at which the authority conclude that the person has a sufficient interest shall be treated for the purpose of these Regulations as the date of receipt of the representations.

Appointment of independent person

5. Where the local authority receive representations under regulation 4 they shall appoint an independent person to take part in the consideration of them, unless regulation 4(4)(c) applies.

Consideration by local authority with independent person

6.—(1) The local authority shall consider the representations with the independent person and formulate a response within 28 days of their receipt.

(2) The independent person shall take part in any discussions which are held by the local authority about the action (if any) to be taken in relation to the child in the light of the consideration of the representations.

Withdrawal of representations

7. The representations may be withdrawn at any stage by the person making them.

Notification to complainant and reference to panel

8.—(1) The local authority shall give notice within the period specified in regulation 6 to—

    (a) the complainant;

    (b) if different, the person on whose behalf the representations were made, unless the local authority consider that he is not of sufficient understanding or it would be likely to cause serious harm to his health or emotional condition;

    (c) the independent person;

    (d) any other person whom the local authority consider has sufficient interest in the case

of the proposed result of their consideration of the representations and the complainant's right to have the matter referred to a panel under paragraph (2).

(2) If the complainant informs the authority in writing within 28 days of the date on which notice is given under paragraph (1) that he is dissatisfied with the proposed result and wishes the matter to be referred to a panel for consideration of the representations, a panel shall be appointed by the local authority for that purpose.

(3) The panel shall include at least one independent person.

(4) The panel shall meet within 28 days of the receipt by the local authority of the complainant's request that the matter be referred to a panel.

(5) At that meeting the panel shall consider—

(a) any oral or written submissions that the complainant or the local authority wish to make; and

(b) if the independent person appointed under regulation 5 is different from the independent person on the panel, any oral or written submissions which the independent person appointed under regulation 5 wishes to make.

(6) If the complainant wishes to attend the meeting of the panel he may be accompanied throughout the meeting by another person of his choice, and may nominate that other person to speak on his behalf.

Recommendations

9.—(1) When a panel meets under regulation 8, they shall decide on their recommendations and record them with their reasons in writing within 24 hours of the end of the meeting referred to in regulation 8.

(2) The panel shall give notice of their recommendations to—

(a) the local authority;

(b) the complainant;

(c) the independent person appointed under regulation 5 if different from the independent person on the panel;

(d) any other person whom the local authority considers has sufficient interest in the case.

(3) The local authority shall, together with the independent person appointed to the panel under regulation 8(3) consider what action if any should be taken in relation to the child in the light of the representation, and that independent person shall take part in any decisions about any such action.

PART III

REVIEW

Monitoring of operation of procedure

10.—(1) Each local authority shall monitor the arrangements that they have made with a view to ensuring that they comply with the Regulations by keeping a record of each representation received, the outcome of each representation, and whether there was compliance with the time limits specified in regulations 6(1), 8(4) and 9(1).

(2) For the purposes of such monitoring, each local authority shall, at least once in every period of twelve months, compile a report on the operation in that period of the procedure set out in these Regulations.

(3) The first report referred to in paragraph (2) shall be compiled within twelve months of the date of coming into force of these Regulations.

PART IV

APPLICATION OF REGULATIONS TO VOLUNTARY ORGANISATIONS AND REGISTERED CHILDREN'S HOMES AND IN SPECIAL CASES

Application to voluntary organisations and registered children's homes

11.—(1) The provisions of Parts I to III of these Regulations shall apply where accommodation is provided for a child by a voluntary organisation, and he is not looked after by a local authority, as if—

(a) for references to "local authority" there were substituted references to "voluntary organisation";

(b) for the definition in regulation 2(1) of "complainant" there were substituted—

""complainant" means

(a) any child who is being provided with accommodation by a voluntary organisation;

(b) any parent of his;

(c) any person who is not a parent of his but who has parental responsibility for him;

(d) such other person as the voluntary organisation consider has a sufficient interest in the child's welfare to warrant his representations being considered by them.";

(c) for the definition in regulation 2(1) of "independent person" there were substituted

""independent person" means in relation to representations made to, or treated as being made to a voluntary organisation, a person who is not an officer of that voluntary organisation nor a person engaged in any way in furthering its objects, nor the spouse of any such person;" and

(d) for the definition in regulation 2(1) of "representations" there were substituted—

""representations" means representations referred to in section 59(4) about the discharge by the voluntary organisation of any of their functions relating to section 61 and any regulations made under it in relation to the child.";

(e) for the reference in regulation 4(1) and (4) to a person to whom section 26(3)(e) may apply or to whom the local authority consider section 26(3)(e) may apply there was substituted a reference to a person who may fall within sub-paragraph (d) in the definition of "complainant" in these Regulations.

(2) The provisions of Parts I to III of these Regulations shall apply where accommodation is provided for a child in a registered children's home, but where a child is neither looked after by a local authority nor accommodated on behalf of a voluntary organisation, as if—

(a) for references to "local authority" there were substituted references to "the person carrying on the home";

(b) for the definition in regulation 2(1) of "complainant" there were substituted—

""complainant" means

(i) any child who is being provided with accommodation in a registered children's home;

(ii) a parent of his;

(iii) any person who is not a parent of his but who has parental responsibility for him;

(iv) such other person as the person carrying on the home considers has a sufficient interest in the child's welfare to warrant his representations being considered by them;"

(c) for the definition in regulation 2(1) of "independent person" there were substituted—

"" independent person" means in relation to representations made to a person carrying on a registered children's home, a person who is neither involved in the management or operation of that home nor financially interested in its operation, nor the spouse of any such person;"

(d) for the definition in regulation 2(1) of "representations" there were substituted—

"" representations" means any representations (including any complaint) made in relation to the person carrying on the registered children's home by a complainant about the discharge of his functions relating to section 64.";

(e) for the reference in regulation 4(1) and (4) to a person to whom section 26(3)(e) may apply or to whom the local authority consider section 26(3)(e) may apply there was substituted a reference to a person who may fall within sub-paragraph (d) in the definition of "complainant" in these Regulations.

Special cases including application to representations by foster parents

12.—(1) Where representations would fall to be considered by more than one local authority, they shall be considered by the authority which is looking after the child or by the authority within whose area the child is ordinarily resident where no authority has that responsibility.

(2) The provisions of Parts I and III of, and of regulation 12(1) of, these Regulations, shall apply to the consideration by a local authority of any representations (including any complaint) made to them by any person exempted or seeking to be exempted under paragraph 4 of Schedule 7 to the Act (foster parents: limits on numbers of foster children) about the discharge of their functions under that paragraph as if—

(a) for the definition in regulation 2(1) of "complainant" there were substituted: "a person exempted or seeking to be exempted under paragraph 4 of Schedule 7 to the Act making any representations;"

(b) for the definition in regulation 2(1) of "representations" there were substituted: "representations referred to in paragraph 6 of Schedule 7 to the Act.";

(c) in regulation 4(1) the words "except from a person to whom section 26(3)(e) may apply" were omitted;

(d) regulation 4(4) and (5) were omitted.

Signed by authority of the Secretary of State for Health.

Virginia Bottomley
Minister of State,
2nd April 1991
Department of Health

EXPLANATORY NOTE

(This note is not part of the Regulations)

These Regulations establish a procedure for considering representations (including complaints) made to local authorities about the discharge by the authority of any of their functions—

(a) under Part III of the Act in relation to a child looked after by them or in need;

(b) where section 24(14) of the Act applies (representations concerning advice and assistance for certain children aged 18 to 21);

(c) under paragraph 4 of Schedule 7 to the Act (foster parents: limits on number of foster children) in relation to exemption from the usual fostering limit.

The Regulations make provision to include consideration of representations by an independent person and for reference of representations to a panel which is to make recommendations to the authority, organisation or person carrying on the home.

The Regulations also make provision for a record to be kept of all representations received and their outcome to monitor the operation of the procedure and for a report on the operation of the procedure to be prepared every twelve months.

The Regulations apply the procedure for considering representations (including complaints) made to voluntary organisations and persons carrying on registered children's homes with modifications.

STATUTORY INSTRUMENTS

1991 No. 892

CHILDREN AND YOUNG PERSONS

Definition of Independent Visitors (Children) Regulations 1991

Made - - - -	*2nd April 1991*
Laid before Parliament	*10th April 1991*
Coming into force	*14th October 1991*

The Secretary of State for Health, in exercise of the powers conferred by paragraph 17(7) of Schedule 2 to the Children Act 1989(**a**) and of all other powers enabling him in that behalf hereby makes the following Regulations:

Citation and commencement

1. These Regulations may be cited as the Definition of Independent Visitors (Children) Regulations 1991 and shall come into force on 14th October 1991.

Independent visitors

2. A person appointed by a local authority as an independent visitor under paragraph 17(1) of Schedule 2 to the Children Act 1989 shall be regarded as independent of the local authority appointing him in the following circumstances:

(a) where the person appointed is not connected with the local authority by virtue of being–

  (i) a member of the local authority or any of their committees or sub-committees, whether elected or co-opted; or

  (ii) an officer of the local authority employed in the Social Services Department of that authority; or

  (iii) a spouse of any such person;

(b) where the child who is to receive visits from the person appointed is accommodated by an organisation other than the local authority, and the person appointed is not–

  (i) a member of that organisation; or

  (ii) a patron or trustee of that organisation; or

  (iii) an employee of that organisation, whether paid or not; or

  (iv) a spouse of any such person.

Signed by authority of the Secretary of State for Health.

Virginia Bottomley
Minister of State,
Department of Health

2nd April 1991

(**a**) 1989 c.41.

EXPLANATORY NOTE

(This note is not part of the Regulations)

These Regulations prescribe the circumstances in which a person appointed as an independent visitor is to be regarded as independent of the local authority appointing him.

Regulation 2(a) provides that certain local authority members, employees and their spouses, are not to be regarded as independent. Regulation 2(b) provides that where the child is accommodated by some organisation other than a local authority, certain persons connected with that organisation shall not be regarded as independent.

STATUTORY INSTRUMENTS

1991 No. 1505

CHILDREN AND YOUNG PERSONS

The Children (Secure Accommodation) Regulations 1991

Made - - - -	*30th June 1991*
Laid before Parliament	*8th July 1991*
Coming into force	*14th October 1991*

Arrangement of Regulations

1. Citation and commencement.
2. Interpretation.
3. Approval by Secretary of State of secure accommodation in a community home.
4. Placement of a child aged under 13 in secure accommodation in a community home.
5. Child to whom section 25 of the Act shall not apply.
6. Detained and remanded children to whom section 25 of the Act shall have effect subject to modifications.
7. Children to whom section 25 of the Act shall apply and have effect subject to modifications.
8. Applications to court.
9. Duty to give information of placement in community homes.
10. Maximum period in secure accommodation without court authority.
11. Maximum initial period of authorisation by a court.
12. Further periods of authorisation by a court.
13. Maximum periods of authorisation by court for remanded children.
14. Duty to inform parents and others in relation to children in secure accommodation in a community home.
15. Appointment of persons to review placement in secure accommodation in a community home.
16. Review of placement in secure accommodation in a community home.
17. Records to be kept in respect of a child in secure accommodation in a community home.
18. Voluntary homes and registered children's homes not to be used for restricting liberty.
19. Revocation of Secure Accommodation (No. 2) Regulations 1983 and the Amendment Regulations.

The Secretary of State for Health, in exercise of the powers conferred by sections 25(2) and (7) and 104(4) of and paragraphs 4(1) and (2)(d) and (i) of Schedule 4, 7(1) and (2)(f) and (3) of Schedule 5 and 10(1) and (2)(j) and (3) of Schedule 6 to the Children Act 1989**(a)** and of all other powers enabling him in that behalf hereby makes the following regulations:

(a) 1989 c.41.

Citation and commencement

1. These Regulations may be cited as the Children (Secure Accommodation) Regulations 1991 and shall come into force on 14th October 1991.

Interpretation

2.—(1) In these Regulations, unless the context otherwise requires—

"the Act" means the Children Act 1989;

"independent visitor" means a person appointed under paragraph 17 of Schedule 2 to the Act;

"secure accommodation" means accommodation which is provided for the purpose of restricting the liberty of children to whom section 25 of the Act (use of accommodation for restricting liberty) applies.

(2) Any reference in these regulations to a numbered regulation shall be construed as a reference to the regulation bearing that number in these Regulations, and any reference in a regulation to a numbered paragraph is a reference to the paragraph bearing that number in that regulation.

Approval by Secretary of State of secure accommodation in a community home

3. Accommodation in a community home shall not be used as secure accommodation unless it has been approved by the Secretary of State for such use and approval shall be subject to such terms and conditions as he sees fit.

Placement of a child aged under 13 in secure accommodation in a community home

4. A child under the age of 13 years shall not be placed in secure accommodation in a community home without the prior approval of the Secretary of State to the placement of that child.

Children to whom section 25 of the Act shall not apply

5.—(1) Section 25 of the Act shall not apply to a child who is detained under any provision of the Mental Health Act 1983(a) or in respect of whom an order has been made under section 53 of the Children and Young Persons Act 1933(b) (punishment of certain grave crimes).

(2) Section 25 of the Act shall not apply to a child—

(a) to whom section 20(5) of the Act (accommodation of persons over 16 but under 21) applies and who is being accommodated under that section,

(b) in respect of whom an order has been made under section 43 of the Act (child assessment order) and who is kept away from home pursuant to that order.

Detained and remanded children to whom section 25 of the Act shall have effect subject to modifications

6.—(1) Subject to regulation 5, section 25 of the Act shall have effect subject to the modification specified in paragraph (2) in relation to children who are being looked after by a local authority(c) and are of the following descriptions—

(a) children detained under section 38(6) of the Police and Criminal Evidence Act 1984(d) (detained children), and

(b) children remanded to local authority accommodation under section 23 of the Children and Young Persons Act 1969(e) (remand to local authority accommodation) but only—

(i) where the child is charged with or convicted of an offence imprisonable in the case of a person aged 21 or over for 14 years or more, or

(ii) where the child is charged with or convicted of an offence of violence, or has been previously convicted of an offence of violence.

(a) 1983 c.20.

(b) 1933 c.12. Section 53(1) was substituted by section 1(5) of the Murder (Abolition of Death Penalty) Act 1965 (c.71). Section 53(2) was amended by the Criminal Justice Act 1948 (c.58) and section 2(1) and Schedule 4 to the Criminal Justice Act 1961 (c.39). Section 53(4) was repealed by the Criminal Justice Act 1967 (c.80), Schedule 7.

(c) A child who is "looked after by a local authority" is defined in section 22(1) of the Act— See also the definition of "care order" in section 105(1) of and Schedule 14 to the Act.

(d) 1984 c.60. Section 38(6) was amended by paragraph 53 of Schedule 13 to the Act.

(e) 1969 c.54. Section 23 was substituted by a new section by paragraph 26 of Schedule 12 to the Act.

(2) The modification referred to in paragraph (1) is that, for the words "unless it appears" to the end of subsection (1), there shall be substituted the following words—

"unless it appears that any accommodation other than that provided for the purpose of restricting liberty is inappropriate because—

  (a) the child is likely to abscond from such other accommodation, or

  (b) the child is likely to injure himself or other people if he is kept in any such other accommodation ".

Children to whom section 25 of the Act shall apply and have effect subject to modifications

7.—(1) Subject to regulation 5 and paragraphs (2) and (3) of this regulation section 25 of the Act shall apply (in addition to children looked after by a local authority)—

  (a) to children, other than those looked after by a local authority, who are accommodated by health authorities, National Health Service trusts established under section 5 of the National Health Service and Community Care Act 1990(a) or local education authorities, and

  (b) to children, other than those looked after by a local authority, who are accommodated in residential care homes, nursing homes or mental nursing homes.

(2) In relation to the children of a description specified in paragraph (1)(a) section 25 of the Act shall have effect subject to the following modifications—

  (a) for the words " who is being looked after by a local authority " in subsection (1) there shall be substituted the words " who is being provided with accommodation by a health authority, a National Health Service trust established under section 5 of the National Health Service and Community Care Act 1990 or a local education authority ".

  (b) for the words " local authorities " in subsection (2)(c) there shall be substituted the words " health authorities, National Health Service trusts or local education authorities ".

(3) In relation to the children of a description specified in paragraph (1)(b), section 25 of the Act shall have effect subject to the following modifications—

  (a) for the words " who is being looked after by a local authority " in subsection (1) there shall be substituted the words " who is being provided with accommodation in a residential care home, a nursing home or a mental nursing home "; and

  (b) for the words " local authorities " in subsection (2)(c) there shall be substituted the words " persons carrying on residential care homes, nursing homes or mental nursing homes ".

Applications to court

8. Subject to section 101 of the Local Government Act 1972(b), applications to a court under section 25 of the Act in respect of a child shall be made only by the local authority which are looking after that child.

Duty to give information of placement in community homes

9. Where a child is placed in secure accommodation in a community home which is managed by an authority other than that which are looking after him the local authority which manage that accommodation shall inform the authority which are looking after him that he has been placed there, within 12 hours of his being placed there, with a view to obtaining their authority to continue to keep him there if necessary.

Maximum period in secure accommodation without court authority

10.—(1) Subject to paragraphs (2) and (3), the maximum period beyond which a child to whom section 25 of the Act applies may not be kept in secure accommodation without the authority of a court is an aggregate of 72 hours (whether or not consecutive) in any period of 28 consecutive days.

(a) 1990 c.19.
(b) 1972 c.70.

(2) Where authority of a court to keep a child in secure accommodation has been given, any period during which the child has been kept in such accommodation before the giving of that authority shall be disregarded for the purposes of calculating the maximum period in relation to any subsequent occasion on which the child is placed in such accommodation after the period authorised by court has expired.

(3) Where a child is in secure accommodation at any time between 12 midday on the day before and 12 midday on the day after a public holiday or a Sunday, and

(a) during that period the maximum period specified in paragraph (1) expires, and

(b) the child had, in the 27 days before the day on which he was placed in secure accommodation, been placed and kept in such accommodation for an aggregate of more than 48 hours,

the maximum period does not expire until 12 midday on the first day, which is not itself a public holiday or a Sunday, after the public holiday or Sunday.

Maximum initial period of authorisation by a court

11. Subject to regulations 12 and 13 the maximum period for which a court may authorise a child to whom section 25 of the Act applies to be kept in secure accommodation is three months.

Further periods of authorisation by a court

12. Subject to regulation 13 a court may from time to time authorise a child to whom section 25 of the Act applies to be kept in secure accommodation for a further period not exceeding 6 months at any one time.

Maximum periods of authorisation by court for remanded children

13.—(1) The maximum period for which a court may from time to time authorise a child who has been remanded to local authority accommodation under section 23 of the Children and Young Persons Act 1969 to be kept in secure accommodation (whether the period is an initial period or a further period) is the period of the remand.

(2) Any period of authorisation in respect of such a child shall not exceed 28 days on any one occasion without further court authorisation.

Duty to inform parents and others in relation to children in secure accommodation in a community home

14. Where a child to whom section 25 of the Act applies is kept in secure accommodation in a community home and it is intended that an application will be made to a court to keep the child in that accommodation, the local authority which are looking after the child shall if practicable inform of that intention as soon as possible—

(a) his parent,

(b) any person who is not a parent of his but who has parental responsibility for him,

(c) the child's independent visitor, if one has been appointed, and

(d) any other person who that local authority consider should be informed.

Appointment of persons to review placement in secure accommodation in a community home

15. Each local authority looking after a child in secure accommodation in a community home shall appoint at least three persons, at least one of whom must not be employed by the local authority by or on behalf of which the child is being looked after, who shall review the keeping of the child in such accommodation for the purposes of securing his welfare within one month of the inception of the placement and then at intervals not exceeding three months where the child continues to be kept in such accommodation.

Review of placement in secure accommodation in a community home

16.—(1) The persons appointed under regulation 15 to review the keeping of a child in secure accommodation shall satisfy themselves as to whether or not—

(a) the criteria for keeping the child in secure accommodation continue to apply;

(b) the placement in such accommodation in a community home continues to be necessary; and

(c) any other description of accommodation would be appropriate for him,

and in doing so shall have regard to the welfare of the child whose case is being reviewed.

(2) In undertaking the review referred to in regulation 15 the persons appointed shall, if practicable, ascertain and take into account the wishes and feelings of—

(a) the child,

(b) any parent of his,

(c) any person not being a parent of his but who has parental responsibility for him,

(d) any other person who has had the care of the child, whose views the persons appointed consider should be taken into account,

(e) the child's independent visitor if one has been appointed, and

(f) the local authority managing the secure accommodation in which the child is placed if that authority are not the authority who are looking after the child.

(3) The local authority shall, if practicable, inform all those whose views are required to be taken into account under paragraph (2) of the outcome of the review and the reasons for such outcome.

Records to be kept in respect of a child in secure accommodation in a community home

17. Whenever a child is placed in secure accommodation in a community home the local authority which manages that accommodation shall ensure that a record is kept of—

(a) the name, date of birth and sex of that child,

(b) the care order or other statutory provision by virtue of which the child is in the community home and in either case particulars of any other local authority involved with the placement of the child in that home,

(c) the date and time of his placement in secure accommodation, the reason for his placement, the name of the officer authorising the placement and where the child was living before the placement,

(d) all those informed by virtue of regulation 9, 14 or 16(3) in their application to the child,

(e) court orders made in respect of the child by virtue of section 25 of the Act,

(f) reviews undertaken in respect of the child by virtue of regulation 15,

(g) the date and time of any occasion on which the child is locked on his own in any room in the secure accommodation other than his bedroom during usual bedtime hours, the name of the person authorising this action, the reason for it and the date on which and time at which the child ceases to be locked in that room, and

(h) the date and time of his discharge and his address following discharge from secure accommodation

and the Secretary of State may require copies of these records to be sent to him at any time.

Voluntary homes and registered children's homes not to be used for restricting liberty

18.—(1) The use of accommodation for the purpose of restricting the liberty of children in voluntary homes and registered children's homes is prohibited.

(2) The contravention of, or failure to comply with the provisions of paragraph (1), without reasonable excuse, shall be an offence against these Regulations(a).

Revocation of Secure Accommodation (No. 2) Regulations 1983 and the Amendment Regulations

19. The Secure Accommodation (No. 2) Regulations 1983(b) and the Secure Accommodation (No. 2) (Amendment) Regulations 1986(c) are hereby revoked.

Signed by authority of the Secretary of State for Health.

Virginia Bottomley
30th June 1991   Minister of State, Department of Health

(a) A person who is guilty of an offence against these Regulations is liable to a fine not exceeding level 4 on the standard scale (paragraph 7(4) of Schedule 5 and paragraph 10(4) of Schedule 6 to the Act).
(b) S.I. 1983/1808.
(c) S.I. 1986/1591.

EXPLANATORY NOTE

(This note is not part of the Regulations)

These Regulations replace the Secure Accommodation (No. 2) Regulations 1983 and the Secure Accommodation (No. 2) (Amendment) Regulations 1986 in consequence of the bringing into force of section 25 of the Children Act 1989 and the repeal of section 21A of the Child Care Act 1980 (c.5) which it replaces. The main changes include the extension of the secure accommodation provisions to children accommodated by health or local education authorities or National Health Service trusts or in residential care, nursing or mental nursing homes. The Regulations also prohibit for the first time the use of voluntary homes and registered children's homes for restricting the liberty of children.

The Regulations provide for approval by the Secretary of State of secure accommodation in community homes (regulation 3); the placement of a child aged under 13 in secure accommodation in community homes (regulation 4); the children to whom section 25 of the Act shall not apply (regulation 5); the modifications subject to which section 25 of the Act shall have effect in relation to detained and remanded children (regulation 6); certain children accommodated by health authorities, National Health Service trusts or local education authorities and in residential care, nursing or mental nursing homes to whom the Act shall apply and have effect subject to modifications (regulation 7); the making of applications to court (regulation 8); the duty to give information of placements in community homes (regulation 9); provision as to the maximum period in accommodation for restricting liberty without court authority (regulation 10); the maximum initial period of authorisation by any court (regulation 11); further periods of authorisation by a court (regulation 12); the maximum periods of authorisation by a court for remanded children (regulation 13); the duty to inform parents and others in relation to children in secure accommodation in a community home (regulation 14); the appointment of persons to review placements in secure accommodation in a community home (regulation 15); the review of placements in secure accommodation in a community home (regulation 16); the records to be kept in respect of a child in secure accommodation in a community home (regulation 17); the prohibition of the use of accommodation for restricting liberty in voluntary homes and registered children's homes and breach thereof (regulation 18); and the revocation of the Secure Accommodation (No. 2) Regulations 1983 and the amendment regulations (regulation 19).

STATUTORY INSTRUMENTS

1991 No. 1507

CHILDREN AND YOUNG PERSONS

The Refuges (Children's Homes and Foster Placements) Regulations 1991

Made - - - -	*30th June 1991*
Laid before Parliament	*8th July 1991*
Coming into force	*14th October 1991*

The Secretary of State for Health, in exercise of the powers conferred by sections 51(4) and 104(4) of the Children Act 1989**(a)** and of all other powers enabling him in that behalf hereby makes the following regulations:—

Citation and commencement

1. These Regulations may be cited as the Refuges (Children's Homes and Foster Placements) Regulations 1991 and shall come into force on 14th October 1991.

Interpretation

2.—(1) In these Regulations unless the context otherwise requires—

"certificate" means a certificate issued under section 51 (refuges for children at risk);

"designated officer" means a police officer for the time being designated for the purpose of these Regulations by the chief officer for the police area within which—

    (a) a home which is provided as a refuge in pursuance of section 51(1) is situated, or

    (b) a foster parent who provides a refuge in pursuance of section 51(2) lives;

"home" means a registered children's home or voluntary home;

"responsible person" in relation to a child means—

    (a) except where a person has care of the child as mentioned in paragraph (b) below—

      (i) a parent of his,

      (ii) a person who is not a parent of his, but who has parental responsibility for him, and

      (iii) any person who for the time being has care of him not being a person providing a refuge;

    (b) any person who for the time being has care of the child by virtue of a care order, emergency protection order or section 46 (removal and accommodation of children by police in cases of emergency) as the case may be.

(2) Any reference in these Regulations to a numbered section is a reference to the section in the Children Act 1989 bearing that number.

Requirements

3.—(1) The provisions of this regulation shall apply while a certificate is in force with respect to a home or a foster parent.

(a) 1989 c.41.

(2) A child may not be provided with a refuge unless it appears to the person providing the refuge that the child is at risk of harm unless the child is or continues to be provided with a refuge.

(3) As soon as is reasonably practicable after admitting a child to a home for the purpose of providing a refuge or after a foster parent provides a refuge for a child, and in any event within 24 hours of such provision, the person providing the refuge for the child shall—

    (a) notify the designated officer that a child has been admitted to the home, or provided with refuge by a foster parent, together with the telephone number by which the person providing the refuge for the child may be contacted,

    (b) if he knows the child's name, notify the designated officer of that name, and

    (c) if he knows the child's last permanent address, notify the designated officer of that address.

(4) Where subsequently the person providing the refuge discovers the child's name or last permanent address he shall immediately notify the designated officer accordingly.

(5) As soon as is reasonably practicable after providing the refuge for the child, and in any event within 24 hours of becoming aware of the identity of the responsible person for the child, the person providing the refuge shall give to the designated officer the name and address of the responsible person.

(6) The requirements of paragraph (7) of this regulation shall apply where the designated officer has been notified or is otherwise aware—

    (a) that a child is being provided with a refuge, and

    (b) of the name and address of a responsible person.

(7) The designated officer shall—

    (a) inform the responsible person

        (i) that the child is being provided with a refuge,

        (ii) by whom the refuge is being provided,

    (b) notify the responsible person of a telephone number by which the person providing the refuge for the child may be contacted,

    (c) not disclose to any person the address of the place at which the refuge is provided.

(8) Where a child ceases to be provided with a refuge, the person who provided him with the refuge shall notify the designated officer.

(9) No child shall be provided with a refuge in any one place for a continuous period of more than 14 days or for more than 21 days in any period of 3 months.

Withdrawal of a Certificate

4.—(1) The Secretary of State may withdraw a certificate at any time

    (a) where a person providing a refuge fails to comply with a requirement of regulation 3 of these Regulations;

    (b) where a person providing a refuge in a home fails to comply with any provision of Part II of the Children's Homes Regulations 1991(**a**);

    (c) where a foster parent providing a refuge fails to comply with any provision contained in the agreement relating to him concerning the matters to which paragraphs 3 to 9 of Schedule 2 to the Foster Placement (Children) Regulations 1991(**b**) apply and any provision contained in the agreement relating to him concerning the matters to which paragraphs 4 to 8 of Schedule 3 to those Regulations apply or with any provision of regulation 11(4) of those Regulations in respect of an emergency placement under those Regulations, or

    (d) where the person providing a refuge or any person assisting him in that respect has had proceedings instituted against him in relation to, or has been convicted of, any criminal offence.

(**a**) S.I. 1991/1506.
(**b**) S.I. 1991/910.

(2) Where a certificate is withdrawn the person carrying on the voluntary home or registered children's home in respect of which, or the foster parent in respect of whom, it was issued shall return it immediately to the Secretary of State.

Signed by authority of the Secretary of State for Health.

Virginia Bottomley
Minister of State,
Department of Health

30th June 1991

EXPLANATORY NOTE

(This note does not form part of the Regulations)

These Regulations make provision in respect of registered children's homes and voluntary homes which are used as refuges and foster parents who provide refuges in accordance with section 51 of the Children Act 1989. Regulation 3 provides for the requirements which are to be complied with while a certificate is in force and regulation 4 makes provision for the withdrawal of certificates by the Secretary of State.

Printed in the United Kingdom for HMSO
Dd302665 6/96 C10 G3397 10170